1 MONTH OF
FREE
READING

at

www.ForgottenBooks.com

By purchasing this book you are
eligible for one month membership to
ForgottenBooks.com, giving you
unlimited access to our entire
collection of over 1,000,000 titles via
our web site and mobile apps.

To claim your free month visit:

www.forgottenbooks.com/free543476

ISBN 978-0-666-04112-8
PIBN 10543476

This book is a reproduction of an important historical work. Forgotten Books uses
state-of-the-art technology to digitally reconstruct the work, preserving the original format
whilst repairing imperfections present in the aged copy. In rare cases, an imperfection in
the original, such as a blemish or missing page, may be replicated in our edition. We do,
however, repair the vast majority of imperfections successfully; any imperfections that
remain are intentionally left to preserve the state of such historical works.

JOURNAL

OF THE

SEVENTY-EIGHTH ANNUAL CONVENTION

OF THE

PROTESTANT EPISCOPAL CHURCH

IN THE

DIOCESE OF NORTH CAROLINA

HELD IN

ST. PAUL'S CHURCH, WINSTON,

MAY 16—20, 1894.

RALEIGH:
F. M. Uzzell, Power Printer and Binder.
1894

JOURNAL

OF THE

SEVENTY-EIGHTH ANNUAL CONVENTION

OF THE

PROTESTANT EPISCOPAL CHURCH

IN THE

DIOCESE OF NORTH CAROLINA

HELD IN

ST. PAUL'S CHURCH, WINSTON,

MAY 16—20, 1894.

———

RALEIGH.
E. M. Uzzell, Power Printer and Binder
1894.

The Seventy–ninth Annual Convention
of the Diocese of North Carolina
is appointed to meet in
Grace Church, Morganton,
Wednesday, May 15, A. D. 1895,
at 10 o'clock a. m.

————————

DIOCESE OF NORTH CAROLINA.

1894.

DIOCESAN OFFICERS.

BISHOP OF THE DIOCESE AND CHAIRMAN EX-OFFICIO OF THE CONVENTION.

The Rt. Rev. JOSEPH BLOUNT CHESHIRE, Jr., D.D., Raleigh.

PRESIDENT OF THE CONVENTION.

The Rev. MATTHIAS M. MARSHALL, D.D., Raleigh.

SECRETARY AND REGISTRAR.

The Rev. JULIAN E. INGLE, Henderson.

ASSISTANT SECRETARY.

Mr. G. C. LAMB, Henderson.

TREASURER OF THE DIOCESE.

Mr. CHARLES E. JOHNSON, Raleigh.

HISTORIOGRAPHER.

Mr. JOHN S. HENDERSON, Salisbury.

STANDING COMMITTEE.

The Rev. Matthias M. Marshall, D.D., President.

The Rev. Robert B. Sutton, D.D.   Mr. P. E. Hines, M.D.
The Rev. Bennett Smedes, D.D.   Mr. Richard H. Battle.

EXAMINING CHAPLAINS.

The Rev. M. M. Marshall, D.D.   The Rev. A. H. Stubbs.
The Rev. Bennett Smedes, D.D.   The Rev. Frederick Towers.
The Rev. A. Burtis Hunter.   The Rev. F. J. Murdoch, D.D.

ARCHDEACON FOR COLORED WORK.

The Rev. William Walker.

4 *Officers and Committees.*

DEANS OF CONVOCATIONS.

The Rev. John A. Deal,	Dean of Asheville.
The Rev. Julian E. Ingle,	Dean of Raleigh.
The Rev. F. J. Murdoch, D.D.,	Dean of Salisbury.
The Rev. Walter J. Smith,	Dean of Tarboro.
The Rev. Wm. R. Wetmore, D.D.,	Dean of Charlotte.

EXECUTIVE MISSIONARY COMMITTEE.

The Bishop of the Diocese.
The Deans of Convocations.

Mr. William L. London.	Mr. H. G. Connor.
Mr. Charles M. Busbee.	Mr. R. H. Battle.
	Mr. John Wilkes.

COMMITTEE ON CANONS.

The Rev. Wm. R. Wetmore, D.D.	Mr. R. H. Battle.
The Rev. James A. Weston.	Mr. J. C. Buxton.
The Rev. McNeely DuBose.	

CHURCH BUILDING COMMITTEE.

The Bishop of the Diocese.

The Rev. Robert B. Sutton, D.D.	Mr. W. E. Ashley.
The Rev. I. McK. Pittenger, D.D.	Mr. W. H. Cheek.
The Rev. Julian E. Ingle.	

TRUSTEES OF THE DIOCESE.

The Bishop of the Diocese.

Mr. Charles E. Johnson.	Mr. R. H. Battle.

TRUSTEES OF THE UNIVERSITY OF THE SOUTH.

The Rev. Francis J. Murdoch, D.D.

Mr. William L. London.	Mr. William A. Smith.

TRUSTEE OF THE GENERAL THEOLOGICAL SEMINARY.

The Rev. William Stanley Barrows, S.T.B.

BOARD OF FELLOWS OF RAVENSCROFT.

The Bishop of the Diocese.

The Rev. Wm. R. Wetmore, D.D.	Term expires 1895.
Mr. T. W. Patton.	" " 1895.
The Rev. Jarvis Buxton, D.D.	" " 1897.
Mr. J. H. Law.	" " 1897.
The Rev. McNeely DuBose.	" " 1899.
Mr. W. W. Jones.	" " 1899.

MANAGERS OF THE THOMPSON ORPHANAGE AND TRAINING INSTITUTION.

The Bishop of the Diocese.

The Rev. James Carmichael, D.D.	Term expires 1896.
Mr. J. Fairfax Payne.	" " 1896.
The Rev. Wm. R. Wetmore, D.D.	" " 1898.
Mr. William A. Smith.	" " 1898.
The Rev. Francis J. Murdoch, D.D.	" " 1900.
Mr. Baxter H. Moore.	" " 1900.

DELEGATES TO THE MISSIONARY COUNCIL.

The Rev. I. McK. Pittenger, D.D.   Mr. Silas McBee.

DEPUTIES TO THE GENERAL CONVENTION.

The Rev. Jarvis Buxton, D.D.	Mr. John Wilkes.
The Rev. M. M. Marshall, D.D.	Mr. R. H. Battle.
The Rev. F. J. Murdoch, D.D.	Mr. S. S. Nash.
	Mr. Silas McBee.

SUPPLEMENTARY DEPUTIES.

The Rev. R. B. Sutton, D.D.	Mr. John S. Henderson.
The Rev. Bennett Smedes, D.D.	Mr. William L. London.
The Rev. Julian E. Ingle.	Mr. W. H. S. Burgwyn.
	Mr. William L. Wall.

ALPHABETICAL LIST OF THE CLERGY.

MAY, 1894.

Those whose names are printed in *italics* were not members of the Convention
An asterisk (*) marks the names of those who were not present

---

The Rt. Rev. JOSEPH BLOUNT CHESHIRE, Jr., D.D., Bishop of the Diocese; P. O., Raleigh.

ALSTON, P. P., Priest in charge of the Chapel of St. Michael and All Angels, Charlotte, officiating also at Lincolnton; P. O., Charlotte.

BARBER, R. W., Rector of St. Paul's Church, Wilkesboro, and Missionary in Wilkes and Surry counties; P. O., Wilkesboro.

BARKER, J. W., Assistant Minister in Franklin Mission; P. O., Franklin, Macon county.

BARROWS, WILLIAM S., S.T.B., Instructor in Ravenscroft Training School, and Priest in charge of Ravenscroft Missions; P. O., Asheville.

BATTLE, GASTON, officiating in St. John's, Battleboro, and the Church of the Advent, Enfield; P. O., Rocky Mount.

BELL, GEORGE H., Missionary in Buncombe county; P. O., Bell.

*BENEDICT, EDWARD, Rector of St. Stephen's Church, Oxford.

*BLAND, CHARLES T., Rector of St. Bartholomew's Church, Pittsboro; in charge also of St. Mark's Mission, Gulf; P. O, Pittsboro.

BOST, SIDNEY S., officiating in Rowan county; P. O., Salisbury.

*Boyle, A. H., residing in Philadelphia, Pa.

*BRONSON, B. S., Master, "Home School for Boys," Warrenton.

BUXTON, JARVIS, D.D., Rector of St. James' Church, Lenoir.

*BYNUM, WILLIAM S., residing at Lincolnton.

*CHESHIRE, JOSEPH BLOUNT, D.D., residing at Tarboro.

DAVIS, J. C., Rector of All Saints' Church, Concord.

DEAL, JOHN A., Priest in charge of Franklin Mission; P. O., Franklin, Macon county.

*DELANY, HENRY B., Instructor in St. Augustine's School and Assistant Minister in St. Augustine's Church, Raleigh.

DuBOSE, McNEELY, Rector of Trinity Church, Asheville.

FERRIS, CHARLES, Priest in charge of the Church of the Holy Cross, Tryon, and Missionary at Columbus; P. O, Tryon.

FETTER, CHARLES, officiating at Christ Church, Milton; St. John's, Madison; Christ Church, Walnut Cove, and Cuningham's Chapel; P. O., Kernersville.

FETTER, FREDERICK A., officiating at St. Mary's, High Point, and the Church of Redemption, Lexington; P. O., High Point.

George, John F., Rector of St. Paul's Church, Winston.

*GREEN, E. P.; P. O., Morganton.

Hilliard, Francis W., Priest in charge of St. Paul's Church, Monroe.

Hoffmann, Charles L., Rector of Calvary Church, Tarboro.

HORNER, JUNIUS M., Rector of St. Paul's Church, Goshen; in charge also of St. Peter's Church, Stovall; P. O., Oxford.

HUNTER, A. BURTIS, Principal of St. Augustine's School, and Rector of St. Augustine's Church, Raleigh.

INGLE, JULIAN E., Rector of the Church of the Holy Innocents, Henderson.

Joseph, H. M., residing in New York.

*KENNEDY, JAMES T., officiating in St. Cyprian's Chapel, Franklin, Macon county.

MARSHALL, M. M., D.D., Rector of Christ Church, Raleigh.

McDUFFEY, H. S , Priest in charge of St. Matthias' Church, Asheville, and St. Stephen's, Morganton; P. O., Asheville.

McKENZIE, B. S., Rector of St. Matthew's Church, Hillsboro, and St. Mary's Chapel, Orange county; P. O., Hillsboro.

McQUEEN, STEWART, Rector of St. Philip's Church, Durham.

Milbank, John F., Rector of Emmanuel Church, Warrenton.

MILLER, JAMES D., officiating in St. Andrew's Church, Greensboro.

*MORRIS, T. A., P. O., Skyland.

MURDOCH, F. J., D.D., Rector of St. Luke's Church, Salisbury; in charge also of Rowan Associate Mission, and of St. James' Church, Iredell county; P. O., Salisbury.

Murphy, J. W., residing in Washington, D. C.

OSBORNE, E. A., Superintendent of the Thompson Orphanage and Training Institution, and Rector of Trinity Church, Statesville; P. O., Charlotte.

OWENS, R. B., officiating in Rowan county; P. O., Salisbury.

PERRY, JOHN W., Rector of St. Luke's Church, Tarboro; in charge also of St. Mark's Chapel, Wilson; P. O., Tarboro.

*PETTIGREW, WILLIAM S., Rector of the Church of the Good Shepherd, Ridgeway, and St. John's, Williamsboro; in charge also of the Mission at Middleburg; P. O., Ridgeway.

PHELPS, GIRARD W., Priest in charge of the Missions at Rutherfordton, Shelby, Marion and Old Fort; P. O., Shelby.

Phelps, *H. H.*, Rector of Calvary Church, Henderson county; P. O., Fletcher.

PICARD, W. T., officiating in the Church of the Saviour, Jackson, and at Rich Square; P. O., Jackson.

PITTENGER, I. McK., D.D., Rector of the Church of the Good Shepherd, Raleigh.

*POSTELL, JAMES H., Missionary in Buncombe county; P. O., Asheville.

· QUIN, CHARLES C., Rector of Calvary Church, Wadesboro; in charge also of Ansonville Mission; P. O., Wadesboro.

RATHBUN, SCOTT B., Rector of St. John's Church, Flat Rock; in charge also of St. James' Church, Hendersonville; P. O., Flat Rock.

RHODES, SAMUEL, Assistant Minister in Ravenscroft Mission, Asheville.

*RICE, W. F., Missionary in Buncombe county; P. O , Grace.

SMEDES, BENNETT, D.D., Rector of St. Mary's School, Raleigh.

SMITH, WALTER J., Rector of Trinity Church, Scotland Neck, and St. Mark's, Halifax; P. O , Scotland Neck.

STICKNEY, FENNER S., Rector of St. Peter's Church, Charlotte.

STUBBS, ALFRED H., Rector of St. Barnabas' Church, Greensboro.

SUTTON, ROBERT B., D.D., Vice-Principal of St. Augustine's School, and Assistant Minister of St. Augustine's Church, Raleigh.

*TOWERS, FREDERICK, Rector of the Chapel of the Cross, Chapel Hill.

VANDERBOGART, ALVIN J., Rector of the Church of the Good Shepherd, Rocky Mount.

*WAINWRIGHT, RICHARD, Priest in charge of Gethsemane Mission, Bowman's Bluff.

WALKER, ROBERT J., Rector of St. Athanasius' Church, Burlington.

WALKER, WILLIAM, Archdeacon in charge of colored work; P. O., Raleigh.

WESTON, JAMES A., Rector of the Church of the Ascension, Hickory.

WETMORE, THOMAS C., officiating in Lincoln and Gaston counties; P. O., Lincolnton.

WETMORE, WM. R., D.D., Rector of St. Luke's Church, Lincolnton, and Missionary in Lincoln and Gaston counties; P. O., Lincolnton.

WINGATE, CHARLES J., Rector of St. Timothy's Church, Wilson.

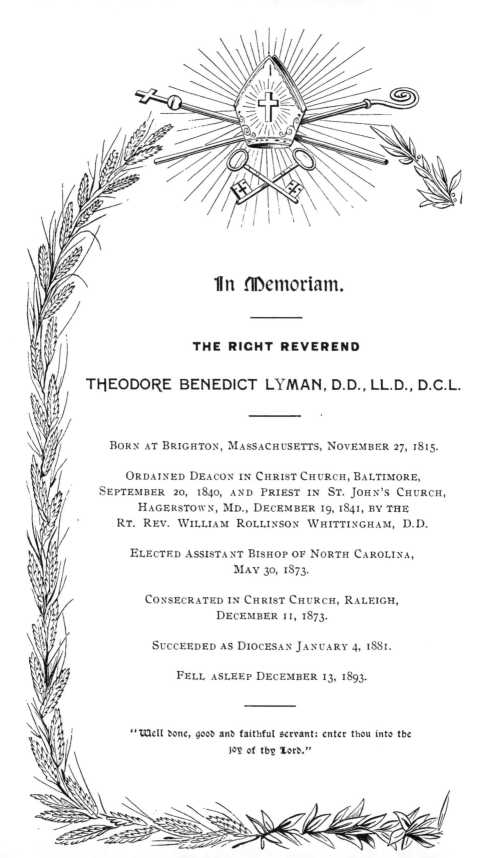

In Memoriam.

THE RIGHT REVEREND

THEODORE BENEDICT LYMAN, D.D., LL.D., D.C.L.

BORN AT BRIGHTON, MASSACHUSETTS, NOVEMBER 27, 1815.

ORDAINED DEACON IN CHRIST CHURCH, BALTIMORE,
SEPTEMBER 20, 1840, AND PRIEST IN ST. JOHN'S CHURCH,
HAGERSTOWN, MD., DECEMBER 19, 1841, BY THE
RT. REV. WILLIAM ROLLINSON WHITTINGHAM, D.D.

ELECTED ASSISTANT BISHOP OF NORTH CAROLINA,
MAY 30, 1873.

CONSECRATED IN CHRIST CHURCH, RALEIGH,
DECEMBER 11, 1873.

SUCCEEDED AS DIOCESAN JANUARY 4, 1881.

FELL ASLEEP DECEMBER 13, 1893.

"Well done, good and faithful servant: enter thou into the
joy of thy Lord."

In Memoriam.

THE REVEREND

FRANKLIN LEONARD BUSH, M.A.

Born in Boston, Massachusetts, August 8, 1843.

Graduated at Harvard University and entered the Berkeley
Divinity School 1864.

Ordained Deacon June 5, 1867, and Priest June 23, 1868,
by the Rt. Rev. John Williams, D.D.

Served for three years as Assistant Minister in St. Peter's,
Philadelphia, and after a sojourn in Europe, labored
in the Diocese of Massachusetts.

Became Rector of St. James Church, Lenoir, N. C., 1878,
and of St. Stephen's, Oxford, 1882.

Since 1883 he has been connected with the Colored work at St.
James Chapel, Pittsboro, which he was largely instrumental in building, and at other points, and has
lately added to his cares the preparation
of Colored Candidates for Holy Orders.

After a brief illness he fell asleep at Raleigh on the Feast
of St. James, July 25, 1893.

"He walked with God: and was not; for God took him."

LIST OF THE CLERGY

ACCORDING TO DATE OF ORDINATION.

BISHOP.

The Rt. Rev. Joseph Blount Cheshire, Jr., D.D.,

CONSECRATED OCTOBER 15, 1893

PRIESTS.

The Rev. Joseph Blount Cheshire, D.D.	ordained	May	9, 1841.
"	Jarvis Buxton, D.D.	"	June	17, 1849.
"	Charles Theodore Bland	"	Nov.	17, 1850.
"	Richard Wainwright Barber	"	May	22, 1852.
"	Thomas Alexander Morris	"	Nov.	24, 1852.
"	Robert Bean Sutton, D.D.	"	Dec.	29, 1852.
"	Joseph Wiggins Murphy	"	Nov.	4, 1855.
"	Francis William Hilliard	"	March	25, 1857.
"	Benjamin Swan Bronson	"	May	31, 1857.
"	William Robards Wetmore, D.D.	"	Sept.	21, 1862.
"	Bennett Smedes, D.D.	"	July	26, 1863.
"	Julian Edward Ingle	"	June	11, 1865.
"	Matthias Murray Marshall, D.D.	"	Sept.	3, 1865.
"	Alfred Houghton Stubbs	"	Sept.	24, 1865.
"	William Walker	"	Jan.	27, 1867.
"	Richard Wainwright	"	June	14, 1867.
"	Girard William Phelps	"	May	23, 1869.
"	Alexander Hannay Boyle	"	Jan.	9, 1870.
"	Francis Johnstone Murdoch, D.D.	"	May	8, 1870.
"	William Shepard Pettigrew	"	June	13, 1870.
"	Johnson-Carmon Davis	"	June	30, 1870.
"	Edward Benedict	"	April	28, 1872.
"	John Archibald Deal	"	Sept.	8, 1872.
"	James Augustus Weston	"	Nov.	12, 1876.
"	Charles James Wingate	"	Jan.	7, 1878.

2

The Rev. Scott Bogie Rathbun ------------- ----ordained June 11, 1879.
"   Charles Ferris ------------------ ---   "   May   3, 1880.
"   Isaac McKendree Pittenger, D.D. ---   "   May   6, 1880.
"   Edwin Augustus Osborne -----------   "   May   22, 1881.
"   John Francis George-- --------------   "   June   7, 1881.
"   Frederick Towers ------------------   "   June   8, 1881.
"   Stewart McQueen-------------------   "   April   30, 1882.
"   Aaron Burtis Hunter---------------   "   May   1, 1882.
"   William Shipp Bynum ------- ------   "   May   5, 1882.
"   Robert Jefferson Walker------------   "   May   12, 1882.
"   George Hamilton Bell ---------------   "   July   15, 1883.
"   Henry Mason Joseph ----------------   "   June   4, 1884.
"   Walter Johnston Smith --- ----------   "   Nov.   15, 1885.
"   McNeely Dubose - -----------------   "   Dec.   16, 1885.
"   Hardy Hardison Phelps-------------   "   Dec.   17, 1886.
"   John William Perry ----------------   "   April   7, 1887.
"   Charles Carroll Quin ---------------   "   Oct.   18, 1887.
"   Henry Stephen McDuffey ------------   "   June   3, 1888.
"   William Stanley Barrows, S T.B. ----   "   June   16, 1889.
"   Charles Lorenzo Hoffmann ----- ----   "   May   18, 1891.
"   Junius Moore Horner---------------   "   May   24, 1891.
"   Edward Philip Green ---------------   "   Nov.   29, 1891.
"   Fenner Satterthwaite Stickney------   "   Nov.   29, 1891.
"   Primus Priss Alston ----------------   "   Jan.   26, 1892.
"   John Frederick Milbank---- --- ----   "   April   29, 1892.
"   Henry Beard Delany ---------------   "   May   2, 1892.
"   Alvin Jones Vanderbogart ----------   "   June   4, 1893.
"   Benjamin Sumner McKenzie --------   "   Feb.   18, 1894.

DEACONS.

The Rev. James Harvey Postell ------------- ----ordered Nov. 28, 1883.
"   William Francis Rice--------------- ---   "   Sept.   8, 1886.
"   William Thomas Picard --------------   "   May   11, 1887.
"   John William Barker ---------------   "   Aug.   24, 1890.
"   James Thomas Kennedy--------------   "   Sept.   7, 1890.
"   Samuel Rhodes -------------------- ---   "   Oct.   18, 1891.
"   Sidney Steuart Bost -----------------   "   May   20, 1892.

The Rev. Robert Bruce Owens --------------------- ordered Nov. 17, 1892.
"   Gaston Battle ------------------------------- "   March 26, 1893.
"   James Daniel Miller------------------------ "   June 27, 1893.
"   Frederick Augustus Fetter ----------------- "   Dec. 21, 1893.
"   Charles Fetter ------------------------------ "   Dec. 21, 1893.
"   Thomas Cogdell Wetmore ----------------- "   Feb. 21, 1894.

CANDIDATES FOR PRIEST'S ORDERS.

The Rev. John William Barker ----------------- admitted Nov. 16, 1891.
"   Gaston Battle ------------------------------- "   March 27, 1893.
"   James Daniel Miller ------------------------ "   Nov. 15, 1890.
"   Frederick Augustus Fetter ----------------- "   Dec. 21, 1893.
"   Charles Fetter ------------------------------ "   Dec. 21, 1893.
"   Thomas Cogdell Wetmore ----------------- "   Feb. 25, 1893.
"   Nathan Adolphus Seagle* ----------------- "   March 25, 1891.
"   George Valerie Gilreath* ------------------ "   July 27, 1891.
William Bentley Crittenden --------------------- "   Nov. 8, 1892.

CANDIDATES FOR DEACON'S ORDERS.

Samuel Alexander Bucher Trott --------------- admitted April 24, 1889.
James Edward King ---------------------------- "   Dec. 21, 1892.
Eugene Leon Henderson ------------------------ "   March 22, 1893.
Thomas Burke Bailey -------------------------- "   May 22, 1893.

POSTULANTS.

Edward L. Whitehead -------------------------- admitted March 15, 1890.
Alfred James Griffin -------------------------- "   May 29, 1891.
John Creighton Seagle ------------------------- "   Sept. 5, 1891.
John Harvey Gilreath -------------------------- "   Sept. 21, 1891.
Isaac Norfleet Neal ---------------------------- "   Feb. 17, 1893.
Charles Scales Burgess ------------------------ "   Sept. 10, 1893.
Thomas Clayton Brown ------------------------- "   March 24, 1894.

*Messrs. George V. Gilreath and Nathan A. Seagle were ordered Deacons May 20, 1894.

LIST OF PARISHES AND MISSIONS

IN THE

DIOCESE OF NORTH CAROLINA,

WITH THE NAMES OF CLERGY IN CHARGE AND LAY DELEGATES, AND
THEIR ALTERNATES, TO THE CONVENTION.

PARISHES in small capitals. *Organized Missions* in italics. Missions
entitled to representatives marked thus. †   Lay delegates present marked
thus. *

Ansonville,	Mission,	Rev. CHARLES C. QUIN.
Asheville,	*St. Matthias* (col.),	Rev. H. S. McDUFFEY.
Asheville,	TRINITY,	Rev. McNEELY DuBOSE.
	T. W. Patton.	*A. J. Lyman.
	*J. H. Law.	H. M. Anderson, M.D.
	Thomas A. Jones.	Ronald MacDonald.
	*R. R. Rawls.	N. S. Rogers.
Battleboro,	St. John's,	Rev. GASTON BATTLE.
Bowman's Bluff,	*Gethsemane*,	Rev. RICHARD WAINWRIGHT.
Brevard,	St. Philip's,	Rev. S. B. RATHBUN.
Bryson City,	St. Stephen's,	Rev. J. W. BARKER
Buncombe County,	St. Andrew's,	} Rev. JAMES H. POSTELL.
Buncombe County,	St. Paul's,	
Burlington,	ST. ATHANASIUS,	Rev. R. J. WALKER.
	J. Locke Erwin.	
	John Q. Gantt.	
Candler's,	St. Clement's,	Rev. GEORGE H. BELL.
Cashier's Valley,	*Good Shepherd*,	Rev. JOHN A. DEAL.
Chapel Hill,	CHAPEL OF THE CROSS,	Rev. FREDERICK TOWERS.
	*K. P. Battle, LL.D.	Charles Baskerville.
	R. S. McRae.	John H. London.
	John Manning, LL.D.	
	George T. Winston, LL.D.	
Charlotte,	St. Mary's,	Rev. E. A. OSBORNE.

Charlotte,	†*St. Michael's* (col),	Rev. P. P. ALSTON.
	John S. Leary.	
Charlotte,	ST. PETER'S,	Rev. F. S. STICKNEY.
	*J. L. Myers.	J. C. Palamountain.
	*John Wilkes.	P. D. Walker.
	H. C. Jones.	C. L. Hunter.
	B. S. Davis.	E. L. Keesler.
Chunn's Cove,	Mission,	Rev. W. F. RICE.
Concord,	ALL SAINTS,	Rev. J. C. DAVIS.
	*B. F. Rogers.	
	W. G. Means.	
	H. S. Puryear.	
	*Paul B. Means.	
Cullowhee,	St. David's,	Rev. J. A. DEAL.
Cuningham's,	Chapel,	Rev. CHARLES FETTER.
Durham,	ST. PHILIP'S CHURCH,	Rev. STEWART McQUEEN.
	W. L. Wall.	E. G. Lineberry.
	W. A. Erwin.	L. W. Wise.
	Charles McGary.	J. M. Manning, M.D.
	*W. J. Griswold.	Samuel Kramer.
Durham,	St. Philip's Chapel (col.), Rev. STEWART McQUEEN.	
Enfield,	ADVENT,	Rev. GASTON BATTLE.
	J. J. Whitaker.	F. W. Pippen.
Flat Rock,	ST. JOHN'S,	Rev. S. B. RATHBUN.
Franklin,	*St. Agnes,*	Rev. J A. DEAL.
Franklin,	St. Cyprian's, (col.), Rev. J. A. DEAL.	
Gaston,	†*St. Luke's.*	
	Ashley Wilkins.	E. W. Wilkins.
Germanton,	†*St. Philip's.*	
Goshen,	ST. PAUL'S,	Rev. J. M. HORNER.
Grace,	†*Beaver Dam Mission,* Rev. W. F. RICE.	
Greensboro,	ST. ANDREW'S,	Rev. J. D. MILLER.
	J. G. Brodnax, M.D.	O. Williams.
	W. R. Gales.	P. C. Pope.
	E. Berkeley.	H. L. Fry.
	*J. D. Glenn.	T. C. Gales.
Greensboro,	ST. BARNABAS,	Rev. A. H. STUBBS.
	William E. Stone.	Thomas Woodroffe.
	David Schenck.	George Woodroffe.
	John M. Dick.	John R. Fitzmaurice.
	John L. Forda.	William H. Snow.

Gulf,	*St. Mark's,*	Rev. C. T. BLAND.
Halifax,	ST. MARK'S,	Rev. W. J. SMITH.
Haw Creek,	Trinity,	Rev. GEORGE H. BELL.
Henderson,	HOLY INNOCENTS,	Rev. JULIAN E. INGLE.
	*G. C. Lamb.	W. H. Cheek.
	*D. Y. Cooper.	Redding Perry.
	J. H. Tucker, M.D.	A. C. Zollicoffer.
	Wm. H. S. Burgwyn.	F. J. Hill.
Henderson County,	CAVALRY,	Rev. H. H. PHELPS.
	Thomas A. Weston.	Overton Price.
	G. W. Fletcher, M.D.	George F. Weston.
	N. J. Lance.	Robert B. Blake.
Henderson County,	Mt. Cavalry Chapel,	Rev. H. H. PHELPS.
Henderson County,	St. Paul's,	Rev. W. S. BARROWS.
Hendersonville,	†*St. James,*	Rev. S B. RATHBUN.
Hickory,	ASCENSION,	Rev. JAMES A. WESTON.
	O. M. Royster.	
	J. McD. Michal.	
	*M. E. Thornton.	
	Frank A. Clinard.	
High Point,	St. Mary's,	Rev. F. A. FETTER.
High Shoals,	St. John's,	Rev. W. R. WETMORE, D.D.
Hillsboro,	ST. MATTHEW'S,	Rev. B. S. McKENZIE.
	D. H. Hamilton.	James Webb, Sr.
	George P. Collins.	W. A. Hayes.
	William B. Mears.	E. A. Rosemond.
	*Paul C. Graham.	James Webb, 3d.
Hot Springs,	*St. John's,*	Rev. W. S. BARROWS.
Iredell County,	ST. JAMES,	REV. F. J. MURDOCH, D.D.
Jackson,	CH. OF THE SAVIOUR,	Rev. W. T. PICARD.
	D. A. Jordan.	G. P. Burgwyn.
	R. B. Peebles.	J. A. Burgwyn.
	R. H. Stancell, M.D.	C. G. Peebles.
	J. B. McRae.	W. W. Peebles.
Kittrell,	ST. JAMES,	Rev. J. B. AVIRETT.
	B. A. Capehart.	G. W. Kittrell.
	C. W. Raney.	A. L. Capehart.
Leaksville,	EPIPHANY.	
	Henry C. Moir.	A. B. Johns, M.D.
	*W. S. Martin, M.D.	S. L. Martin, M.D.
Leicester,	St. Paul's.	

Lenoir,	ST. JAMES,	Rev. JARVIS BUXTON, D.D.
	W. W. Scott, M.D.	J. C. Blair, M.D.
	S. L. Patterson.	A. A. Kent.
	Edmund Jones.	T. B. Lenoir.
Lexington,	Redemption,	Rev. F. A. FETTER.
Lincoln County,	Our Saviour,	
Lincoln County,	St. Paul's,	
Lincoln County,	St. Stephen's,	Rev. WM. R. WETMORE, D.D.
Lincoln and Gaston Missions,		
Lincolnton,	St. Cyprian's (col.),	
Lincolnton,	ST. LUKE'S,	Rev. WM. R. WETMORE, D.D
	*J. C. Cobb.	
	*Silas McBee.	
	Blair Jenkins.	
	W. A. Hoke.	
Littleton,	*Chapel of the Cross.*	
Louisburg,	ST. PAUL'S,	Rev. J. B. AVIRETT.
	*F. S. Spruill.	R. H. Davis.
	Thomas White.	J. K. White.
	H. A. Crenshaw.	W. P. Neal.
Louisburg,	Mission (col),	Rev. WM. WALKER.
Madison,	†*St. John's,*	Rev. CHARLES FETTER.
	T. R. Pratt.	J. M. Galloway.
Marion,	St. John's,	Rev. G. W. PHELPS.
Mecklenburg Co.,	St. Mark's,	Rev. E. A. OSBORNE.
Micadale,	St. Mary's,	Rev. W. S. BARROWS.
Middleburg,	*Heavenly Rest,*	Rev. W. S. PETTIGREW.
Milton,	Christ Church,	Rev. CHARLES FETTER.
Monroe,	†*St. Paul's,*	Rev. F. W. HILLIARD.
	*S. J. Welsh, M.D.	M. E. McCauley.
Morganton,	. GRACE.	
	Theodore Gordon.	T. George Walton.
	*W. T. Powe.	D. C. Pearson.
	*John H. Pearson.	C. F. McKesson.
Morganton,	St Stephen's (col),	Rev. H. S. McDUFFEY.
Noise,	St. Philip's (col.),	Rev. WILLIAM WALKER
Nonah,	*St. John's,*	Rev. J. W. BARKER.
Old Fort,	Mission,	Rev. G. W. PHELPS.
Orange County,	St. Jude's,	Rev. B. S. McKENZIE.
Orange County,	†*St. Mary's,*	Rev. B. S. McKENZIE.

Oxford,	St. Stephen's,	Rev. Edward Benedict.
	Gowan Dusenbury.	W. C. Reed.
	R. W. Lassiter.	H. A. Taylor.
	*J. G. Hall.	W. H. White.
Pittsboro,	St. Bartholomew's,	Rev. C. T. Bland.
	*William L. London.	
	L. J. Haughton.	
	H. A. London.	
	A. D. Lippitt.	
Pittsboro,	†*St. James* (col.),	Rev. William Walker.
Raleigh,	Christ Church,	Rev. M. M. Marshall, D.D.
	*C. E. Johnson.	C. McKimmon.
	*C. M. Busbee.	H. B. Battle, Ph.D.
	*R. H. Lewis, M.D.	R B. Raney.
	*V. E. Turner, M.D.	R. W. Rogers.
Raleigh,	Good Shepherd,	Rev. I. McK. Pittenger.
	*R. H. Battle.	C. G. Latta.
	*J. B. Batchelor, LL D.	W. E. Foster.
	*S. P. Child.	Walter Woollcott.
	William Woollcott.	Jesse G. Ball.
Raleigh,	St. Augustine's (col.),	Rev. A. B. Hunter.
	Wm. B. Crittenden.	W. F. Debnam.
Raleigh,	St. Mary's Chapel,	Rev. Bennett Smedes, D.D.
Raleigh,	St. Saviour's,	Rev. M. M. Marshall, D.D.
Reidsville,	St. Thomas.	
	A. H. Galloway.	R. J. Mayo.
	A. M. Whitsett.	*N. K. Smith.
Ridgeway,	Good Shepherd,	Rev. W. S. Pettigrew.
	William L. Baxter.	
	Stephen L. Crowder.	
	Thomas G. Plummer.	
	Charles Petar, Jr.	
Ringwood,	St. Clement's.	
	H. S. Harrison.	C. A. Williams.
	F. H. Taylor.	J. L. Tyree.
	L. Vinson.	J. M. Weller.
Rockwood,	Redeemer,	Rev. William F. Rice.
Rocky Mount,	Good Shepherd,	Rev. A. J. Vanderbogart.
	Jacob Battle.	Buckner Davis.
	E. G. Muse.	W. B. Jordan.
	D. W. Thorpe.	L. V. Bassett.
	F. Y. Ramsay.	J. A. Brogden.

Rowan County,	CHRIST CHURCH,	
Rowan County,	ST. ANDREW'S,	} Rev. F. J. MURDOCH, D.D.
Rowan County,	St. Jude's,	

Rowan County,	ST. MARY'S,	Rev. F. J. MURDOCH, D.D.
	J. H. McKenzie.	N. P. Slive.
	J. A. Owens.	T. J. McKenzie.
	W. L. Harris.	J. L. Harris.
	E. B. McKenzie.	R A. Morse.

Rowan County,	St. Matthew's,	} Rev. F. J. MURDOCH, D.D.
Rowan County,	ST. PAUL'S,	

Rutherfordton,	ST. JOHN'S,	Rev. G. W. PHELPS.

Salisbury,	ST. LUKE'S,	Rev. F. J. MURDOCH, D.D.
	J. S. Henderson.	J. M. Hill.
	S. F. Lord	T. F. Young.
	C. A. Overman.	C. S. Burgess.
	A. H. Brogden.	S. J. M. Brown.

Salisbury,	St. John's,	} Rev. F. J. MURDOCH, D.D.
Salisbury,	St. Peter's,	

Saluda,	Transfiguration,	Rev. W. S. BARROWS.
Sanford,	Mission,	Rev. C. T. BLAND.

Scotland Neck,	TRINITY,	Rev. WALTER J. SMITH.
	S. M. Alexander.	P. E. Smith.
	R. H. Smith.	J. T. Applewhite.
	A. L. Purrington.	T. W. Fenner.
	J. Y. Savage.	J. S. Paull.

Shelby,	Redeemer,	Rev. G. W. PHELPS.
Smithfield,	Mission.	
Statesville,	TRINITY,	Rev. E. A. OSBORNE.
Stovall,	St. Peter's,	Rev. J. M. HORNER.
Sylva,	Mission,	Rev. W. S. BARROWS.

Tarboro,	CALVARY,	Rev. C. L. HOFFMANN.
	*Fred. Philips.	H. H. Shaw.
	*M. A. Curtis.	J. L. Jenkins.
	Ed. Pennington.	J. W. Cotten.
	Henry Johnston.	C. F. Clayton.

Tarboro,	ST. LUKE'S,	Rev. J. W. PERRY.
	Jordan H. Dancy.	Levi Thigpen.
	*Thomas Newton.	N. B. Brown.
	David W. Harris.	Allen Taylor.
	Warren H. Peyton.	James H. Harrison.

Tryon,	Holy Cross,	Rev. CHARLES FERRIS.

Tryon,	Mission (col.),	Rev. WILLIAM WALKER.
Wadesboro,	CALVARY,	Rev. CHARLES C. QUIN.
	*W. A. Smith.	J. A. Little.
	T. B. Wyatt.	J. I. Dunlap.
	J. A. Lockhart.	J. E. Hill.
	W. L. Steele.	J. M. Little.
Walnut Cove,	†*Christ Church*,	Rev. CHARLES FETTER.
Warren County,	St. Luke's (col.),	Rev. WILLIAM WALKER.
Warrenton,	All Saints (col.),	Rev. JOHN F. MILBANK.
Warrenton,	EMMANUEL,	Rev. JOHN F. MILBANK.
	*A. B. Cayce.	
	*W. G. Rogers.	

Watauga and Mitchell Counties.
Boone, St. Luke's.
Valle Crucis, St. John's.
Blowing Rock.
Bakersville.
Cranberry.
Linville.

Waynesville,	†*Grace*,	Rev. W. S. BARROWS.
Weldon,	GRACE.	
	D. E. Stainback.	T. A. Clark.
	William M. Cohen.	*J. E. Shields, M.D.
Wilkesboro,	ST. PAUL'S,	Rev. R. W. BARBER.
	John T. Reden.	
	*A. B. Galloway.	
Wilkes County,	Gwyn's Chapel,	Rev. R. W. BARBER.
Williamsboro,	ST. JOHN'S,	Rev. W. S. PETTIGREW.
	William T. Hardy.	
	R. H. Royster.	
	Nat. D. Boyd.	
	Walter B. Thomas.	
Wilson,	St. Mark's (col.),	Rev. J. W. PERRY.
Wilson,	ST. TIMOTHY'S,	Rev. C. J. WINGATE.
	H. G. Connor.	J. B. Stickney.
	*T. C. Davis.	E. G. Rawlings.
	John E. Woodard.	T. N. Jones.
Winston,	ST. PAUL'S,	Rev. JOHN F. GEORGE.
	*H. D. Law.	*A. B. Daingerfield.
	*J. C. Buxton.	J. A. Coles.
	*E. C. Edmunds.	H. H. S. Handy.
	A. Coleman.	W. R. Leak.
Yadkin Valley,	Chapel of Rest and Chapel of Peace,	Rev. Jarvis Buxton, D.D.

JOURNAL OF PROCEEDINGS.

The seventy-eighth Annual Convention of the Diocese of North Carolina assembled in St. Paul's Church, Winston, at 10 o'clock A. M. on Wednesday, the 16th day of May, 1894.

The Bishop of the Diocese called the Convention to order and offered prayers.

The Secretary called the roll, and thirty-five of the Clergy, and Lay Delegates from sixteen Parishes, answered to their names. The Convention was thereupon declared duly organized.

On motion of the Rev. Dr. Marshall, the Rt. Rev. Dr. Rondthaler, of Salem, was invited to an honorary seat in the Convention, and, being introduced by Bishop Cheshire, made a brief address of welcome to the members of the Convention.

A recess was then taken in order to attend Divine Service at 11 o'clock.

The Litany was said by the Rev. John A. Deal, and the Bishop of the Diocese proceeded to the celebration of the Holy Communion. The Rev. Dr. Buxton read the Epistle and the Rev. Dr. Marshall, the Gospel. The Rev. Charles J. Wingate preached the sermon from the texts, St. John X, 15, and II, 25: "As the Father knoweth me, even so know I the Father," and "He knew what was in man."

The Bishop was assisted in the distribution of the elements by the Rev. John F. George, rector of the Parish.

The offerings of the congregation were appropriated to the New York Bible and Common Prayer-Book Society.

At the conclusion of Divine Service, the Bishop took the chair and announced the first business to be the election

of a President of the Convention. The Rev. C. C. Quin
nominated the Rev. M. M. Marshall, D.D. There being no
other nomination, the Secretary was, on motion, instructed
to cast the vote of the Convention, and Dr. Marshall was
declared elected.

The election of a Secretary being next in order, Mr. John
Wilkes nominated the Rev. Julian E. Ingle. There being no
other nomination, the Chairman was, on motion, requested
to cast the vote of the Convention, and he was declared
elected.

On motion of Mr. J. C. Buxton, amended by Mr. John
Wilkes, it was

Resolved, That the daily sessions of the Convention shall begin with
Morning Prayer at 9 o'clock, and that a recess shall be taken from 12:30
to 3 o'clock P. M.

On motion, it was

Resolved, That Clergymen of the Diocese, not being members of the
Convention, visiting Clergymen, and Candidates for Orders, present in
the house, be invited to honorary seats in the Convention.

On motion, the Convention then took a recess until 3:30
o'clock P. M.

WEDNESDAY, May 16, 3:30 P. M.

The Convention re-assembled and was called to order by
the President. The roll having been called, the Bishop
took the chair.

The Secretary announced the appointment of Mr. G. C.
Lamb, of Henderson, as Assistant Secretary.

The Rev. Dr. Marshall presented the following

REPORT OF THE STANDING COMMITTEE.

The Standing Committee met for organization on the 22d of May, 1893,
when the Rev. M. M. Marshall, D.D., was elected President, and the
Rev. Robert B. Sutton, D.D., Secretary.

St. Clair Hester, a Candidate for Orders and a student of the General Theological Seminary, was recommended to be ordered Deacon by the Bishop of New York with the consent and approval of the Bishop of this Diocese. Thomas Burke Bailey (colored) was recommended to be received as a Candidate for Holy Orders; the Rev. Alvin Jones Vander bogart (Deacon) was recommended for ordination to the Priesthood, the time to be fixed by the Bishop, in his discretion, and the consent of the Committee was given to the consecration of the Rev. William Lawrence, D.D , Bishop-elect of the Diocese of Massachusetts, and to the consecration of the Rev. Thomas Frank Gailor, D D., Assistant Bishop-elect of the Diocese of Tennessee.

June 5, 1893. The Committee gave its consent to the consecration of the Rev. Ellison Capers, D.D., Assistant Bishop-elect of the Diocese of South Carolina.

July 4, 1893. Messrs. Frederick A. and Charles Fetter were recommended to be ordered Deacons at any time on or after December 21, 1893. At this meeting the testimonials and certificate of the election of the Rev. Joseph Blount Cheshire, Jr., D.D., Rector of St. Peter's Church, Charlotte, to be Assistant Bishop of this Diocese, were presented, accredited and duly signed by all the members of the Committee. The President was requested to send copies of said testimonials and certificate to the several Standing Committees and ask their assent to his consecration.

The Rt. Rev. T. B. Lyman, D.D., LL.D., Bishop of the Diocese, having previous to the election given his consent in writing to the election of an Assistant Bishop, and having stated the duties which "he assigns to the Assistant Bishop when duly elected and consecrated," according to the provisions of Title I, Canon XIX, section 5 of the Digest, this consent and assignment of duty was laid before the Committee, and the President was requested to put it on file.

October 10, 1893. The President reported that up to the 15th of September he had received the consent of twenty-seven of the fifty-three Standing Committees, and that he had at once informed the Presiding Bishop of the fact; that on the 7th of October the Assistant Bishop-elect had telegraphed him that the consent of a majority of the Bishops had been given to his consecration and that the 15th of October had been appointed for that sacred function in Calvary Church, Tarboro.

The President read an invitation from General Cotten, Chairman of the Committee of Arrangements of Calvary Church, Tarboro, inviting the Standing Committee to attend the consecration services. On motion, the invitation was accepted with thanks, and the President was requested to inform General Cotten of the fact.

The Bishop asked the approval of the Committee in the proposed appropriation of certain Missionary Funds conditionally placed in his hands, as follows: $75 to the Rev. James D. Miller and $50 to the Rev. Samuel Rhodes, which request was unanimously granted.

The President also presented a communication from the Rev. Thomas S. Bacon, of Buckeystown, Maryland, alleging that the Rev. A. C. A. Hall, M.A. (Oxon.), Bishop-elect of Vermont, was unsound in doctrine, and requesting to be allowed time to produce his proofs. The President was requested to ask the Rev. Dr. Bacon for his evidence, and the meeting adjourned.

November 9, 1893. A communication from the Rev. T. S. Bacon with reference to the Bishop-elect of Vermont was read and carefully considered. It was then unanimously resolved, his testimonials and credentials having been found in due and canonical form, that the consent of this Committee be given to the consecration of the Rev. Arthur Crawshay Alliston Hall, M.A. (Oxon.), Bishop-elect of the Diocese of Vermont.

December 14, 1893. The Committee, at the request of Bishop Cheshire, met at the Rectory of Christ Church, Raleigh, and adopted the following resolution:

"The Standing Committee having learned with very great regret and sorrow of the death of the late Rt. Rev. Theodore Benedict Lyman, D.D., LL.D., D.C.L., the fourth Bishop of this Diocese, on the morning of the 13th instant, at his residence in this city, therefore

"*Resolved*, That the Rev. M. M. Marshall, D.D., the Rev. Bennett Smedes, D.D., and the Secretary be requested to draw up and present to the next meeting of this Committee an expression of our deep feeling at the sad event which deprives each one of us of a personal friend and the Diocese of a faithful and laborious Bishop.

The President presented a communication from the Standing Committee of the Diocese of Georgia expressing their deep regret that they were deprived of the pleasure of giving their consent to the consecration of Bishop Cheshire in consequence of misplaced papers and the consequent delay in having the matter brought before them.

The Bishop having asked counsel of the Committee in the matter, it was resolved as the sense of this Committee that the Rt. Rev. Joseph Blount Cheshire, Jr., D.D., having become Bishop of the Diocese in consequence of the death of Bishop Lyman, should cancel certain of his appointments and remain in the city in order to look over such papers and records as the late Bishop may have left with reference to the Diocese.

January 4, 1894. The Secretary read the report of the Committee appointed at the last meeting to make a minute of the sentiments of this Committee on the death of our late Bishop, as follows:

"This Committee has heard with profound sorrow of the departure of our greatly revered and dearly beloved Bishop, the Rt. Rev. T. B. Lyman, D.D., LL.D , D.C.L., and desire to put on record our appreciation of his worth and services for so many years both as a Bishop and as a man.

"He was the devout Christian, the earnest, forcible preacher, the warm friend, the liberal giver. Through his generosity numbers of churches in weak places have been completed and others much adorned; and not a few of his Clergy have been cheered by his thoughtful kindness in their hour of need.

"We thank our Heavenly Father that his departure was in peace and with so little suffering.

"We deeply sympathize with his widow and his children in their great bereavement, and implore Almighty God to sanctify it to their spiritual good.

"*Resolved,* That the above be spread on the minutes of this body, and that a copy be transmitted to the afflicted widow."

At this meeting, also, Thomas C. Wetmore was recommended to be ordered Deacon on the Wednesday after the first Sunday in Lent, February 14th, or on any day thereafter at the Bishop's convenience.

February 14, 1894. The Rev. Benjamin Sumner McKenzie (Deacon) was recommended for ordination to the Priesthood.

March 13, 1894. The Committee gave its consent to the consecration of the Rev. John Brockenbrough Newton, M.D., Assistant Bishop-elect of the Diocese of Virginia.

April 24, 1894. George V. Gilreath was recommended to be ordered Deacon at any time on or after July 27, 1894, and Nathan A. Seagle was also recommended for ordination to the Diaconate.

The application of S. A. B. Trott (colored) for recommendation to be ordered Deacon was presented to the Committee; but the papers having been found to be defective, action in this case was deferred. The President was requested to prepare the report of the Committee for the past year and present it to the approaching Diocesan Convention.

April 27, 1894. At the request of the Bishop of the Diocese, and for reasons satisfactory to the Committee, the required term of candidateship in the case of George V. Gilreath, applicant for Deacon's Orders, was recommended to be shortened by the space of two months and seven days under the provisions of Section 3, Canon VII, Title I of the Digest.

Respectfully submitted for the Committee,

M. M. MARSHALL,
President.

On motion of Mr. R. H. Battle, the Rev. Dr. Marshall was granted leave of absence in order that he might attend the funeral of a member of his Parish.

Mr. R. H. Battle presented the following

REPORT OF THE TRUSTEES OF THE DIOCESE.

The Trustees to hold property for the Diocese of North Carolina submit their annual report as follows:

They have received the following deeds of conveyance for the benefit of the Diocese not heretofore reported:

1. Deed from John T. Patrick, for himself and as attorney for others, for lot, 100 feet square, on New York Avenue in the town of Southern Pines, Moore county, dated May 15, 1889, and registered November 14, 1890, in Register's office for Moore, in Deed Book No. 2, at page 523.

2. Deed from Rebecca M. Kimberly, Thomas M. Kimberly and others, for one acre in Beaver Dam Township, Buncombe county, "for the purpose of establishing a church, rectory and school-house," etc., dated August 18, 1891, and registered in Buncombe county, in Book 83 of Deeds, at page 142, June 17, 1893.

3. Deed from John W. Scott and wife, for lot No. 38 in the town of Sanford, Moore county, 100 feet squaie, dated December 11, 1893, and registered in Moore, in Book No. 11, at page 236, December 26, 1893

4. Deed from Lillie A. Rose to J. F. Payne, S. S. McCauley and C. M. T. McCauley, for lot No. 68 in the town of Monroe, Union county, containing 36,642 square feet, for expressed consideration of $1,000, dated June 16, 1885, and registered in Union, in Book 15, at page 200, June 17, 1885.

5. Deed for same lot from J. F. Payne, S. S. McCauley and C. M. T. McCauley to Trustees of the Diocese, dated December 21, 1893, and registered in Union, January 6, 1894, in Book 24, at page 259.

6. Deed for lot of about one-half an acre, on Morehead street, in the town of Burlington, Alamance county, from William A. Erwin and wife, dated December 1, 1892, and registered in Alamance, September 15, 1893, in Book No. 16, at page 280.

7. Deed from W. C. Dunlop and wife, for 30½ acres in Sheffield Township, Moore county, dated January 10, 1894, and registered January 15, 1894, in Moore, in Book No. 10, at page 314.

8. Deed from Mary A. Stedman and husband, Nathan A. Stedman, for lot on Main street, in the town of Germanton, Stokes county, 94 by 140 feet, dated February 8, 1894, and registered April 2, 1894, in Book No. 35, at page 389, in Stokes.

Mr. J. T. Patrick has applied to the Trustees for a reconveyance to him and his associates of the lot in Southern Pines, numbered 1 in the foregoing list. The ground of his application is that the lot was conveyed as a site for a church building, and with the condition, orally expressed at the time, that there should be such building erected on it in a reasonable time, and that that was the consideration and inducement of the conveyance, and that subsequently the late Rev. Mr. Thorne made a trade with him for another lot for the erection of a church, with the understanding that the one previously conveyed should be reconveyed to him. He expresses the purpose, if such reconveyance is made, to donate the lot to a charitable organization. Under the circumstances the Trustees are of opinion that the reconveyance should be made, and they recommend that they be authorized to make it.

The Trustees, for a statement in respect to the invested funds and securities in their hands or subject to their control, respectfully refer to the Treasurer's report to this Convention at pages 19 *et seq.*

Respectfully submitted,

Jos. BLOUNT CHESHIRE, JR.,
CHAS. E. JOHNSON,
R. H. BATTLE,

WINSTON, N. C., May 16, 1894. *Trustees, etc.*

On motion of Mr. Battle, it was

Resolved, That for the reasons set forth in the report of the Trustees of the Diocese, the said Trustees be authorized to execute to John T. Patrick, or to such other person or persons as he shall designate, a deed of quitclaim for the lot in Southern Pines, N. C., conveyed to the Trustees by deed dated May 15, 1889.

The Bishop announced the appointment of the Regular Committees, as follows:

On Canons:

The Rev. Wm. R. Wetmore, D.D.	Mr. R. H. Battle.
The Rev. James A. Weston.	Mr. J. C. Buxton.
The Rev. McNeely DuBose.	

On the State of the Church:

The Rev. F. J. Murdoch, D.D.	Mr. Fred. Philips.
The Rev. Walter J. Smith.	Mr. John H. Pearson.
The Rev. A. B. Hunter.	

On Finance:

The Rev. R. B. Sutton, D.D.	Mr. R. S. Tucker.
The Rev. Bennett Smedes, D.D.	Mr. Chas. G. Latta.
	Mr. F. P. Haywood, Jr.

On Elections:

The Rev. R. W. Barber.	Mr. J. S. Myers.
The Rev. C. C. Quin.	Mr. S. F. Lord.
	Mr. F. S. Spruill.

4

On New Parishes:

The Rev. Girard W. Phelps.	Mr. Wm. S. Martin.
The Rev. Charles Ferris.	Mr. Wm. A. Smith.
	Mr. Thos. C. Davis.

On Unfinished Business:

The Rev. Wm. Walker.	Mr. Paul C. Graham.
The Rev. Gaston Battle.	Mr. N. K. Smith.
	Mr. J. E. Shields, M.D.

The Rev. Dr. Murdoch moved to refer to the Committee on Canons a resolution to amend Chapter II, Canon I, Section 1, of the Canons of the Diocese, by changing the word *four* to *five*, and by inserting the words *of Salisbury* after the words *of Raleigh.*

The motion was agreed to.

Mr. Charles E. Johnson presented his report as Treasurer of the Diocese. (See Appendix C).

The Rev. Dr. Sutton presented the following

REPORT OF THE COMMITTEE ON FINANCE.

The Finance Committee beg leave to report that they have examined the several accounts of the Treasurer and find them all correct, and that the several balances named in his report are on deposit in the Citizens National Bank of Raleigh. They also find that all the securities specified on page 3 of Appendix C are in his hands and are kept securely in a box lodged in the Citizens National Bank of Raleigh.

For further particulars attention is called to the annual statement of the Treasurer submitted herewith and marked Appendix C.

The Finance Committee recommend that the schedule of assessments remain the same as shown in the Treasurer's report, with the exception of Calvary Church, Wadesboro, which should be placed at $50 for the present year.

The Committee unanimously recommend that the notes given for the increase of the Permanent Episcopal Fund be collected; that one-fourth be used for the Current Episcopal and Contingent Fund, and the remainder applied to a fund for the purchase of an Episcopal Residence in the city of Raleigh.

The Committee, therefore, beg leave to offer the following resolutions:

"*Resolved 1,* That the Trustees of the Diocese be authorized to purchase from Mrs. Susan Robertson Lyman, widow of the late Bishop Lyman, for an Episcopal Residence, part of the lot formerly occupied by Bishop Lyman in the city of Raleigh, fronting 164 feet on North street, at the corner of Wilmington and North streets, and running back in a rectangular form as far as may be about 350 feet, at the price of $9,000, payable in such manner and upon such terms as may be agreed upon between the Trustees and Mrs. Lyman.

"*Resolved 2*, That upon the purchase of the said lot for an Episcopal Residence, the Bishop of the Diocese shall be privileged to occupy the same as his home free of rent; the Treasurer of the Diocese to pay the insurance on the buildings, but all ordinary repairs to be paid for by the Bishop as tenant."   For the Committee,

ROBT. B. SUTTON,
Chairman.

The report was, on motion of Mr. John Wilkes, made the order of the day for 11 o'clock on Thursday morning.

The Rev. Julian E. Ingle moved that a committee of three be appointed to present to the Convention resolutions of respect to the memory of the late Rev. Franklin L. Bush. The motion was agreed to, and the Chair appointed as such committee the Rev. A. B. Hunter, the Rev. I. McK. Pittenger and Mr. W. L. London.

Mr. R. H. Battle offered the following resolution:

Resolved, That Article III, section 3 of the Constitution of the Diocese, be amended by substituting the word *six* for the word *twelve*, so as to read, *six calendar months.*

Mr. J. B. Batchelor moved to amend by changing the words *six calendar months* to *one calendar month.*

The resolution and amendment were, on motion, referred to the Committee on Canons.

The Rev. William Stanley Barrows offered the following resolution, which, on his motion, was referred to the Committee on Canons:

Resolved, That hereafter all deeds conveying property to the Trustees of the Diocese of North Carolina be printed in full in the Journal of Convention.

The Secretary moved the appointment of a Special Committee to consider certain changes in the form of the Parochial Reports, and to report the same to this Convention. The Chair appointed the Rev. A. J. Vanderbogart, Mr. G. C. Lamb and Mr. James D. Glenn.

On motion, the Convention adjourned.

At 8 o'clock P. M. Evening Prayer was said by the Rev. John F. Milbank and a sermon was preached by the Rev. Stewart McQueen.

SECOND DAY.

St. Paul's Church, Winston,
Thursday, May 17, 1894.

The Convention met at 9 o'clock.

Morning Prayer was said by the Rev. Messrs. J. W. Barker and John F. George.

The Convention was called to order by the Bishop.

The calling of the roll was, on motion, dispensed with, and the minutes of yesterday's proceedings were read and approved.

Upon nomination of Mr. John Wilkes, the Rev. F. J. Murdoch, D.D., was, on motion, elected President *pro tempore* of the Convention.

The Bishop read his Annual Address. (See Appendix A).

On motion of the Rev. William R. Wetmore, D.D., the address was referred to the Committee on the State of the Church.

Mr. R. H. Battle presented the following paper:

THE RT. REV. THEODORE BENEDICT LYMAN, D.D., LL.D., D.C.L.

REPORT OF A COMMITTEE APPOINTED AT A MEETING OF THE CLERGY AND LAITY ATTENDING THE FUNERAL OF THE LATE BISHOP LYMAN, THE RT. REV. JOSEPH BLOUNT CHESHIRE, Jr, D D, PRESIDING, DECEMBER 15, 1893.

The Committee appointed to draft resolutions expressive of the feeling of the Clergy and Laity of the Diocese of North Carolina in reference to the death of the late Bishop Lyman, do report:

Theodore Benedict Lyman was born at Brighton, Mass., on the 27th day of November, 1815. He was educated at Hamilton College, at Clinton, New York. Graduating from the General Theological Seminary in New York City in the summer of 1840, he was ordained Deacon in Christ Church, Baltimore, by the Rt. Rev. William R. Whittingham, D.D., Bishop of Maryland, September 20, 1840. He was ordained Priest by the same Prelate on December 19th of the following year at Hagerstown, Md , where he was Rector of St. John's Church for a period of ten years. During this time he was largely instrumental in the establishment of St. James College, a Church institution of large influence far beyond the limits of the State of Maryland. In 1843 he received and declined a call to the rectorate of St. James Church, Wilmington, N. C.

In 1850 he was called to the rectorship of Trinity Church, Pittsburgh, Pa., where he remained for another period of ten years of efficient service.

In 1860 he took his family abroad, and, after making a tour of Europe and establishing a Chapel for Americans in Florence, settled in Rome and established regular services for the American community in that city in spite of some opposition from the papal authorities; and having resigned his Parish in Pittsburgh, he continued his residence abroad until the year 1870, when he accepted the charge of Trinity Church, San Francisco. While resident in Rome he was elected Dean of the General Theological Seminary, but declined that important position. He represented the Diocese of California in the General Convention of 1871, and rendered the Church conspicuous service by the introduction of a resolution whereby the question of certain ritual observances, which deeply agitated the minds of members of the Convention, and of Churchmen generally throughout the country, was postponed, and never revived.

At the Annual Convention of the Diocese of North Carolina in 1873, upon the recommendation of Bishop Atkinson, he was elected Assistant Bishop, and consecrated in Christ Church, Raleigh, on the 11th day of December following; the Presiding Bishop on that occasion being the Rt. Rev. Dr. Whittingham, who was assisted in the consecration by Bishops Atkinson and Lay. Upon the death of Bishop Atkinson on the 4th day of January 1881, Bishop Lyman succeeded to his office as Diocesan.

In 1883 the Diocese was divided, and he chose to continue in charge of the Diocese of North Carolina.

In 1886 he was appointed by the Presiding Bishop of the Church to the Episcopal charge of the American Congregations on the Continent of Europe, and spent several months in visiting them.

At the Annual Convention held in May, 1893, owing to his age and occasional attacks of illness, which impaired his strength, he recommended the election of an Assistant Bishop, and at an adjourned meeting of the Convention in June following, the Rev. Dr. Joseph Blount Cheshire, Jr., was chosen as his Coadjutor. On the 15th of October Bishop Lyman presided at the consecration of Dr. Cheshire in Calvary Church, Tarboro.

On the 20th of December 1891, the fiftieth anniversary of his ordination to the Priesthood was celebrated in the Churches of Raleigh, and he delivered an address setting forth the principal events of his life and ministry. He had just passed the twentieth year of his consecration to the Episcopate when he died at his home in Raleigh, on the morning of December 13, 1893. His last work was an effort to prepare an address to be delivered in Christ Church, Raleigh, on the eve of the anniversary, but a sudden attack of illness prevented its completion. His funeral took place from Christ Church at 1 o'clock on Friday, December 15th, and was attended by Bishops Watson, Randolph and Cheshire, together with twenty-six of the Clergy and a large number of the Laity. He was buried in Oakwood Cemetery, at Raleigh, in accordance with his wish expressed shortly before his death.

Bishop Lyman was twice married; in his early manhood to Miss Anna Albert, of Baltimore, and in February, 1893, to Miss Susan B. Robertson, of Charleston, S. C. By his last will and testament, a considerable portion of his property was given to the Church and its charities.

The degree of Doctor of Divinity was conferred upon Bishop Lyman by St. James' College, Maryland, and that of Doctor of Laws by the University of North Carolina; and his *Alma Mater*, Hamilton College, conferred upon him the degree, uncommon in this country, of Doctor of the Canon Law. All his preferments and honors were entirely unsought by him, and no better proof than this could be given of his high character for ability, learning and influence in the Church and in society. His success as a Rector of his several important Parishes, and as Chaplain of an Embassy in Rome, was marked, and indicated that tact, as well as eloquence as a preacher and zeal in the discharge of his pastoral duties, was one of his characteristics; and the full list and *personnel* of the Clergy of this Diocese, and the fact that his twenty years of service as Bishop have witnessed the building of about sixty churches, are evidence that he was no less successful as a Chief Pastor.

Possessed of a fine physique, with a deep and commanding voice, he read the services most impressively, and his sermons, whether he spoke with or without manuscript, were delivered with unction and with power. Those who were privileged to hear him often must have observed that his sermons, whether exegetical or doctrinal, were sound, logical, eloquent and convincing, and it was plain that he recognized it as the great mission of a preacher to present "Jesus Christ and Him crucified" to sinful man, as his only hope of salvation.

As a Churchman, Bishop Lyman was eminently sound and conservative. While he delighted in orderly, and even ornate, services, he had little toleration for what is known as ritualistic practices. By example and precept he taught that both extremes were to be avoided; that thereby none could be offended and the reasonable should be attracted.

In private life Bishop Lyman, while ever sufficiently dignified, was cordial, genial and companionable. In conversation he was interesting and instructive, giving to others freely, but without vanity, the benefit of his wide and varied experience and observation in this country and in the Old World. His generous hospitality, at his beautiful home in Raleigh, is known far and wide, to Laity and to Clergy. During the larger part of his term of service amongst us he was in receipt of a handsome private income, and it is said by those who have reason to know that he gave back to the Diocese more than all the salary he received from it. Our missionaries and poorer churches can tell the story of his unselfish generosity.

Though in his seventy-ninth year when he died, and though, for a few years past he suffered, occasionally, much from insomnia, he retained his physical strength remarkably, almost to the last, and his mental force suffered no abatement. Those who heard him preach on Thanksgiving Day and the second Sunday before his death, were struck with the power of his thought and the force of his delivery. He died in harness, and he was mercifully spared the long period of helplessness which is the lot of many who attain to such an age, and which he much dreaded. Having finished well his life's work, he was permitted speedily, and after but little suffering, to rest from his labors; therefore

Resolved 1, That the Clergy and Laity of this Diocese are justly proud of this record of the labors of our late beloved Bishop for over half a century in the sacred ministry of the Church, and for a score of years as our Chief Pastor, and that for the results of his labors in the Diocese we should thank God and take courage.

2. That the influence of his example should be to inspire each and all of us with a resolve to labor more zealously in the Master's service, and to see to it that none of the Mission Stations established, or supported partly by him, shall languish or perish, but that others shall be added and adequately supported.

3. That while we cannot grieve for the removal to a higher life of one so full of years as well as of honors as we would for one taken nearer life's meridian, the Diocese will sorely miss Bishop Lyman's earnest zeal, his eloquent voice and his generous hand, and, personally, we will long mourn the departure of a dear friend, as well as a beloved spiritual father.

4. That these resolutions and preamble be reported to the next Annual Convention for such action as may be thought appropriate.

Jos. Blount Cheshire, Jr.,
I. McK. Pittenger,
R. B. Sutton,
J. A. Weston,
R. H. Battle,
C. M. Busbee,
H. A. London,
Geo. T. Winston.

Mr. Battle also offered the following resolutions, which were adopted :

Resolved, That the preamble and resolutions of the Committee be approved and adopted as the action of the Convention and published in the Journal; that a memorial page to Bishop Lyman be set apart and that a lithographic likeness of him be inserted in the Journal.

Resolved, That the sense of the Convention be taken by a rising vote

On motion of Mr. Silas McBee, it was

Resolved, That this Diocese will, at some future and fit season, erect to the memory of Bishop Lyman a monumental Church.

On motion of Mr. Charles M. Busbee, it was agreed that the report of the Finance Commitee be made the order of the day at 3, and the report of the Executive Missionary Committee at 4 o'clock this afternoon.

On motion of Mr. F. S. Spruill, a memorial of the Vestry of St. James Church, Kittrell, asking a reduction in its assessment, was referred to the Committee on Finance.

Mr. John Wilkes presented the reports of the Woman's Auxiliary, the Junior Auxiliary, St. Peter's Home and Hospital and the Good Samaritan Hospital, which were referred to the Committee on the State of the Church.   (See Appendix B).

At the instance of the Rev. B. S. McKenzie, the Brotherhood of St. Andrew was invited to hold a public meeting in St. Paul's Church this evening at 8 o'clock.

After the use of the Collect for All Saints' Day, and other prayers by the Bishop, the Convention, on motion, took a recess.

————

THURSDAY, May 17, 3 P. M.

The Convention re-assembled, the Bishop in the chair.

The Rev. Dr. Murdoch presented an application from St. Paul's Parish, Rowan county, for admission into union with the Convention of the Diocese.   The application was, on motion, referred to the Committee on New Parishes.

On motion of the Rev. Dr. Wetmore, the Rev. R. W. Barber was excused from further attendance.

A message was received from the Secretary of the Council of the Diocese of Virginia, as follows:

To the Secretary of the Convention of the Diocese of North Carolina, Winston, N. C.:

The Council of the Diocese of Virginia sends Christian greetings to the Convention of the Diocese of North Carolina.

EVERARD MEADE,
Secretary.

The Secretary of the Convention was instructed to send a suitable reply.

At this point the Bishop retired from the chair, which was taken by the Rev. Dr. Murdoch.

The order of the day being called for, Mr. Charles E. Johnson moved the passage of the resolutions appended to the report of the Finance Committee.

Mr. R. H. Battle moved to amend the resolutions so that they should read as follows:

1. *Resolved*, That the notes given for the increase of the Permanent Episcopal Fund be collected; that one fourth of the amount be used for the Current Episcopal and Contingent Fund and the remainder added to the Permanent Episcopal Fund.

2. *Resolved*, That the Trustees of the Diocese be authorized to purchase, out of the Permanent Episcopal Fund, from Mrs. Susan Robertson Lyman, widow of the late Bishop Lyman, for an Episcopal Residence, part of the lot formerly occupied by Bishop Lyman, in the city of Raleigh, fronting 164 feet on North street, at the corner of Wilmington and North streets, and running back in a rectangular form as far as may be about 350 feet, at the price of $9,000, payable in such manner and upon such terms as may be agreed upon between the Trustees and Mrs. Lyman.

3. *Resolved*, That upon the purchase of the said lot for an Episcopal Residence, the Bishop of the Diocese shall be privileged to occupy the same as his home free of rent—the Treasurer of the Diocese to pay the insurance on the buildings, but all ordinary repairs to be paid for by the Bishop as tenant.

The amendment was, on motion, agreed to, and the resolutions as amended were adopted.

5

On motion, the Convention proceeded to the election of a Treasurer. The Rev. Dr. Sutton nominated Mr. Charles E. Johnson, and, in the absence of any other nomination, the Secretary was, on motion, instructed to cast the vote of the Convention, and Mr. Johnson was declared elected.

The hour having arrived for the consideration of the order of the day, the Rev. Scott B. Rathbun presented the following

REPORT OF THE EXECUTIVE MISSIONARY COMMITTEE.

The Executive Missionary Committee respectfully submits this report of the work for the past year, which has been regulated in accordance with the following resolution, adopted on the third day of the last Convention, and found on page 48 of the Journal of 1893:

Resolved, That the Executive Missionary Committee be authorized and directed to employ an agent and secretary, to be designated as the Executive Secretary of Diocesan Missions, and to pay him out of the Missionary Funds of the Diocese such annual compensation as they may deem proper. It shall be the duty of such Secretary, at least once each quarter, to call a meeting of the Committee at such time and place as may be designated by the Chairman; to attend the same and to keep the records thereof; also to acquaint himself, as far as possible, with the condition and needs of the Missionary field, and to urge upon the Rectors of Parishes and the people thereof, personally or otherwise, a more zealous and systematic contribution to the Missionary Fund of the Diocese.

Accordingly, at its first meeting, held during the session of the same Convention, it elected the Rev. F. S. Stickney to this office, and fixed the salary at $500 for six months' service. At the same time it confirmed a list of appropriations, submitted by the Treasurer, aggregating $1,500 for the current year.

At the next meeting of the Committee, held in Calvary Church, Tarboro, October 15, 1893, the resignation of the Rev. Mr. Stickney was received and accepted, and the Rev. Scott B. Rathbun was elected Executive Secretary. The salary was fixed at $400 and expenses, for the equivalent of five months' service, to be performed at any time within the year, as might appear most advantageous to the work. The Treasurer reported, through the Bishop, that few contributions to the Missionary Fund were being received, and that there was no balance in the treasury with which to meet the quarter's stipends then due. Examination of the records showed that many of the Parishes were not complying with the provisions of the Canon in regard to offerings for Diocesan Missions, that this method of collecting funds had proved itself inadequate to our needs, and that the amount contributed to this purpose was growing less each year.

It was, therefore, evident to all that some radical change was necessary if we were to meet even those extremely limited obligations which had already been assumed for the current year.

Accordingly, the Committee decided to adopt a system of monthly pledges and endeavor to interest therein every member of all the Parishes and Mission Stations in the Diocese, and as a first step in this direction the Executive Secretary was instructed to forward to every Clergyman in charge of a congregation a copy of the following letter, together with a statement of the plan proposed, and such further appeal as he might deem advisable, or a request to be permitted to present this subject in person to some of the larger congregations.

In pursuance of these instructions, the Secretary prepared and mailed, on October 23, 1893, fifty-seven copies of this

PASTORAL LETTER OF THE BISHOPS.

"Tarboro, October 16, 1893.

"Rev. and Dear Brother:—The Treasurer of the Diocesan Board of Missions reports a most lamentable state of affairs; no balance in the treasury and stipends due upon which our hard-worked Missionaries depend for daily bread. *Our duty is clear.* Every effort should be put forth to remedy this condition at the earliest possible day.

" With this end in view, and in accordance with the action of the last Diocesan Convention, the Executive Missionary Committee has elected as Executive Secretary the Rev. Scott B. Rathbun, who will endeavor to put in operation certain measures which, the Committee believes, will result in infusing new life into our Missionary work, *provided* the Clergy give requisite support and co-operation.

" We earnestly commend this subject to your consideration and ask that you do everything in your power to assist in establishing and executing a systematic plan of offerings for this work. The plan which the Secretary will communicate to you has our hearty approval.

"Please accord him hearty co-operation.

"Faithfully yours,
"Theo. B. Lyman,
"*Bishop of North Carolina.*
"Jos. Blount Cheshire, Jr.,
"*Assistant Bishop.*"

From eighteen of the Clergy to whom this letter was sent the Secretary requested the privilege of presenting the subject to their congregations in person at an early day; to the balance he inclosed blanks for subscriptions and a copy of the following letter, requesting that they should endeavor to put the plan in operation at once, without waiting for a personal visit from him:

"FLAT ROCK, N. C., October 20, 1893.

"MY DEAR BROTHER:—There should be no need of addressing the Clergy on the importance of our Missionary work, nor of arguing the point of our *duty* in sustaining it; but they may need to be reminded that the failure of the Laity to appreciate *their* duty in the premises is too often caused by the neglect of their Pastors to urge it upon them. They know but little of the extent of our Mission field, or of the character and needs of the work which we have in hand.

"Those needs are great, but would be more generously supplied were they thoroughly understood. Every man, woman and child within our jurisdiction would be willing, nay, *eager* to do their utmost towards this work could they once be impressed with its importance, and for this the Church naturally looks to her Clergy.

"Shall she look to *you* in vain?

"Do your people say: 'Ours is Missionary ground itself, and should be expected to require aid, not give it'? True; yet we must not overlook the great moral influence of the spectacle of every baptized member of Christ recognizing individual responsibility for the spread of His Gospel and giving freely toward this cause, even though that gift be small, and return to one's own door to accomplish the object of its mission. Such *general* offerings *only* will infuse spirit and energy into our now lifeless and half-hearted Missionary efforts. This conscientious giving of weaker Stations must inevitably stimulate the wealthier Parishes to larger gifts, and this "bread cast upon the waters" will surely return to those Mission fields, not "after many days," but in the very near future.

"But to produce adequate results this giving must be steady and systematic, not spasmodic, that the Committee may lay plans with some degree of confidence and prosecute them without those disastrous interruptions, through unexpected lack of funds, which have been so common in the past.

"With this end in view the Committee desires that you present this duty, in its strongest light, to all your people. Organize in each Parish and Station a Diocesan Missionary Guild (or Committee) of two or more ladies who will undertake the responsibility of securing monthly pledges on the inclosed blank, collecting and forwarding the same on the first of each month. Surely there can be but few baptized members of the Church who would not be glad to pledge themselves for at least five cents per month for this cause; but with this small amount, even from communicants only, our work could be more than doubled at once. Many, doubtless, would make much larger pledges, but the *influence* of these smaller gifts will be incalculable.

"To increase the general interest and keep all our people informed as to the progress of the work, it is proposed to publish a new monthly journal, in which offerings will be acknowledged and to which contributions of news items are solicited from all interested. We hope to be able to send a copy into every family represented on these subscription lists. Please send a brief account of your work and the most pressing needs of your field for early publication.

"Let us one and all "awake out of sleep," accept our responsibilities and endeavor to do our full duty as "members incorporate in the mystical Body of Christ." Please report progress at an early day.

"Faithfully yours,

"SCOTT B. RATHBUN,

" *Executive Secretary.*"

Thus prior to the 25th of October the joint appeals of the Secretary, the Committee and the Bishops were in the hands of fifty-seven individuals, representing ninety Parishes and Stations from which aid for our Missionary Work could reasonably be expected; but when the Committee held its next meeting three months later at Raleigh, January 17, 1894, only sixteen of this number had made any response whatever to these communications, and of these only eight promised speedy and full co-operation in the plans adopted by the Board; the Secretary was accordingly directed to communicate again with those who had failed to reply, asking that they inform him at once as to what they proposed to do in regard to this system of pledges.

At this meeting the Committee considered it necessary, in spite of the discouraging report of the Treasurer, to add to the list of appropriations at the rate of $300 per annum, making a total now pledged of $1,800 per annum, besides the salary of the Secretary.

These appropriations are distributed among twelve Missionaries, as follows: $700 to five in the Convocation of Asheville, $500 to one in the Convocation of Raleigh, $400 to four in the Convocation of Charlotte and $200 to two in the Convocation of Tarboro. Eight of these stipends are at the rate of $100 per annum, two at $150, one at $200 and one at $500.

At this meeting also the *Messenger of Hope* was indorsed and recommended as a valuable assistant in furthering the work of Missions, and the manager was directed to send a sample copy into every family in the Diocese with a request to subscribe. The Committee hope that this paper will receive that substantial support which is necessary to its continuance, and to this end recommend a very easy plan by which this may be accomplished, viz., that the Convocations, Brotherhood of St. Andrew and the Woman's Auxiliary each pledge themselves to furnish a definite number of subscribers sufficient to insure the permanence of this useful adjunct to our Mission Work. The undertaking is easily within the reach of all these organizations and lies directly in line with their regular work.

In accordance with the instructions of the Committee, the Secretary, on January 22, 1894, sent a second letter to those of the Clergy who failed to respond to former communications, asking them to inform the Committee, at their earliest convenience, what they had done, were doing or proposed to do in regard to this system of monthly pledges; but although seven months have now elapsed since the date of the first letter, more than half of the Clergy have not yet found it convenient to furnish this important information; a fact which needs no further comment, but serves to illustrate some of the difficulties under which this Committee labors.

The Executive Secretary has presented the subject personally to eighteen congregations and the system has been adopted by twenty-six, in most cases with greatly encouraging results; from these it seems manifest that the general introduction of this pledge system, with reasonable co-operation on the part of the Clergy, would largely increase the funds at the disposal of the Missionary Treasury.

With a view to securing greater efficiency in the operation of our Missionary machinery the Committee recommend the following amendments to the Canons bearing upon this subject:

1. *Resolved*, That Chapter I, Canon VIII, Section 1, be amended to read:

In addition to the Standing Committee there shall be elected annually the following Committees, of which the Bishop shall be Chairman *ex-officio*, viz.: An Education Committee, to consist of three; a Church Building Committee, to consist of five; and an Executive Missionary Committee, composed as follows: The Bishop, the Deans of Convocations and the Treasurer of the Diocese, *ex-officio;* four Laymen to be elected by the Convention and an Executive Secretary to be elected by the Committee, any four of whom shall constitute a quorum.

The balance of section 1 to remain as now.

2. *Resolved*, That to Chapter I, Canon VIII, Section 3, be added as follows:

It shall be the duty of the Executive Secretary to call a meeting of the Committee at least once each quarter, at such time and place as the Chairman may designate; to attend the same and keep the records thereof; to acquaint himself as far as possible with the condition and needs of the Missionary field, and to urge upon both Clergy and Laity throughout the Diocese, personally or otherwise, a more zealous and systematic contribution to the Missionary Fund. His salary shall be determined by the Committee and shall be paid from the Missionary Treasury.

3. *Resolved*, That Chapter I, Canon XIV, be amended to read:

SECTION 1. It shall be the duty of every Clergyman of the Diocese to make collections in all congregations under his charge, at least once in each year, in aid of the Education Fund, the Church Building Fund and the Relief Fund of the Diocese.

Sec. 2. It shall also be the duty of the Minister in charge of each congregation in the Diocese to obtain through the agency of the Laity, from every member of the same, if possible, an individual subscription, payable monthly, to the Diocesan Missionary Fund, and to provide for the prompt and regular collection and remittance of the same to the Treasurer.

4. *Resolved,* That Chapter II, Canon I, Section 1, be amended to read:

The Diocese shall be divided into *five* Missionary Convocations, with boundaries to be determined by the Convocations with consent of the Bishop, and to be styled the Convocations of Tarboro, of Raleigh, of Salisbury, of Charlotte and of Asheville.

By order of the Committee,

SCOTT B. RATHBUN,
Executive Secretary.

Mr. William L. London moved to refer all proposed changes to the Committee on Canons, to report at 10 o'clock to-morrow morning.

On motion of Mr. C. E. Johnson, unanimous consent was given for the consideration of the amendments without reference to the Committee on Canons.

The Resolution 1 of the Committee being under consideration, Mr. John Wilkes moved to amend by substituting *five* for *four* wherever the word occurs in the resolution.

The amendment was, on motion, agreed to, and the resolution as amended was adopted.

On motion of Mr. William L. London, Resolution 2 was amended so as to read as follows:

Resolved, That to Chapter I, Canon VIII, Section 3, be added the following words, viz.:

The duties of the Executive Secretary shall be such as the Committee may from time to time designate. His salary shall be determined by the Committee and shall be paid from the Missionary Treasury.

The resolution as amended was adopted.

In lieu of Resolution 3 of the Committee, it was, on motion of Mr. C. E. Johnson,

Resolved, That Chapter I, Canon XIV, be amended so as to read as follows:

Section 1. It shall be the duty of every Clergyman of the Diocese to make a collection in the Parish or Parishes under his charge at least once in each year in aid of the Education Fund, the Church Building Fund and the Relief Fund of the Diocese.

Sec. 2. It shall also be the duty of the Minister in charge of each congregation in the Diocese to obtain, through the agency of the Laity, from every member of the same, if possible, an individual subscription, payable monthly, to the Diocesan Missionary Fund.

Sec. 3. It shall be the duty of the Clergyman, or of some proper officer of each Parish, to remit promptly to the Treasurer of the Diocese the amounts collected as herein provided.

The fourth resolution proposed by the Committee was, on motion, referred to the Committee on Canons.

On motion of Mr. R. H. Lewis, M.D., it was

Resolved, That it is the sense of this Convention that the word *collection* in Chapter I, Canon XIV, Section 1, means any collection at a public service.

Mr. R. H. Battle presented the following preamble and resolution :

Whereas, This Convention has by unanimous vote decided that, at some future time, a Church shall be erected as a memorial of the Rt. Rev. T. B. Lyman, D.D., LL.D., D.C L., late Bishop of the Diocese of North Carolina; and

Whereas, The family and friends of Bishop Lyman have expressed their willingness to contribute towards the erection of a permanent Church for the congregation of the Church of the Good Shepherd in Raleigh, to be a memorial of Bishop Lyman; and

Whereas, This is the Church to which Mrs. Lyman, who was a large and liberal contributor to the Church in North Carolina, as well as to that individual congregation, belonged, and to which she and the Bishop were devotedly attached; and

Whereas, A large number of the Church people in North Carolina have already expressed their desire to contribute to such a memorial; therefore be it

Resolved, That this Convention recommends that the people of the Diocese shall unite in the erection of a Church in Raleigh as a memorial of Bishop Lyman.

The resolution was, on motion, adopted.

Mr. J. S. Myers offered the following preamble and resolution, which were not adopted :

WHEREAS, The creation of debt by a congregation militates against its spiritual and material welfare; therefore be it

Resolved, That the various congregations of this Diocese be and are hereby urged to refrain from the erection or improvement of Church property till the means for doing so are visible.

Mr. Paul B. Means, in behalf of the Parish of All Saints, Concord, offered the following resolution, which, on his motion, was referred to the Committee on Canons:

Resolved, That before any assessments are made against any Parish or Organized Mission, the Committee on Finance shall consult with the Delegates representing such Parish or Mission.

On motion, the Convention adjourned.

At 8 o'clock P. M. a meeting was held in St. Paul's Church in the interest of the Brotherhood of St. Andrew, at which addresses were delivered by the Bishop, the Rev. J. F. George, the Rev. Dr. Murdoch and Messrs. C. M. Busbee and Silas McBee.

THIRD DAY.

ST. PAUL'S CHURCH, WINSTON,
FRIDAY, May 18, 1894.

The Convention met at 9 o'clock.

The Litany was said by the Rev. H. H. Phelps.

The Convention was called to order by the Bishop.

The calling of the roll was, on motion, dispensed with, and the minutes of yesterday's proceedings were read and approved.

On motion of Mr. F. S. Spruill, leave of absence was granted to the Rev. Mr. McKenzie.

On motion of Mr. William A. Smith, the Convention accepted with thanks an invitation to visit the Salem Academy at 4 o'clock to-morrow afternoon.

6

The Rev. William Walker presented the following

REPORT OF THE COMMITTEE ON UNFINISHED BUSINESS.

The Committee on Unfinished Business beg leave to report that they
find a resolution amending Article XII, Section 1, of the Constitution, to
be found on page 65 of the Journal, is subject to ratification by this Convention, and that two matters reported by the Committee on Unfinished
Business of last year have not been disposed of, viz : "That no report has
been made by the Committee on the change of site of the Ravenscroft
High School, nor by the Committee appointed to confer with Trustees of
the University of the South in relation to the affiliation of our Diocesan
School with the University."	W. WALKER,

Chairman.

The Rev. Dr. Wetmore presented the following

REPORT OF THE MANAGERS OF THE THOMPSON ORPHANAGE
AND TRAINING INSTITUTION.

The managers of this, the noblest of the Church's charities in the
Diocese, with unfeigned gratification, report that continued and increasing prosperity marks this Institution.

Notwithstanding the financial depression of the times, contributions
that have come in during the year compare very favorably with those of
past years   The income for the support of the children has steadily
increased from $3,700 (speaking in round numbers) in 1890, to $5,400 in
1894.

The Farm, including now a Dairy in successful operation, has become,
under efficient management, more than ever helpful in the maintenance
of the children.

The wise administration of the faithful and devoted Superintendent,
assisted by his able and willing subordinates, is increasing more and
more the usefulness of this Institution.   This is apparent to us who make
our official visits to the Orphanage and inquire into its working.   The
highest commendation of character and manners is bestowed upon the
children by those who know them.

With much gratitude we record three very important donations made
to the Orphanage during the past six months: First, The Trustees of
St. John's Hospital, on the closing of that, gave us, to be used in the
work of this Institution as a permanent memorial of Bishop Atkinson,
$2,500.   This sum had been raised through the efforts of Miss Rebecca
Cameron by the children of the State for "the Bishop Atkinson Memorial Cot" in the Hospital.   With this money we are now erecting an
annex to Thompson Hall and in making other much-needed improve-

ments, all of which will add very materially to the capacity of the buildings and vastly increase the comfort and welfare of the children. Second, Mrs. M. A. Southerland, late of Pittsboro, has given us by her will, an interest in lands thought to be very valuable. Third, Our late revered, generous-hearted Bishop, one of the last of whose official acts was to preside at a meeting of this Board, and who on that occasion manifested more than his wonted interest in the Orphanage, by his will, made a few days after that meeting, has left us a valuable legacy. It is impossible at present to estimate the money value of either of these testamentary gifts.

We devoutly hope that others will follow their noble examples. What better charity can one find wherein to bestow his money than the erection of that "Industrial Hall," for which our worthy Superintendent has been appealing year after year for so long?

It is noteworthy that there never has been any very serious case of sickness at the Orphanage. During the eight years of its existence there has been only one death among the 125 children received, and that death was the result of an accident.

Appended, and made a part of this report, is the Annual Report of the Superintendent, omitting an itemized statement of contributions.

Influenced by the past, why should we not expect the Thompson Orphanage to take a still deeper hold upon the hearts of the people of both Dioceses, that contributions will flow in still larger amounts, that other legacies will be left, and that with God's blessing upon it, even in the near future, its sphere of usefulness will be greatly enlarged?

For these things let all hopefully pray to the Giver of all good.

W. R. WETMORE,

W. A. SMITH,

For the Managers.

EIGHTH ANNUAL REPORT OF THE REV. E. A. OSBORNE, SUPERINTENDENT OF THE THOMPSON ORPHANAGE AND TRAINING INSTITUTION.

Divine Providence has continued to favor the work by opening the hearts of the people to make frequent and generous offerings and greatly prospering our efforts.

The number of children has been greater, and the contributions, both in money and in kind, have been larger than during any previous year.

Although the cotton crop was almost a failure, the aggregate products of the farm were larger than ever before. This was owing to the sale of vegetables, milk and butter. We now have a Dairy in successful operation, which furnishes an abundance of milk for the children and some for market This affords splendid training for the boys, and, in addition, makes fine manure for the land.

The school under Miss Capehart has been well taught, and the children show decided improvement. The two Matrons, Miss Mackay and

Mrs. Sargent, have been most faithful and efficient in their work, and Mr. Jamison, the Foreman, has been untiring in his duties. The children have also shown much appreciation of our efforts, and faithfulness to their duties. We have had sixty-six children in the Orphanage during the year, of whom nineteen were from the Diocese of East Carolina and forty-seven were from North Carolina. We have discharged fifteen children during the year, of whom seven were from the Diocese of East Carolina and eight from the Diocese of North Carolina. Of those discharged four have good positions and are earning from seventy-five cents to one dollar a day, while others have good homes with fair prospects of usefulness. We now have fifty-two children, of whom twelve are from East Carolina and forty are from North Carolina. We have received 125 children since the work began. The health of the children has been remarkably good.

Church people and others in both Dioceses, and even in other Dioceses, show much interest in the Institution, which is doing incalculable good, not only for its inmates, but also for our people generally, by enlisting their sympathies and energies in so noble a work.

We have been made glad by a donation of $2,500 by St. John's Guild, Raleigh, being the fund known as the Bishop Atkinson Memorial Cot Fund. This is being used for building a new dining-room, pantry, etc., and adding two new dormitories, a Matron's room, room for the sick, and other much-needed apartments. The Guild also gave us a most valuable supply of household and kitchen furniture, bedding, etc. We are also gratified to mention that two important legacies have been left us during the year—the first by Mrs. M. A. Southerland, and the other by our late beloved and honored Diocesan, Bishop Lyman. These will amount to several thousand dollars when the estates are fully administered.

Our present needs are an Industrial Hall for boys, which will cost $600, and two cottages, one for the Foreman and one for a gardener, costing each $600. These are much needed and will be valuable investments for the Institution.

I desire to express heart-felt thanks for innumerable acts of kindness and sympathy shown by all who have aided in this blessed work. The Bishop and Rectors in each Diocese have been exceedingly kind, and Laymen everywhere have been kind and generous. Dr. Jones, and since his resignation Dr. Petree, have been untiring in their attention to our sick, while Drs. Alexander, Bland and Graham have cheerfully rendered valuable services in their respective departments, three of them as dentists and the last as oculist. We are also under many obligations to the railroad companies of our State, and to the Southern Express Company, for many favors, and likewise to the editors of newspapers, who have always been ready to assist us.

FINANCIAL STATEMENT.

Balance from last year---$ 901 04
Contributions during the year----------------------------------- 3,223 75
Messenger of Hope -- 191 81
Cash products of the farm-------------------------------------- 880 74
Rents -- 215 30
Farm products reserved for use ------------------------------ 200 00
Butter and milk reserved for use--------------------------------- 365 00
Value of manure reserved ------------------------------------- 100 00
Farm products reserved for stock------------------------------- 245 00
Total products of farm ------------------------------------ 2,006 04

    Total ---$6,322 64

EXPENSES.

Salaries ---$1,800 00
Current expenses of farm --------------------------------- 885 38
Permanent improvements, Dairy, cows, etc.----------- 395 40
Messenger of Hope --- 194 23
Current expenses for provisions, clothing, books, etc.--- 1,433 14
Balance on hand - -- 704 49
Farm products consumed --------------------------------- 200 00
Butter and milk consumed---------------------------------- 365 00
Produce consumed by stock------------------------------- 245 00
Permanent value of manure to land ----------------- 100 00
                                                           —————$6,322 64

To the above should be added $2,560 from St. John's Guild, referred to in my report.   Respectfully,

                                        E. A. OSBORNE,
April 30, 1894.   *Superintendent.*

The report was, on motion, referred to a Special Committee of three. The Bishop appointed the Rev. McNeely DuBose, Mr. C. A. Overman and Mr. R. H. Lewis, M.D., as members of that Committee.

The Rev. Dr. Wetmore presented the following

REPORT OF THE COMMITTEE ON CANONS.

The Committee on Canons beg leave to report as follows in regard to the three matters referred to them yesterday:

First: We do not think it advisable to spread upon the Journal of our Convention copies of all deeds to Church property. In our judgment this would be no additional aid in securing proper titles to real estate, while it would greatly enlarge the size of the Journal and increase the cost of its publication. We believe an entirely sufficient safeguard is provided by Section 2 of Canon XI, Chapter I.

Second: We recommend the change proposed by the resolution of Dr. Murdoch in regard to creating a new Convocation. The Convocation of Charlotte is much larger than any other, both in territory and in the number of its Clergy. If this is divided into two, the new Convocation as well as the old will be about as large as the others.

Third: We have carefully considered the proposition to reduce the time of Canonical residence of a Clergyman before he shall be allowed to a seat and a vote in the Convention, and have come to the conclusion that the period should be reduced. While we cannot consent, as far as we are concerned, to reduce the period to the smallest time that has been named, we do think that a Clergyman coming to us by letters dimissory should be entitled to a seat in the Convention and to take part in any debate as soon as he is received by the Bishop.

In view of the above we offer the following resolutions and ask their adoption:

1. *Resolved*, That Section 1 of Canon I, Chapter II, be amended by changing the word "four" in first line into "five," and by inserting the words "of Salisbury" between "of Raleigh" and "of Charlotte."

2. *Resolved*, That Section 3, Article III, of the Constitution be amended by substituting the word "six" for the word "twelve" in the third line, and by adding after the words "the same" in the sixth line, "and every Clergyman Canonically connected with the Diocese and resident therein for any less time shall be entitled to a seat and to speak in the Convention."

W. R. WETMORE,
Chairman.

The first resolution appended to the report was, on motion, adopted.

The second resolution was divided. The first part being under consideration, Mr. C. M. Busbee asked unanimous consent to allow a gentleman present, not a member of this body, to address the Convention.

The Chair, deeming such action under the circumstances unconstitutional, decided that the suggestion was out of order, but asked that an appeal might be taken so that the Convention should decide the question. This being done, the decision of the Chair was sustained.

The first part of the resolution, referring to the term of

residence required of clerical members of the Convention, was lost by the non-concurrence of orders, as follows:

Clergy—*Ayes*, 19; *noes*, 22. *Parishes*—*Ayes*, 15; *noes*, 6; *divided*, 1.

Of the Clergy—*Ayes:* The Rev. Messrs. Davis, DuBose, Ferris, C. Fetter, Horner, Hunter, Ingle, McQueen, Perry, Picard, Pittenger, Rathbun, Rhodes, Vanderbogart, Wm. Walker, Weston, T. C. Wetmore, W. R. Wetmore, Wingate. *Noes:* The Rt. Rev. J. B. Cheshire, Jr., the Rev. Messrs. Barker, Barrows, Battle, Bell, Bost, Buxton, Deal, Marshall, McDuffey, Miller, Murdoch, Osborne, Owens, G. W. Phelps, Quin, Smedes, Smith, Stickney, Stubbs, Sutton, R. J. Walker.

Of the Laity—*Ayes:* Asheville, Trinity—Messrs. J. H. Law, R. R. Rawls; Henderson, Holy Innocents—Mr. G. C. Lamb; Leaksville, Epiphany—Mr. W. S. Martin; Lincolnton, St. Luke's—Mr. Silas McBee; Louisburg, St. Paul's— Mr. F. S. Spruill; Morganton, Grace—Mr. J. H. Pearson; Raleigh, Good Shepherd—Mr. S. P. Child; Reidsville, St. Thomas—Mr. N. K. Smith; Tarboro, Calvary—Messrs. Fred. Philips, M. A. Curtis; Tarboro, St. Luke's—Mr. Thomas Newton; Warrenton, Emmanuel—Messrs. A. B. Cayce, W. G. Rogers; Weldon, Grace—Mr. J. E. Shields; Wilkesboro, St. Paul's—Mr. A. B. Galloway; Wilson, St. Timothy's—Mr. T. C. Davis; Winston, St. Paul's—Messrs. H. D. Law, J. C. Buxton. *Noes:* Charlotte, St. Peter's— Messrs. J. S. Myers, J. Wilkes; Hillsboro, St. Matthew's— Mr. P. C. Graham; Pittsboro, St. Bartholomew's—Mr. Wm. L. London; Raleigh, Christ Church—Messrs. C. E. Johnson, C. M. Busbee; Salisbury, St. Luke's—Messrs. S. F. Lord, C. A. Overman; Wadesboro, Calvary—Mr. W. A. Smith. *Divided:* Concord, All Saints—*Aye*, Mr. B. F. Rogers; *no*, Mr. P. B. Means.

The second part of the resolution, allowing to certain Clergy of the Diocese a seat and voice, but not a vote in the Convention, subject to ratification by the next Convention, was adopted by the following vote:

Clergy—Ayes, 36; *noes,* 5.   *Parishes—Ayes,* 22; *divided,* 1.

Of the ,Clergy—Ayes: The Rt. Rev. J. B. Cheshire, Jr., the Rev. Messrs. Battle, Bost, Buxton, Deal, DuBose, Ferris, F. A. Fetter, C. Fetter, Horner, Hunter, Marshall, McDuffey, McQueen, Miller, Murdoch, Osborne, Owens, Perry, G. W. Phelps, Picard, Pittenger, Quin, Rathbun, Rhodes, Smedes, Smith, Stubbs, Sutton, Vanderbogart, R. J. Walker, Wm. Walker, Weston, T. C. Wetmore, W. R. Wetmore, Wingate. *Noes:* The Rev. Messrs. Barker, Barrows, Bell, Davis, Ingle.

Of the Laity—Ayes: Asheville, Trinity—Messrs. J. H. Law, R. R. Rawls; Charlotte, St. Peter's—Mr. J. S. Myers; Concord, All Saints—Mr. P. B. Means; Durham, St. Philip's—Mr. W. J. Griswold; Henderson, Holy Innocents—Mr. G. C. Lamb; Hillsboro, St. Matthew's—Mr. P. C. Graham; Leaksville, Epiphany—Mr. W. S. Martin; Lincolnton, St. Luke's—Mr. Silas McBee—Louisburg, St. Paul's—Mr. F. S. Spruill; Morganton, Grace—Mr. J. H. Pearson; Pittsboro, St. Bartholomew's—Mr. W. L. London; Raleigh, Christ Church—Messrs. C. E. Johnson, C. M. Busbee, R. H. Lewis; Raleigh, Good Shepherd—Mr. S. P. Child; Reidsville, St. Thomas—Mr. N. K. Smith; Tarboro, Calvary—Messrs. Fred. Philips, M. A. Curtis; Tarboro, St. Luke's—Mr. Thomas Newton; Wadesboro, Calvary—Mr. W. A. Smith; Warrenton, Emmanuel—Messrs. A. B. Cayce, W. G. Rogers; Weldon, Grace—Mr. J. E. Shields; Wilkesboro, St. Paul's—Mr. A. B. Galloway; Wilson, St. Timothy's—Mr. T. C. Davis; Winston, St. Paul's—Messrs. H. D. Law, J. C. Buxton.   *Divided:* Salisbury, St. Luke's—*Aye,* C. A. Overman; *no,* S. F. Lord.

The Rev. Dr. Wetmore presented the following

REPORT OF THE COMMITTEE ON CANONS.

The Committee on Canons, having considered the difficult and delicate matter in relation to assessments referred to them in the resolution of Mr. Means, offer the following resolution:

Resolved, That whenever the knowledge comes to the Chairman of the Committee on Finance, through a reliable channel, that any congregation feels that the assessment placed upon it is not of proper amount, he shall enter into correspondence with the Minister in charge or the Senior Warden in regard to such assessment.

W. R. WETMORE,
For Committee.

Mr. Paul B. Means offered the following resolution:

Resolved, That Chapter I, Canon VIII, Section 8, of the Canons of the Diocese, be amended by the insertion, after the semicolon following the word *purposes* in the fourth line thereof, the following: But they shall report no such assessment on any Church or organized Mission until they have satisfied the Clergy and Lay Delegates present when said report shall be made from such Church or organized Mission, what the assessment and its purpose will be, and thus give such representatives of said Church or organized Mission an opportunity to be heard thereon.

On motion of the Rev. Dr. Murdoch, the whole matter was referred to a Special Committee of three, to report to the next Convention. The Bishop appointed on this Committee the Rev. Dr. Wetmore, Mr. Paul B. Means and Mr. John Wilkes.

On motion of Mr. C. E. Johnson, it was

Resolved, That the Bishop be requested and authorized to prepare and make public a programme of meetings and services to be held during the term of the next Convention, subject to any modification or change by the Convention.

Mr. Johnson also offered the following resolution, which was adopted:

Resolved, That the expenses in attending the Convention incurred by Clergymen who have been received into the Diocese since the last meeting of the Convention, and who have been given honorary seats in this Convention, be paid by the Treasurer.

The Rev. Wm. Stanley Barrows offered the following resolution, which, on motion, was referred to the Committee on Finance:

Resolved, That the Trustees of the Diocese be advised to invest the permanent funds of the Diocese in good business real estate as they may from time to time be able advantageously to secure the same.

The Rev. Dr. Murdoch presented the following

REPORT OF THE COMMITTEE ON THE STATE OF THE CHURCH.

The Parochial Reports handed to us yield the following statistics:

Number of families 1,925. Number of persons 8,168. Baptisms, infant 424; adult 116; total 540. Confirmations 509. Communicants 4,716. Marriages 119. Burials 200. Sunday-school teachers 507; scholars 4,211. Parish School teachers 20; scholars 432. Church edifices 112. Rectories 29. Contributions $35,824.76. Value of Church property $401,376.

These numbers will doubtless be increased when all the reports reach the hands of the Secretary.

The Committee will this year depart from the usual custom of calling attention to the various institutions of the Church and speak of other things which seem to demand our attention

And first, with devout thankfulness to God, we would point out the greatly increased measure of hopefulness that pervades all our deliberations. God does not ordinarily do great things for His people unless they have sufficient faith in His promises to enable them to hope and confidently expect the promised blessings. We look on this greater hopefulness as a sure sign that great blessings are at hand, and that God will do for us such noble works as He did in the days of our fathers and in the old time before them.

Second: We rejoice at the many signs that there is a growing spirit of prayer that God would prosper the work of our hands upon us. The increasing number of the members of the Brotherhood of St. Andrew and of the Daughters of the King, orders pledged to daily prayer, and the larger number of monthly Missionary meetings held chiefly for the purpose of prayer, are outward and visible signs of an increasing spirit of intercession among our people. We beseech you brethren that it may abound more and more, and that each of you may clearly determine and resolve by God's Grace, "For Zion's sake I will not hold my peace, and for Jerusalem's sake I will not rest until the righteousness thereof go forth as brightness and the salvation thereof as a lamp that burneth."

Third: The matter that lies heaviest on our hearts is the support of our Diocesan Missionaries. The amount on which these devoted men have to live is so small as to render it impossible for them to devote themselves wholly to the work of the ministry. Never will they have sufficient time for reading and prayer unless we lift from them the care of providing for their families. What a short-sighted policy it is to send them out as teachers and not give them the means to provide the necessary tools of teachers— books; to cut them off from the touch and in a measure from the fellowship of the Church by depriving them of the Church papers; to have them unable to attend Clerical meetings for want of money. Let us try during the coming year, with one consent, to make a revolution in this matter. Let us make this the one great work of the year so far as gifts and offerings are concerned. Let us feel assured that as Hezekiah prospered in the work which he did for the house of the Lord, so we will prosper in this if like him *we do it*, and if we do it with all our hearts.

Fourth: We have set before us in the Book of Common Prayer the ideal of a Church—an ideal as perfect as human infirmity will allow. But this ideal cannot influence our fellow-men until it is embodied and set before their eyes in living men and women. Let us strive to make our own Church, and by Church we mean our Diocese, as near as possible a perfect manifestation of the spirit of the Prayer-Book; to this end let us try to carry out all the rubrics and directions of the Prayer-Book. Let Laymen ask for all those services, notices and admonitions which their Clergy may forget to offer, and let them comply loyally on their part with every direction which their Clergy may give them out of that book. Let us try to make ourselves, by God's grace, the one Diocese in the world which shall better than any other carry out the Prayer-Book, the whole Prayer-Book, and nothing but the Prayer-Book, since the Prayer-Book represents accurately the meaning of the Bible.

Lastly: We cannot without deep distress remember the many places in which the work of the Church is hindered by insubordination to authority, by dissensions and open quarrels. God's work cannot prosper where Satan has the mastery. We ask you brethren of the Clergy and Laity to convey to every Parish and Mission Station our affectionate entreaty that all our people would be one. We ask you to remind them that the one recorded prayer of our Lord Jesus for each of us Churchmen in the Diocese of North Carolina was, "Neither pray I for these Apostles alone, but for them also which shall believe on me through their word that they all may be one; as Thou Father art in me and I in Thee that they also may be one in us, that the world may know that Thou hast sent me and hast loved them as Thou hast loved me." Let us join all our prayers and bend every effort to end all dissensions and to make our Church as a city that is in unity in itself, assured that then all the tribes will go up, even all the tribes of the Lord, to testify unto Israel and to give thanks unto the Lord.

All of which is respectfully submitted,

F. J. Murdoch,
A. B. Hunter,
W. J. Smith,
Fred. Philips,
John H. Pearson,
Committee.

On motion of Mr. C. E. Johnson, it was resolved that the report of the Committee should be printed and distributed, and that the Clergy be requested to read it to their congregations.

A communication was received from the Young Men's Christian Association offering the hospitalities of their rooms to the members of the Convention. The Secretary expressed to the Association the thanks of the Convention.

FRIDAY, May 18, 3 P. M.

The Convention re-assembled, the Bishop in the chair.

On motion, leave of absence was given to the Rev. McNeely DuBose, the Rev. R. J. Walker, the Rev. J. M. Horner and Mr. S. J. Welsh, M.D., and it was agreed that no further leave should be given except in case of sickness.

The Rev. Dr. Wetmore presented the following

REPORT OF THE BOARD OF FELLOWS OF RAVENSCROFT.

The Board of Fellows of Ravenscroft respectfully report:

The School for Boys, under the management of Mr. Ronald MacDonald, as Head Master, has won for itself an excellent reputation. We have offered to continue to Mr. Ronald MacDonald the lease of the property free of rent for another term of five years, on condition of his keeping the building in repair and paying for the insurance on the same.

The Rev. W. S. Barrows, S T.B., Instructor in the Training School for the Ministry, has had the direction of the Theological Students, and at the same time he and Rev. Samuel Rhodes have been conducting in an acceptable manner the work of the Associate Mission.

The Rev. Samuel Rhodes, Rev. W. F. Rice, Mr. John H. Gilreath and Mr. John C. Seagle have been pursuing their studies under Mr. Barrows.

We regret to learn that Mr. Barrows, who is an earnest, faithful and efficient worker, intends to leave the Diocese.

The Board of Fellows ask the adoption by the Convention of the following resolutions:

1. *Resolved*, That the Board of Fellows of Ravenscroft be composed of six members, three Clergymen and three Laymen, to be elected as provided for in Resolution 1, page 41, Journal of 1885, and that so much of said resolution of 1885, and only so much as interferes with this—that is to say, "the Board of Fellows shall be composed of seven members, of

whom the Principal of the School shall be a member *ex-officio,*" is hereby rescinded.

2. *Resolved,* The Board of Fellows shall make all needful rules and by-laws for the management of "Ravenscroft."

3. *Resolved,* The officer at the head of the Training School shall be elected by the Board of Fellows upon nomination by the Bishop.

4. *Resolved,* Resolutions 2 and 3, on page 41, Journal of 1885, are hereby rescinded. W. R. WETMORE,

For the Board of Fellows of Ravenscroft.

The report was, on motion, referred to a Special Committee to report to this Convention. The Bishop appointed as members of this committee the Rev. Dr. Murdoch, the Rev. Mr. Stickney and Mr. Fred. Philips.

The Rev. Dr. Wetmore nominated the Rev. F. J. Murdoch, D.D., and Mr. B. H. Moore, of Charlotte, as members of the Board of Managers of the Thompson Orphanage.

No other nominations being made, the Secretary was instructed to cast the vote of the Convention, and these gentlemen were declared elected.

On motion, the Secretary was requested to convey to the Rev. Frederick Towers the sympathy of his brethren of the Clergy and Laity in the bereavement which prevented his attendance at the Convention.

The Rev. A. B. Hunter presented the report of St. Augustine's School, which, on his motion, was referred to the Committee on the State of the Church. (See Appendix B).

The Rev. Mr. Hunter, from the Committee appointed for the purpose, presented the following resolutions of respect to the memory of the late Rev. F. L. Bush, which were adopted by the Convention:

Resolved, That the Convention of the Diocese of North Carolina desires to place on record its sense of loss in the death of the Rev. Franklin Leonard Bush, on July 25, 1893. He was a thoroughly trained scholar, learned in the Scriptures and in the teachings of the Church, a devout man and thoroughly devoted to his priestly work. St. James Church, Pittsboro, erected under his care and largely by his exertions, will ever be a monument to his interest in work among the colored people. His modesty and humility and his saintly life will ever be an esteemed heritage for this Diocese.

Resolved, That a copy of this resolution be sent to the family of our
departed brother, and that a memorial page be inserted in the Journal.

Mr. William A. Smith presented the report of the Diocesan Trustees of the University of the South, as follows:

Many changes have been made in the *personnel* of the Faculty of the
University. We have a new Vice-Chancellor, Dean. Chaplain and Professor of Divinity and Ecclesiastical History.

Notwithstanding the great depression throughout the southern section
of our country, we are much gratified to be able to report that the Theological Department has largely increased; and students in this department could not be accommodated in St. Luke's Hall and were forced to
seek rooms elsewhere.

The Medical Department and the Law Class have also increased, while
the number of students in the regular Academic Department has remained
about the same.

The report of Dr. F J. Murdoch, acting as agent for the University of
the South, shows that the Theological Department has received contributions from only twelve Churches and one individual, amounting to
just eighty cents more than one-half of the apportionment of this
Diocese.

Cannot we appreciate the great importance of this department of the
institution and rise to the measure of duty toward it?

Receipts have been as follows:

Christ Church, Raleigh	$ 21 31
St. Luke's Church, Salisbury	1 70
Grace Church, Morganton	2 59
St. Agnes Church, Franklin	2 75
Ascension Church, Hickory	2 00
Mr. W. A. Smith	5 00
Holy Innocents Church, Henderson	5 00
Trinity Church, Asheville	53 50
Rev. W. J. Smith's Churches	6 45
St. Peter's Church, Charlotte	27 00
St. James Church, Lenoir	2 00
St. Luke's Church, Lincolnton	21 50
	$ 150 80

F. J. MURDOCH,
W. L. LONDON,
W. A. SMITH,
Trustees.

The report was, on motion, referred to a Special Committee consisting of the Rev. J. M. Horner, the Rev. Stewart McQueen, Mr. F. S. Spruill and Mr. H. D. Law.

The Rev. G. W. Phelps presented the following

REPORT OF THE COMMITTEE ON NEW PARISHES.

The Committee on New Parishes, to whom was referred the application of St. Paul's Parish, Rowan county, for admission into union with the Convention, offers the following resolution:

Resolved, That the new Parish, now within the bounds of St. Luke's Parish, Salisbury, to be known as St. Paul's Parish, Rowan county, be admitted into union with the Convention of the Diocese of North Carolina; the Canon applicable to such cases having been duly complied with.

GIRARD W. PHELPS,
Chairman.

The resolution offered by the Committee was, on motion, adopted.

The Rev. A. J. Vanderbogart, from the Committee to whom was referred the Form of Parochial Reports, presented the following report:

The Committee to whom was referred the Form of Parochial Reports, with a view to its conformity to recent requirements of the General Convention, and the provision of further facilities for obtaining accurate information in regard to the condition of the Diocese, present the accompanying Form and offer the following resolution:

Resolved, That the Form presented by the Committee be adopted by the Convention.

ALVIN JONES VANDERBOGART,
J. D. GLENN,
G. C. LAMB,
Committee.

On motion of the Rev. Wm. S. Barrows, the Form proposed was amended by the insertion of the item *Baptized persons,* and the resolution was adopted. (For Form of Report see Appendix D).

Mr. Wm. A. Smith offered the following resolution, which was adopted:

Resolved, That the Bishop of the Diocese, and the Trustee of the General Theological Seminary for this Diocese, be authorized to prepare and present to the Trustees of the Seminary a memorial in the name and on behalf of the Convention of the Diocese of North Carolina, requesting said Trustees to allow this Diocese to use the proceeds of the North Carolina Scholarship in the General Theological Seminary for the support of Candidates for Orders in the Theological Department of the University of the South, or elsewhere, in the discretion of the Bishop of this Diocese.

The Rev. McNeely DuBose offered the following resolution, which was adopted:

Resolved, That a Committee of five be appointed to consider the advisability of requesting the General Convention to set apart the western portion of this Diocese as a Missionary Jurisdiction, and that they report to the next Convention.

The Bishop appointed on the Committee called for, the Rev. McNeely DuBose, the Rev. James Buxton, D.D., the Rev. M. M. Marshall, D.D., Mr. Fred. Philips and Mr. Silas McBee.

The Rev. Julian E. Ingle presented the following preamble and resolution, which, on motion, were adopted:

WHEREAS, There exists a doubt as to the relation of certain congregations to the Convention of the Diocese; and

WHEREAS, Certain Parishes, being no longer in a condition to discharge as such their obligations to the Diocese, desire leave to dissolve their Parochial Organizations and to be recognized as Organized Missions in union with the Convention; therefore

Resolved, That a Committee of three be appointed to communicate with such Parishes and congregations, and to report the facts to the next Convention.

The following persons were appointed by the Bishop as members of the Committee: The Rev. J. E. Ingle, the Rev. J. M. Horner and Mr. G. C. Lamb.

Mr. J. S. Myers offered the following resolution, which was adopted:

Resolved, That every Missionary of this Diocese shall, at each Annual Convention, make orally a personal report of his work for the past year, and what encouragement he may have for a continuance of his efforts for the ensuing year.

The Rev. Dr. Murdoch presented the following

REPORT OF THE EDUCATION COMMITTEE.

The amount contributed to this fund during the past year by the various congregations of the Diocese was $45.35; the expenditures, including Treasurer's commission, was $137.26; and there is a debit balance of $48.55. It is evident that without larger contributions but little can be accomplished by this fund.   F. J. MURDOCH,
                                                                Chairman.

The Rev. Dr. Murdoch moved that the ratification of the amendment of Article XII, section 1, of the Constitution of the Diocese, which was passed by the last Convention, be postponed until the next Convention. The motion was unanimously agreed to—thirty-four Clergy and sixteen Parishes voting in its favor.

Mr. John H. Pearson moved that the next Annual Convention be held in Grace Church, Morganton, on Thursday, May 16, 1894.

The Rev. Stewart McQueen moved to amend by inserting in the place of the words *Grace Church, Morganton,* the words *St. Philip's Church, Durham.*

It was also moved to amend by striking out the words *Thursday, May 16,* and inserting *Wednesday, May 15,* and this motion was agreed to.

It was then agreed that the sense of the Convention in regard to the place of meeting should be determined by ballot, and the Bishop appointed as Tellers the Rev. Messrs. Quin and Battle. The ballots having been counted, the Tellers reported that Morganton had been chosen as the place of meeting of the next Annual Convention.

The Rev. C. C. Quin nominated as members of the Standing Committee for the ensuing year the Rev. M. M. Marshall, D.D., the Rev. R. B. Sutton, D.D., the Rev. Bennett Smedes, D.D., Mr. P. E. Hines, M.D. and Mr. R. H. Battle. In the absence of other nominations, the Secre-

8

tary was instructed to cast the ballot of the Convention, and they were declared elected.

The Rev. Dr. Murdoch nominated the following persons as elective members of the Executive Missionary Committee: Messrs. W. L. London, C. M. Busbee, H. G. Connor, R. H. Battle and John Wilkes. There being no other nominations, the Secretary was instructed to cast the ballot of the Convention, and they were declared elected.

The Rev. M. M. Marshall, D.D., nominated as Historiographer of the Diocese, Mr. John S. Henderson, of Salisbury. There being no other nomination, the Secretary was instructed to cast the ballot of the Convention, and Mr. Henderson was declared elected.

Mr. Charles E. Johnson offered the following resolution, which was adopted:

Resolved, That the Convention hereby expresses its high appreciation of the work and labor of Bishop Cheshire as Historiographer of the Diocese.

The Rev. Dr. Murdoch nominated as members of the Education Committee the Rev. E. A. Osborne, the Rev. F. S. Stickney and Mr. Silas McBee. There being no other nominations, the Secretary was instructed to cast the ballot of the Convention, and they were declared elected.

The following persons were nominated as members of the Church Building Committee: The Rev. R. B. Sutton, D.D., the Rev. I. McK. Pittenger, the Rev. Julian E. Ingle, Mr. W. E. Ashley and Mr. W. H. Cheek. In the absence of other nominations, the Secretary was instructed to cast the ballot of the Convention, and they were declared elected.

The Convention then adjourned.

At 8 o'clock a Missionary meeting was held in St. Paul's Church, at which addresses were made by Bishops Capers and Cheshire, the Rev. Messrs. Deal, Pittenger and Barrows and Dr. R. H. Lewis.

FOURTH DAY.

St. Paul's Church, Winston,
Saturday, May 19, 1894.

The Convention met at 9 o'clock.

Morning Prayer was read by the Rev. Messrs. John A. Deal and J. F. George.

The chair was taken by the Rev. Dr. Murdoch and the Convention called to order.

The calling of the roll was, on motion, dispensed with, and the minutes of yesterday were read and approved.

The Rev. Stewart McQueen, from the Special Committee appointed to consider the report of the Diocesan Trustees of the University of the South, presented the following report:

The Committee to whom was referred the report of the Trustees of the University of the South beg leave to report as follows:

They regret exceedingly to note that so many of the Clergy fail to observe the standing resolution of the Convention which recommends a yearly offering for the Theological Department at Sewanee. It should be observed that the University Trustees ask aid for this Department only. Students in Divinity are entitled to all of its privileges without charge. Besides this, the Bishop has the right to appoint two students from this Diocese, in the Academic Department, who receive free tuition.

In a word, this Diocese *receives* two or three times as much from the University *as it pays towards the support of its Theological Department.* Even if we contributed for that Department the whole amount asked for, which is only three hundred dollars a year, we would still be in debt to the University. Only twelve out of the sixty-seven Clergy in the Diocese took an offering during the past year for Sewanee. Surely, if the Clergy felt the interest in the Theological Department which they ought to feel, more of them would observe the resolution of the Convention on this subject.

There are now between seventy-five and one hundred men in Holy Orders who are *alumni* of Sewanee. This represents no inconsiderable proportion of the Clergy in the South, where, indeed, most of them are at work. In this Diocese four of the Clergy, and three of them are Rectors of three of the best Parishes we have, were students at Sewanee.

In view of the above the Committee offer the following resolution:

Resolved, That this Convention earnestly urges the Clergy of the Diocese to take at least one offering annually, at the usual Sunday morning service, for the support of the Theological Department of the University of the South.   STEWART McQUEEN,
                                                    For the Committee.

The resolution appended to the report was, on motion, adopted:

The Rev. Wm. S. Barrows moved a resolution that three members be added to the Committee appointed to consider the expediency of the creation of a new Missionary Jurisdiction in the western part of the State of North Carolina. After some discussion the resolution was laid upon the table.

The President of the Convention appeared and took the chair.

Mr. John Wilkes offered the following resolution, which was adopted by a rising vote:

Resolved, That the thanks of this Convention are hereby tendered to the Rector and congregation of St. Paul's Church, and to the citizens of Winston-Salem generally, for their generous hospitality in the entertainment of this body, the Woman's Auxiliary, Daughters of the King, and of visitors in attendance on our sessions.

On motion of Mr. Wilkes, it was

Resolved, That the Treasurer be instructed to pay to the Sexton of St. Paul's Church, Winston, the sum of five dollars for services rendered the Convention.

Dr. R. H. Lewis, from the Committee appointed to consider the report of the Managers of the Thompson Orphanage, reported the work to be in a prosperous condition under the efficient management of the Rev. Mr. Osborne.

The Rev. F. J. Murdoch, D.D., from the Committee appointed to consider the report of the Board of Fellows of Ravenscroft, submitted the following report:

The Committee to whom was referred the report of the Board of Fellows of Ravenscroft report that they have examined that report and approve it, with the exception that in place of Resolution 1 of the Board of Fellows they recommend that Resolution 1, page 41, Journal 1885, be amended by substituting for the first two lines the words, "That the Board of Fellows shall be composed of seven members, of whom the Bishop of the Diocese shall be a member and Chairman of the Board *ex-officio*," and that the words in the eighth and ninth lines, "of which Board the Bishop of the Diocese shall be Chairman *ex-officio*," be stricken out.   F. J. MURDOCH,
Chairman.

The recommendations contained in the report were, on motion, adopted.

The Convention then took a recess.

———

SATURDAY, May 19, 3 P. M.

The Convention re-assembled, the President in the chair.

The Rev. Wm. R. Wetmore, D.D., at the request of the Executive Missionary Committee, made a statement in regard to the appropriation of the Missionary Funds, and on his motion it was

Resolved, That it be left to the discretion of the Executive Missionary Committee to determine the amount to be given out of the Missionary Funds of the Diocese to the Chapel of the Cross, Chapel Hill.

The Rt. Rev. Ellison Capers, D.D., Bishop of South Carolina, was presented to the Convention by the Bishop of the Diocese, and addressed its members.

On motion of the Secretary, it was

Resolved, That the members of the Convention of the Diocese of North Carolina desire to express their great gratification in having with them the Rt. Rev. the Assistant Bishop of our sister Diocese of South Carolina, and their thanks for his kind consent to deliver an address in memory of our late beloved Diocesan.

There being no further business before the Convention, the minutes were read and approved, and it was

Resolved, That at the conclusion of the service on Sunday morning the Convention shall stand adjourned *sine die.*

The Convention then adjourned to meet at 11 o'clock to-morrow morning for Divine Service.

FIFTH DAY.

St. Paul's Church, Winston,
Trinity Sunday, May 20, 1894.

Morning Prayer was said at 11 o'clock by the Rev. Julian E. Ingle and the Rev. Charles Ferris.

The sermon was preached by the Rt. Rev. Ellison Capers, D.D., Assistant Bishop of South Carolina, from the text: "His Lord said unto him: well done, thou good and faithful servant: thou hast been faithful over a few things, I will make thee ruler over many things; enter thou into the joy of thy Lord." St. Matt. XXV, 21.

Subject: The Life and Character of the Rt. Rev. Theodore Benedict Lyman, D.D., LL.D., D.C.L., late Bishop of North Carolina.

At the conclusion of the sermon, the Bishop of the Diocese admitted to the Order of Deacons Messrs. George Valerie Gilreath and Nathan Adolphus Seagle, on presentation of the Rev. Wm. Stanley Barrows, S.T.B. He then proceeded in the celebration of the Holy Eucharist, in which he was assisted by Bishop Capers, the Rev. George V. Gilreath and others.

The Benediction having been pronounced by the Bishop of the Diocese, the Convention met for final adjournment.

On motion of the Rev. Dr. Buxton, a Committee was appointed to express to Bishop Capers the thanks of the Convention for his sermon, and to ask a copy of the same for publication. The Bishop appointed as such Committee the Rev. James Buxton, D.D., the Rev. I. McK. Pittenger and the Rev. Nathan A. Seagle. It was also ordered that 1500 copies of the sermon and 900 copies of the Journal should be printed. .

The Convention then adjourned *sine die.*

JOS. BLOUNT CHESHIRE, J<small>R</small>.,

Bishop of North Carolina.

J<small>ULIAN</small> E. I<small>NGLE</small>,

    Secretary of the Convention.

APPENDIX A.

ADDRESS OF THE BISHOP.

Brethren of the Clergy and Laity:

I cannot bring into any order or method in my own mind, much less can I put into words, the feelings which this occasion calls up. To no one can it seem stranger than it does to myself that I should occupy this place, and thus address you from the chair of Ravenscroft, of Atkinson, and of him so lately taken from us. I can only ask your prayers, that He who chooses the weak things of this world to confound the strong may strengthen me for the work laid upon me, and that I may never forget the rule which our Lord lays down for him who occupies this chief place, namely, that he must be the servant of all.

Of the late Bishop of this Diocese, the Rt. Rev. Theodore Benedict Lyman, Doctor in Divinity and of Laws, I should think it a privilege to speak somewhat at large, did space permit. Happily this duty will be performed for us by one more competent than myself to do justice to the theme. It is enough that I should say here that I will always strive to imitate, and I trust that I may in some measure approach, the unremitting diligence with which he applied himself to the labors of his high office, and the intelligence and zeal which he brought to the administration of the affairs of the Diocese.

When called by the voice of the Diocese to the office of Assistant Bishop, I felt myself constrained to accept the call, not from any sense of fitness in myself, but simply because such a call seems to me to carry with it an imperative obligation to accept, unless the hand of God should plainly point in another direction: a dispensation was laid upon me. Trusting in that Providence which ordered the result, and counting on the sympathy and support of my brethren of the Clergy and Laity, I take courage for the heavy burden of labor, care and responsibility laid upon me.

I think it is perhaps proper that I should make some note of my Consecration, since he who would naturally have recorded this interesting event has been taken from us. It would hardly be fitting that such a service should not be formally commemorated in the official records of the Diocese.

The election of an Assistant Bishop for this Diocese having been completed by the canonical action of the Bishops and of the Standing Committees, the Presiding Bishop, at my request, appointed the Consecration to take place in Calvary Church, Tarboro, on the twentieth Sunday after Trinity, October 15th, and appointed as Consecrator the Bishop of North Carolina, assisted by the Bishops of East Carolina and South Carolina, with my friend, the Bishop of Kentucky, as preacher. The Bishops of Florida and of Louisiana kindly attended, as my presenters, and the venerable Bishop of Tennessee honored the Bishop-elect and graced the occasion by his presence. More than thirty of the Clergy of this Diocese, and of our sister Diocese of East Carolina, were present, and a large congregation of the Laity of both Dioceses. The services were felt by all to be in a high degree solemn and beautiful, and the sermon by the Bishop of Kentucky well fitted to impress upon all hearers the truth and power of the Church's position, and the value of the Episcopate as a witness to the truth of the Gospel of Christ. All were impressed with the noble simplicity and propriety with which Bishop Lyman, who presided on this occasion, conducted the long and trying service. Little did we suppose as we looked on him that he was so near the end of his earthly ministry!

On the evening of the same day I performed my first episcopal act, a visitation to St. Luke's Church, Tarboro, a colored congregation. After Evening Prayer by the Rev. Messrs. Hunter and Delany, I preached and the Bishop of Louisiana made an address.

Wednesday, October 18th, I spent in visiting members of the congregation of Trinity Church, Scotland Neck. Thursday I visited the Parish School of St. Luke's Church, Tarboro, conducted the opening service and catechised the children.

The twenty-first Sunday after Trinity, October 22d, in Calvary Church, Tarboro, I celebrated the Holy Communion at half past seven, assisted by the Rector, the Rev. Charles L. Hoffmann; and at the midday service I preached.

9

In the afternoon of the same day in a hall at Lawrence, about twelve miles north of Tarboro, after a brief service I confirmed six persons and addressed them. A severe rain-storm interfered very much ' with the attendance of the people at this place, and so delayed our return to Tarboro that we were too late for the evening service appointed in the church.

On the 23d I returned with my family to Charlotte, where on the 25th I assisted the Rector, Mr. Stickney, in a funeral, and on the 26th performed a marriage service. I left home for the western part of the Diocese October 27th, and the next day, the feast of SS. Simon and Jude, opened my visitation in St. Clement's Chapel, Candler's, Buncombe county, where I met the Convocation of Asheville. At 11 A. M. I celebrated the Holy Communion, assisted by the Rev. John A. Deal, Dean, the Rev. McNeely DuBose preaching the sermon. In the afternoon I attended a business meeting of the Convocation.

The twenty-second Sunday after Trinity, October 29th, in the same place, there were present of the Clergy Messrs. Deal, Barrows, Bell, Barker and Rhodes. After Morning Prayer by the Rev. Messrs. Barrows and Barker I confirmed four persons and addressed them, preached, and administered the Holy Communion, assisted by Mr. Deal. In the afternoon I drove in to Asheville.

October 30th, at Beaver Dam Mission, two miles north of Asheville, the Rev. William F. Rice, Deacon in charge, after Morning Prayer by Messrs. Rice and Barrows, I preached, confirmed four persons and addressed them, and administered the Holy Communion. After dinner I accompanied Messrs. Rice and Barrows to the house of a sick man five miles distant, and confirmed him in private. At eight o'clock the same evening, in Asheville, in the Church for colored people, the Rev. Henry S. McDuffey, Priest in charge, after Evening Prayer by Messrs. McDuffey and DuBose, I preached, confirmed five persons and addressed them.

October 31st I went to Murphy, Cherokee county, accompanied by the Rev. Mr. Deal. At seven o'clock in the evening, in the Methodist Church in Murphy, Mr. Deal read such parts of the service as were practicable under the circumstances, and I preached. We own a good lot in this town, but no building, and we have very few of our people here.

November 1st, All Saints, we arrived at Bryson City in time to have service at 11 A. M. Mr. Deal read Morning Prayer, I read the Litany, preached and celebrated the Holy Communion. At night, after Evening Prayer by Mr. Deal, I preached to a large congregation. We have a few zealous members here, and a church building, which is now, as I am informed, occupied for public worship, though not entirely completed.

Thursday, November 2d, I accompanied Mr. Deal to Franklin, by way of Dillsboro, and was kindly entertained by him for a week. The day after our arrival I had a slight attack of sickness, which, though not serious, made it necessary that I should recall my appointments for High-lands and Cashier's Valley. I regretted this very much, but found that it was necessary. My indisposition continued to such an extent that I was not able even to go to the churches in the immediate vicinity. Therefore November 5th, the twenty-third Sunday after Trinity, the candidates from St. Agnes' Chapel, Franklin, and from St. Cyprian's, near by, were presented for confirmation in Mr. Deal's study, and I there confirmed three white persons and one negro; and the next day in the same place I confirmed three persons from St. John's, Nonah. I addressed both classes briefly.

Mr. Deal has under his direction the Rev. John W. Bar-ker, Deacon, who has been assisting him in St. Agnes and the other Missions near Franklin, and a colored Deacon, the Rev. James T. Kennedy, who has charge of St. Cyprian's Chapel, with the Parish School and Industrial School attached, for the benefit of the negro population, which is more numerous here than I had supposed. Besides the church, Mr. Deal is also much interested in an effort to establish a girls' school in Franklin, and has in St. Agnes' School the beginning of an admirable institution. The ladies who have charge of it are in every way worthy of the confidence of those who have girls to educate, and I most sincerely hope that St. Agnes' School may receive such patronage and assistance that it may prove in all that mountain region a center of light and influence for the education of the young, and for the dissemination of the Gospel as this Church hath received the same.

Six miles beyond Franklin is St. John's Church, Nonah, and further across the mountains is Highlands, where is a promising Mission. The Mission at Cashier's Valley has been also under Mr. Deal's care, though for awhile he had a resident Deacon there. Bryson City, in Swain county, is also part of his charge. While none of these places have strong congregations, yet it is apparent that a vast amount of labor and effort must have been expended in bringing the work into its present condition, and it seems to me that foundations have been well and solidly laid. Valuable property has been acquired and excellent buildings erected, both churches and schools. In no part of the Missionary field has this preliminary work been better done. The property of St. Cyprian's Mission is most admirably suited for its purpose, and its work among the colored people has been on the whole excellent. St. Agnes' School has already been alluded to.

Friday, November 10th, I was driven by Mr. Barker, from his house near Franklin, where I had spent the night, to the house of Mr. Davies, at Cullowhee, where we were met the next day by the Rev. Mr. Barrows. The twenty-fourth Sunday after Trinity, in St. David's Church, Cullowhee, after Morning Prayer by Messrs. Barrows and Barker, I confirmed one person, preached, and administered the Holy Communion.

Immediately after the service at St. David's I was driven to the residence of Mr. Dillard Love, where we had dinner, and after dinner went to the village called Sylva, where, in a public hall fitted up as a chapel, Mr. Barrows read Evening Prayer, and I preached.

Monday, November 13th, I proceeded with Mr. Barrows to Waynesville, and in the afternoon, in St. Mary's Chapel, Micadale, near Waynesville, Mr. Barrows said Evening Prayer, and I preached.

The next day, in Grace Church, Waynesville, I preached, confirmed three persons, and addressed them, and administered the Holy Communion, assisted by Mr. Barrows.

I proceeded to Asheville by the afternoon train, and at 4 P. M., in Trinity Church, after Evening Prayer by the Rector, assisted by the Rev. Scott B. Rathbun, I confirmed five persons, and immediately after the service went with Mr. DuBose to a private house and confirmed two persons, a sick lady and her sister.

Wednesday, November 15th, in the Church of the Redeemer, three miles north of Asheville, on a hill overlooking the French Broad River, the Rev. Mr. Rice, Deacon in charge, read the Litany; I confirmed (and addressed) three persons, and administered the Holy Communion, assisted by Mr. Barrows. I dined with Dr. Willis, whose liberality has erected this beautiful stone chapel, and after dinner was driven back to Asheville by him.

The same evening, from eight to ten o'clock, at the house of Mr. Melvin Carter, where I was staying, I had the pleasure of meeting most of the men of Trinity Church, Asheville, besides many other gentlemen of the city, and a smaller number of ladies, who had been invited by my hospitable hosts to meet me, in order that I might have an opportunity of making the acquaintance of the people of Asheville. It was to me a great pleasure to meet so many of our own communion in social intercourse, and also to make the acquaintace of many who, if not of our own particular household, were yet so kind as to feel an interest in us, and to give me a kind welcome to their city and their good wishes for the success of my work.

Thursday, November 16th, in the Church of the Transfiguration, Saluda, after Morning Prayer by Mr. Barrows and Rev. Dr. McCullough, of South Carolina, I confirmed one person, preached, and administered the Holy Communion, assisted by Dr. McCullough. After the service in the church I proceeded to the residence of the Bishop of South Carolina, who has a summer house here, and had the pleasure of ministering to that godly and noble man in a private celebration of the Holy Communion, he being at that time too unwell to go out to the church. I was deeply sensible of my privilege in being able thus to show my affection and respect for Bishop Howe, and I was truly grateful to find him enjoying at least such health as allowed him a very large measure of domestic and social happiness with his family and friends, though the Church is deprived of his active exertions in the work of his office. I am glad to be able to add that since I saw him last November I hear that his health has still further improved.

Friday, November 17th, in St. James' Church, Hendersonville, after Morning Prayer by the Rev. Mr. Rathbun, I confirmed one person, preached, and administered the Holy Communion.

In the afternoon I enjoyed a delightful drive across the mountains with Mr. Rathbun to Bowman's Bluff, where the next day, in Gethsemane Church, after Morning Prayer by Mr. Rathbun, I confirmed two persons, preached, and administered the Holy Communion. The Rev. Richard Wainwright, Priest in charge of this church, was present, but was unable to take part in the service, except to present the Candidates for Confirmation. In the afternoon, accompanied by Mr. Rathbun, I proceeded to Brevard, where the next day, the twenty-fifth Sunday after Trinity, November 19th, in St. Philip's Church, after Morning Prayer by Mr. Rathbun, I preached, and administered the Holy Communion.

November 20th, at a private house in Henderson county, in the presence of a congregation there gathered, I baptized an infant, using the office of Public Baptism. The distance to the nearest church, the season of the year, and the want of regular services in the church, seemed to justify this service.

Tuesday, November 21st, I drove from Asheville to the Chapel at Haw Creek, and was much grieved to find the minister, the Rev. George H. Bell, confined to his bed with a severe attack of neuralgia, from which he had then been suffering about ten days. I therefore had the service at the Chapel myself, preached, confirmed six persons and addressed them.

The next day, at Old Fort, in the church just erected, after Morning Prayer by the Rev. Girard W. Phelps, I confirmed two persons and addressed them, preached, and administered the Holy Communion.

Thursday, November 23d, at Marion, in St. John's Church, after Morning Prayer by Mr. Phelps, I confirmed and addressed five persons, preached, and administered the Holy Communion.

The same evening, in the new church for the colored congregation in Morganton, after Evening Prayer by the Rev. Edward P. Green and the Rev. James T. Kennedy, I preached, confirmed four persons and addressed them.

Friday, November 24th, I consecrated this church by the name of St. Stephen's Church. The Petition for Consecration was read by the Rev. Henry S. McDuffey, of Asheville, the Priest in charge, through whose zeal and energy this important work for the colored people of Morganton had been accomplished, and the Sentence of Consecration by the Rev. William Walker. Morning Prayer was read by the Rev. McNeely DuBose and the Rev. Mr. Kennedy. I preached, and administered the Holy Communion. The church is a very convenient and appropriate structure, with a commodious school-room in the basement, and is in every way fitted for its sacred and beneficent purposes. In the afternoon I assisted the Rev. Mr. Green in a funeral.

At 7:30 P. M., in the public hall used for the present by the congregation of Grace Church, after Evening Prayer by the Rector, the Rev. Mr. Green, I preached. I was glad to see that so much progress had been made upon the new parish church. The walls had been completed, the roof put on, and the floor laid. The building is of stone, well constructed, of good size and pleasing proportions, and when·completed will be one of the handsomest churches in the Diocese. I most earnestly hope that it may soon be so far finished as to be used for public worship.

The Sunday next before Advent, November 26th, in St. James' Church, Lenoir, after Morning Prayer by the Rev. Dr. Buxton, I confirmed two persons, preached, and administered the Holy Communion. The same day at 4 P. M., at the Chapel of Rest, in the Happy Valley, Dr. Buxton read Evening Prayer, and I preached, and confirmed two persons.

Having thus completed my first series of visitations in accordance with the direčtions of Bishop Lyman, the next day I returned to Charlotte, in order to spend a few days with my family, and also that I might have an opportunity of conferring with the Bishop, who was to spend part of the week in that city.

Wednesday, Thursday and Friday, November 29th–December 1st, I spent a good part of the time with the Bishop in Charlotte, receiving much kindly advice and encouragement in connection with my new duties, and enjoying free and confidential conferences with him upon the condition and prospects of the work in the Diocese. He was most deeply interested in hearing about the congregations and Missions in the mountains, in which he had always taken so lively an interest, but which for some time he had not been able to visit. I could not, however, fail to be struck with the great change which had taken place in him since I had last seen him, only six weeks before, and I urged him to return to his home in Raleigh and not to attempt any further visits to parishes or friends until he should feel stronger.

Thursday, November 30th, St. Andrew's Day, being also by appointment of the civil authority Thanksgiving Day, I attended the service in St. Peter's Church, Charlotte, and had the pleasure of listening to the earnest and wholesome sermon preached by the Bishop upon the duty of the people not only to obey but to respect and honor the powers that be. It was the last time it was my privilege to hear him preach, and it was a sermon well worth hearing and remembering.

Friday, December 1st, I attended a meeting of the Managers of the Thompson Orphanage, of which I had been from its organization one of the presbyter members, and for part of the time the Secretary. I thought it right to tender my resignation, but the Board declined to receive it. Much important business was transacted, and the noble work going on in that institution was brought before the Board in a way which impressed us all with the solemn responsibilities resting upon the Diocese in connection therewith. The Bishop seemed specially aroused to the character and the demands of the work, which had not been so familiar to him as to those who have been brought into closer contact with it. I cannot but feel that it was this meeting, and the full investigation of the condition and needs of the Orphanage which there took place, which caused him to remember it so generously in his last will and testament.

The first Sunday in Advent, December 3d, I made a visitation to St. Barnabas' Church, Greensboro, and after Morning Prayer by the Rev. Alfred H. Stubbs, Rector, I confirmed six persons, preached, and administered the Holy Communion. In the afternoon I confirmed in private a sick man and his wife, who were prevented from coming to the church by the bad weather. At night, in St. Andrew's Church, South Greensboro, after Evening Prayer by the Rev. James D. Miller, Deacon in charge, and Mr. Stubbs, I preached.

Thursday, December 7th, in St. Mark's Church, Mecklenburg county, after Morning Prayer by Messrs. Osborne and Stickney, I confirmed and addressed seven persons, preached, and administered the Holy Communion.

Friday, December 8th, in St. James' Church, Iredell county, after Morning Prayer by the Rev. Robert Bruce Owens, Deacon serving under Dr. Murdoch, I confirmed and addressed five persons, preached, and administered the Holy Communion.

The Bishop having informed me, when I was with him in Charlotte, of his intention of celebrating the twentieth anniversary of his Consecration by a special service on Sunday, the 10th of December, I felt it a duty as well as a pleasure that I should be present on that occasion. I therefore recalled the appointments made for Saturday and Sunday in Rowan county, and proceeded at once to Raleigh. I arrived Saturday morning in time to breakfast with the Bishop and Mrs. Lyman. I was much shocked to see the Bishop in what seemed to me a very serious condition of bodily weakness, and I joined his wife in trying to persuade him to send at once for his physician, and to give up all thoughts of being present at the service appointed for Sunday night. He was even then preparing the address which he purposed to deliver upon the occasion, and with characteristic courage and persistence he declined to give up his purpose, but declared that he would be perfectly able to deliver it. A few hours later, however, he felt obliged to send for his physician, who at once forbade him to think of leaving the house for some days. By his direction, therefore, I did what I could to arrange for the proper observance of the interesting anniversary. The second Sunday in Advent, December 10th, in the forenoon, in the Church of the Good Shepherd, Raleigh, after Morning Prayer by the Rector, Rev. Mr. Pittenger, I preached.

In Christ Church, at 8 P. M., we celebrated the twentieth anniversary of the Consecration of Bishop Lyman by an interesting and impressive service. The Bishop of East Carolina honored the occasion with his presence, and by permission of Bishop Lyman I requested him to preside. After Evening Prayer had been said by the Rev. Mr. Pittenger and the Rev. Dr. Smedes, Bishop Watson made a brief address, and introduced the several speakers. Dr. Marshall read a contemporary account of Bishop Lyman's

10

Consecration, and addresses were made by Mr. Pittenger and myself. I concluded the service with prayers and the Benediction. A very large and attentive congregation crowded the capacious edifice, and a solemn interest was given to the services by the consciousness that he in whose honor they were held was detained at home by the increasing burden of care and labor so faithfully borne for his people.

Monday, December 11th, at St. Mary's School, I took part with Dr. Smedes in the Morning Prayers in the Chapel, and made an address to the girls. Monday evening the Bishop received his friends from seven until ten o'clock, and, though unable to be present in the company, enjoyed in his own room the consciousness that he was exercising hospitality and giving pleasure to many. I saw him last about ten o'clock, when I bade him good-bye to return to my visitations in Rowan county. His last words to me were of kindly personal regard and fatherly counsel, with assurances of his full approval of whatever I might feel that the interest of the Church called upon me to do when I could not consult with him, together with a special request that I would so far as possible supply his place in one or two appointments which he could not fulfil in person. I saw him no more in the flesh.

Tuesday, December 12th, at St. Matthew's Chapel, Franklin Township, Rowan county, after Morning Prayer by the Rev. Dr. Murdoch, I confirmed five persons, preached, and administered the Holy Communion. In the evening of the same day, in St. Peter's Chapel, Salisbury, after Evening Prayer by the Rev. Benjamin S. McKenzie and the Rev. Sidney S. Bost, I preached, confirmed six persons presented by Dr. Murdoch, and addressed them.

Wednesday, December 13th, at St. Jude's Chapel, Locke Township, after Morning Prayer by Dr. Murdoch and Mr. Bost, I confirmed one person, preached, and administered the Holy Communion.

Returning to Salisbury, I found telegrams awaiting me informing me of the death of Bishop Lyman that morning about half past eight o'clock. As no train left Salisbury for Raleigh until late in the evening, I filled my appointment at St. John's Chapel, Salisbury, for 7:30 P. M., and after Evening Prayer by Messrs. Bost and Owens I preached, and confirmed two persons.

December 14th, upon arriving in Raleigh, after consulting with a number of the Clergy and Laity, I sent telegrams to such of the Clergy as we thought could reach Raleigh in time for the funeral, requesting them to be present, and I took upon myself the responsibility of promising that their expenses should be paid by the Diocese.

The funeral was appointed for Friday at noon, December 15th. The body was borne from the house to Christ Church upon the shoulders of eight pupils of St. Augustine's School, who requested the honor of being the bearers of the mortal remains of him who had so deeply at heart the interests of the negroes of his Diocese, and especially of that institution for their education.

The body was preceded by the Clergy of the Diocese, the Bishop of Southern Virginia, the Bishop of East Carolina and myself, all vested. The late Bishop's Chaplain, the Rev. Charles C. Quin, carried his Pastoral Staff before the coffin. After the coffin came a long procession composed of the family and friends, the Governor and other chief officers of the State, citizens of Raleigh, and Churchmen from other parts of the Diocese.

At the entrance into the Church-yard the sentences were begun by the Bishop of Southern Virginia, who continued the service to the lesson, which was read by Dr. Marshall, President of the Convention and of the Standing Committee. The Creed and Prayers were said by Bishop Watson. The body was then borne to the cemetery in the same order as from the house. The Committal at the grave was said by myself, the earth being cast upon the coffin by the Rev. A. B. Hunter. I may be allowed to express here my own gratitude and that of the Diocese for the presence with us on this occasion of the Bishops of East Carolina and of Southern Virginia, and also of the Rev. Dr. Barten, of the latter Diocese.

Immediately after returning from the grave a meeting was held in Christ Church of the Clergy and Laity of the Diocese, at which addresses were made by myself (in calling the meeting to order), by the Bishop of Southern Virginia and others, and a committee was appointed to prepare resolutions to be reported to this Convention in regard to the death of Bishop Lyman.

The necessity of making some inquiry into the affairs of

the Diocese, and the character of my new duties and obligations, kept me for some days in Raleigh. I was therefore obliged to cancel my remaining appointments. During three days I sought the advice of the Standing Committee, and other Diocesan officers, and endeavored to gather up the threads which had dropped from the more experienced and stronger hands of my predecessor. I met with much kind assistance from all the members of Bishop Lyman's family, who made diligent search among his effects and turned over to me all things in any way pertaining to the Diocese, together with many useful blanks and other articles which were doubtless the personal property of the Bishop.

The third Sunday in Advent, December 17th, in Christ Church, Raleigh, I took part in the service with Dr. Marshall and Dr. Sutton, and preached. In the evening, at the Church of the Good Shepherd, after Evening Prayer by the Rector and Mr. Ingle, I preached. Monday, December 18th, at 8 P. M., in Christ Church, I presided at a meeting of the Laity of the two parishes, whom I had, with consent of the Rector of Christ Church, invited to meet me there in order that I might set before them the condition of the Missionary work of the Diocese, and explain the new scheme of systematic offerings put forth by the Executive Missionary Committee. The very bad weather prevented a large attendance, but I spoke briefly to those present, and was followed by Mr. Charles E. Johnson, the Rev. Scott B. Rathbun, Dr. Marshall, Mr. Richard H. Battle and Mr. Charles M. Busbee.

Wednesday, December 20th, in a private house in Hillsboro, I confirmed in private a sick woman, and at half past eight o'clock, in St. Andrew's Church, South Greensboro, after Evening Prayer by the Rev. James D. Miller, I preached, and confirmed eight persons.

Thursday, December 21st, St. Thomas' Day, in St. Andrew's Church, I held my first ordination. The appointment had been made by Bishop Lyman, and part of his last conversation with me was to urge me not to fail to supply his place on this day, when he found that he would not himself be able to fulfil his appointment. Morning Prayer was said by Mr. Miller, and the Rev Dr. Murdoch preached an exceedingly able and instructive sermon. The candidates were presented by the Rev. Alfred H. Stubbs, and I ordained to the Diaconate Frederick A. Fetter, M.A., and Charles Fetter, M.A., sons of the late Professor Manuel Fetter, of the University of North Carolina, and both of them graduates of that institution. After a good many years spent in teaching, in which they have gained wide reputation in this State, they have now devoted themselves most zealously to the work of the holy ministry. The rest of the service I said myself, being assisted in the Holy Communion by the Rev. Dr. Murdoch. The afternoon of the same day I confirmed a sick woman in private.

The fourth Sunday in Advent, December 24th, in All Saints' Church, Concord, the Rev. J. C. Davis, Rector, said Morning Prayer, and I preached. In the evening, in the same Church, after Evening Prayer by the Rector, I preached, confirmed six persons and addressed them.

Christmas Day, in St Peter's Church, Charlotte, after Morning Prayer and a sermon by the Rev. Fenner S. Stickney, Rector, I celebrated the Holy Communion. In the evening I visited the Thompson Orphanage and made a brief address to the children at their Christmas-tree festival.

December 27th I attended a committee meeting to consider business of the Thompson Orphanage.

December 28th, at Dallas, in Gaston county, I confirmed a sick man in private, presented by Dr. Wetmore. In the afternoon, in Lincolnton, I confirmed in private a sick woman, and at night, in St. Luke's Church, Lincolnton, after Evening Prayer by Dr. Wetmore, I preached, and confirmed one person.

The Sunday after Christmas, December 31st, in St. Peter's Church, Charlotte, I assisted the Rector in the services, and preached.

In the afternoon I made a visitation to the Church of St. Michael and All Angels, the Rev. Primus P. Alston, Priest in charge, and after Evening Prayer by Messrs. Stickney and Alston I preached, confirmed eight persons and addressed them. After the service I confirmed a colored person, member of St. Michael's, in private, on a sick-bed.

The first Sunday after the Epiphany, January 7th, in a school-house in Gaston county, near the residence of Mrs. Laura E. Johnston, I preached and celebrated the Holy Communion.

The second Sunday after the Epiphany, January 14th, in St. Mark's Church, Mecklenburg county, I had service and preached.

From Tuesday, January 16th, to Thursday, the 18th, I attended the several meetings of the Convocation of Raleigh, in the Church of the Good Shepherd, Raleigh.

Wednesday, January 17th, I attended a meeting of the Executive Missionary Committee in the vestry-room of Christ Church.

The same evening, in Christ Church, I took part with the Rector in a marriage service, at his request pronouncing the Blessing.

Thursday, January 18th, I confirmed in private a sick person presented by Dr. Marshall.

Saturday, January 20th, on my arrival in Oxford, I had the pleasure of attending a very interesting meeting of the parish branch of the Junior Auxiliary, under the direction of Miss Horner.

Septuagesima Sunday, January 21st, in St. Stephen's Church, Oxford, I celebrated the Holy Communion at 7:30 A. M. At 11 A. M. I took part with the Rev. Edward Benedict in the service, and preached. At night, after Evening Prayer by Mr. Benedict and the Rev. Junius M. Horner, I preached, confirmed ten persons and addressed them. Next morning I confirmed a sick person in private.

Monday, January 22d, in St. Philip's Church, Durham, after Evening Prayer by the Rev. Stewart McQueen, I preached and confirmed five persons.

Tuesday, January 23d, in the Chapel of the Cross, Chapel Hill, after Evening Prayer by the Rev. Frederick Towers, Rector, I preached, and confirmed three persons. The next morning I conducted the morning service in the University Chapel, and afterwards spent an interesting hour in inspecting the University in the pleasant company of my friend, President Winston. Every North Carolinian should feel proud and grateful as he contemplates the past history and the present prospects of our great University.

The evening of the same day, in St. Athanasius' Church, Burlington, after Evening Prayer by the Rev. Robert J. Walker, Rector, I preached, confirmed three persons and addressed them. Immediately after this service I proceeded with Mr. Walker to a school-house in which he holds services for colored people, and there I confirmed three negro men presented by Mr. Walker, and made a short address.

Thursday, January 25th, the Feast of the Conversion of St. Paul, in the same church, I preached and administered the Holy Communion, assisted by the Rector.

Friday, January 26th, in St. Mary's Church, High Point, Morning Prayer was said by the Rev. Frederick A. Fetter. I baptized two adults, preached, and administered the Holy Communion. In the afternoon I baptized an infant in a private house, but in presence of a congregation of people gathered together, the weather not permitting the child to be carried out. At night Mr. Fetter said Evening Prayer, and I preached, confirmed nine persons and addressed them.

Saturday, January 27th, in St. Thomas' Church, Reidsville, the Rev. James D. Miller, of St. Andrew's Church, Greensboro, said Morning Prayer, and I made an address. In the afternoon I prepared a short Lenten Pastoral, which I addressed to the Clergy and Laity of the Diocese.

Sexagesima Sunday, January 28th, in the same church, the Rev. Mr. Miller said the Litany. I preached, confimed five persons and addressed them, and administered the Holy Communion.

In the afternoon I baptized in private houses two infants in the presence of a congregation, and with the public service. The weather would not admit of the children being brought to the church, and there was no Minister in charge of the parish, which, in my judgment, created a case of necessity required by the rubric. At night in the church I said Evening Prayer and preached.

Monday, January 29th, in Christ Church, Milton, I confirmed one person, preached, and administered the Holy Communion, assisted by the Rev. Charles Fetter, Deacon in charge. At night Mr. Fetter said Evening Prayer, and I preached. The congregations at both services were large and attentive, and I could not but rejoice to see the impression made in this community during the ministry of our brother, who, though young in the work, is strong in zeal and devotion. I did not go on to Cuningham's, as I found that Mr. Fetter had thought it necessary to cancel that appointment, which I had left to his discretion.

Tuesday, January 30th, I administered the Holy Communion in private to a sick person in Milton.

In spending the night in Danville I took the opportunity of calling on the venerable Dr. Dame, who has done so much to serve our church people on the border near him. I spent some hours very delightfully in his company.

Thursday, February 1st, in the Church of the Epiphany, Leaksville, I said Morning Prayer, baptized two infants, preached, and administered the Holy Communion. At night I said Evening Prayer, baptized an adult, preached, and confirmed three persons.

There is no Minister in charge of Leaksville and Rockingham, and all efforts to obtain one have so far failed. I trust some suitable man may soon be found to take up the work in these two interesting and important parishes.

Friday, February 2d, the Feast of the Purification, in a free church at Stoneville, Rockingham county, I held a brief informal service and preached to a small congregation.

The same evening, in St. John's Church, Madison, I said Evening Prayer and preached.

Saturday, in the same church, at 11 A. M., I said Morning Prayer, confirmed one person, preached, and administered the Holy Communion.

Quinquagesima Sunday, February 4th, in Christ Church, Walnut Cove, I said Morning Prayer, confirmed three persons, preached, and administered the Holy Communion. There being no Minister in charge of this place or Madison, I directed Mr. Charles Fetter to give one Sunday each month to each place, and to continue his present arrangement with Milton and Cuningham's, so that his time is now fully employed.

Tuesday, February 6th, at Mount Airy, I held service in the forenoon in the school-room of Miss Graves, preached, and celebrated the Holy Communion. In the evening, in the Methodist Church, I said Evening Prayer and preached to a large congregation. I cannot refrain from noticing here the hearty and devout character of these services, the full and intelligent responses, and the excellent singing. We have but a small number of communicants in Mount Airy, but they seemed most intelligent and zealous. I believe, on the whole, I have not heard such responses and such appropriate and excellent music anywhere on my visitation, considering the disadvantages under which we labor of having no place of worship and no regular ministrations. It is a matter of very great regret to me that my efforts to provide regular services. here have so far proved unsuccessful.

Ash Wednesday, February 7th, by an unfortunate mistake my appointment for service at King's Cabin was misunderstood, and when I reached that station on the Cape Fear & Yadkin Valley Railway I found no congregation and no place to hold the service. I walked across the fields and woods a mile or so to a small hamlet called Five Forks, and found that the appointment should have been made for that place.

The same afternoon I proceeded to Germanton, where I was met by the Rev. Alfred H. Stubbs, of Greensboro, who had come at my request to assist in the consecration of the church. Thursday, February 8th, I consecrated St. Philip's Church, Germanton, the Sentence of Consecration being read by the Rev. Mr. Stubbs, who also preached the sermon. I baptized an adult and an infant, confirmed one person, and administered the Holy Communion.

In the afternoon I took the train for Davie county, and spent Friday, the 9th, at Cooleemee, the residence of Mrs. Hairston.

Saturday, February 10th, in the forenoon, at St. Andrew's Church, Rowan county, I confirmed two persons, preached, and administered the Holy Communion, assisted by the Rev. Sidney S. Bost, Deacon. At three o'clock in the afternoon, at St. George's Chapel, Woodleaf, after Evening Prayer by Mr. Bost, I preached.

The first Sunday in Lent, February 11th, at Christ Church, Rowan county, the Litany was said by the Rev. Mr. Bost. I confirmed three persons, addressed them, preached, and administered the Holy Communion.

Monday, February 12th, after attending Morning Prayer in St. Peter's Church, Charlotte, I confirmed in private a sick man and his wife, presented by Mr. Stickney.

Wednesday, February 14th, Ember Day, in St. Luke's Church, Lincolnton, I ordained to the Diaconate Mr. Thomas Cogdell Wetmore. There were present of the Clergy the Rev. Wm. R. Wetmore, D.D., Jarvis Buxton, D.D., James A. Weston, Edwin A. Osborne, Charles C. Quin, Edward P. Green, of this Diocese, and the Rev. Wm. A. Guerry, of the Diocese of South Carolina. The candidate was presented by his father, the Rev. Dr. Wetmore, Rector of the parish, and the sermon was preached by the Rev. Mr. Weston.   Before the beginning of the ordination service proper I confirmed one person.

Thursday, February 15th, I attended a special meeting of the Board of Fellows of the Ravenscroft Associate Mission and Training School, held in the Library of Shoenberger Hall, Asheville.   The business transacted will come before the Convention in the report of the Board of Fellows.

The second Sunday in Lent, February 18th, in St. Luke's Church, Salisbury, I advanced to the Priesthood the Rev. Benjamin Sumner McKenzie, of St. Matthew's Church, Hillsboro.   The candidate was presented by the Rev. Dr. Murdoch, who preached the sermon.   There were also present of the Clergy the Rev. Alfred H. Stubbs, Scott B. Rathbun, Charles C. Quin and Fenner S. Stickney, Priests, and Messrs. Bost and Owens, Deacons.   All the Priests present joined with me in the imposition of hands.

At 3:30 P. M., in St. Mary's Church, Rowan county, after Evening Prayer by Dr. Murdoch, I preached, and confirmed one person.

At 8 P. M. in St. Paul's Chapel, Salisbury, after Evening Prayer by Messrs. Stubbs and Owens, I confirmed seven persons.

Tuesday, February 20th, I assisted the Rev. Mr. Stickney in his Lenten Services in St. Peter's Church, Charlotte, and confirmed a sick man in private.

Thursday, February 22d, in Asheville I laid the cornerstone of the new church for the colored congregation under the charge of the Rev. Mr. McDuffey.   A large congregation of both races was present, and addresses were made by Mr. John L. Love, of the colored congregation; by Mr. Thomas L. Patton, Mayor of Asheville, and by the Rev. William S. Barrows.   There were present of the Clergy Messrs. DuBose, Rathbun, Barrows, McDuffey, Rice and Rhodes.   The church for colored people has heretofore been known as Trinity Chapel.   By the consent of the persons interested I named the new structure St. Matthias.   I did this because it seems to me very undesirable to call so many of our churches by the same name.   There are many most appropriate designations entirely unused in this Diocese, while we go on with perplexing iteration bestowing the names of St. John, St. Paul, Trinity, etc.

The third Sunday in Lent, February 25th, I made a visitation to Wilson. At 11 A. M., in St. Timothy's Church, Morning Prayer was said by the Rev. Charles J. Wingate, Rector. I preached, and administerted the Holy Communion. At 4 P. M., in St. Mark's Chapel, for colored people, after Evening Prayer by the Rev. John W. Perry, I preached. At 8 P. M., in St. Timothy's Church, Evening Prayer was said by the Rector, and I preached, and confirmed two persons. The next morning at ten o'clock I confirmed in the same church three persons, and made an address to the congregation.

Monday, February 26th, at 4:30 P. M., in the Church of the Good Shepherd, Rocky Mount, I took part with the Rector, the Rev. Alvin J. Vanderbogart, in Evening Prayer, and made an address. The next day, after Morning Prayer by the Rector,· I confirmed two persons, preached, and administered the Holy Communion. Immediately after the service I confirmed a sick man in private.

Wednesday, February 28th, in the Chapel of St. John, Battleboro, after Evening Prayer by the Rev. Gaston Battle, Deacon, I preached, and confirmed two persons.

The fourth Sunday in Lent, March 4th, in Calvary Church, Tarboro, after Morning Prayer by the Rev. Charles L. Hoffmann, Rector, I preached, and administered the Holy Communion.

At 3:30 P. M., in St. Mary's Chapel, Edgecombe county, Mr. Hoffmann said Evening Prayer and baptized an adult; I preached, and confirmed the person just baptized.

At 7:30 P. M., in Calvary Church, Mr. Hoffmann said Evening Prayer, and I preached, and confirmed six persons.

Monday, March 5th, in St. Luke's Church, the colored congregation, the Rev. John W. Perry, Rector, said Evening Prayer. I preached, and confirmed seven persons.

Tuesday, March 6th, in a hall at Lawrence, Edgecombe county, Mr. Hoffmann said Evening Prayer, and baptized three persons. I preached, and confirmed the persons just baptized.

Wednesday, March 7th, in the chapel of Calvary Church, Mr. Hoffmann said Evening Prayer, and I made an address to the congregation.

Friday, March 9th, at Crowell's Cross-roads, Halifax county, in a private house, I preached, confirmed three persons, and administered the Holy Communion, assisted by the Rev. Walter J. Smith, who has occasional services at this point.

At 7:30 P. M., in Trinity Church, Scotland Neck, I presided at a Missionary meeting, and made a brief address, introducing the Rev. Scott B. Rathbun, Secretary of the Executive Missionary Committee, who addressed the congregation upon the condition and needs of our Missionary work.

The fifth Sunday in Lent, March 11th, in the same church, the Rev. Mr. Smith said Morning Prayer, and I preached and administered the Holy Communion. In the afternoon at the old church in the church-yard just out of the town, Mr. Smith said Evening Prayer, and I preached to a large congregation. All seemed deeply affected by the services and by the hallowed associations of the place. This parish has been sadly visited during the past year or two. A large number of its most devout members, including two Senior Wardens, have been called to rest, and many households have felt the sadness of these separations. In the evening, in the present parish church, Mr. Smith said Evening Prayer, and I preached, and confirmed four persons.

Monday, March 12th, in a hall in the village of Tillery, Halifax county, Mr. Smith said Morning Prayer, and I preached. A few of our people live in this vicinity, and Mr. Smith, who has a monthly appointment here, has begun a fund for the erection of a chapel. The same evening, in St. Mark's Church, Halifax, after Evening Prayer by Mr. Smith, who has also taken this parish in connection with his other work, I preached. The next morning, in the same church, Mr. Smith baptized an adult, whom I confirmed. I also preached and administered the Holy Communion.

Thursday, March 15th, in St. Clement's Church, Ringwood, I said Morning Prayer, preached, and administered the Holy Communion in the forenoon; and in the evening I again conducted the service, preached, and confirmed one person. This parish is without a Minister.

Friday, March 16th, in the Church of the Advent, Enfield, Mr. Vanderbogart said Evening Prayer and I preached. The next morning I celebrated the Holy Communion, assisted by Mr. Vanderbogart, and later in the day baptized an infant in the same church. This place has also been for some months without services. I have directed the Rev. Gaston Battle to give one Sunday each month to this parish.

Palm Sunday, March 18th, in Grace Church, Weldon, I said Morning Prayer, preached, and administered the Holy Communion. In the afternoon I visited the Sunday-school for colored children taught by a few of the good women of this parish. In the evening, in the church, after Evening Prayer by Mr. Vanderbogart, who kindly came up from Rocky Mount on the afternoon train to assist me, I preached and confirmed two persons presented by Mr. Vanderbogart.

Monday, March 19th, in the Church of the Saviour, Jackson, the Rev. Mr. Picard said Morning Prayer and I preached, and administered the Holy Communion. In the evening Mr. Picard again read the service and I preached.

Tuesday, in St. Luke's Church, in Northampton county (near Gaston), the Rev. William Walker said Evening Prayer and I preached. In the same church the next morning I baptized and confirmed an adult, and administered the Holy Communion, assisted by Mr. Walker.

Accompanied by Mr. Walker, I proceeded the same day to Littleton, and in the evening, in the Chapel of the Cross, Mr. Walker said Evening Prayer and I preached. I was glad to be able to remain here a day or two, and to have several services for the congregation, which had for some time been without stated ministrations.

Maunday Thursday, in the same church, after the Litany by Mr. Walker, I baptized an adult. Mr. Walker preached and I administered the Holy Communion. In the evening I said Evening Prayer, preached, confirmed two persons and addressed them. Good Friday, in the same church, I said Morning Prayer, the Litany, and the Ante-Communion, and preached. The five congregations at Ringwood, Weldon, Jackson, Gaston and Littleton have all been without regular ministrations for several months. I am exceedingly anxious to find suitable Ministers to undertake the work in this important and promising field.

The evening of Good Friday, in Emmanuel Church, Warrenton, after Evening Prayer by the Rev. John F. Milbank,

Rector, I preached, confirmed five persons and addressed them. Easter Even, in the same church, at 7:30 A. M., I administered the Holy Communion, assisted by the Rev. Mr. Milbank.

In the afternoon, in the church of the Holy Innocents, Henderson, I took part with the Rev. Julian E. Ingle, Rector, in Evening Prayer.

Easter Day, March 25th, in the same church, after Morning Prayer by the Rector, I preached and administered the Holy Communion. In the evening the Rector said Evening Prayer, and I preached, and confirmed ten persons and addressed them

In the evening, I had the pleasure of meeting many of the people of the parish, who had been invited by the Rector to meet me at his house. I trust that hereafter I may be able to see more of the people of all the parishes than has been possible during this hurried visitation.

Easter Monday, March 26th, in the Church of the Good Shepherd, Ridgeway, the Rev. William S. Pettigrew, Rector, said Evening Prayer and I preached. The next morning, in the Chapel of Heavenly Rest, Middleburg, Mr. Pettigrew said Morning Prayer; I preached, confirmed five persons, and administered the Holy Communion.

Wednesday, March 28th, in St. John's Church, Williamsboro, after Morning Prayer by Mr. Pettigrew, I preached, and administered the Holy Communion.

Thursday, March 29th, on my way to the church, I visited a very aged man, who had been baptized by Mr. Horner, and confirmed him on his sick-bed. At 11 A. M., in St. Peter's Church, Stovall, the Rev. Junius M. Horner said Morning Prayer, and I preached, and administered the Holy Communion.

Friday, March 30th, in St. Paul's Church, Goshen, Mr. Horner said Morning Prayer, and I preached and administered the Holy Communion. In the afternoon Mr. Horner kindly took me back to Oxford with him, and I returned to Henderson on my way to Louisburg.

The first Sunday after Easter, April 1st, in St. Paul's Church, Louisburg, Morning Prayer was said by the Rev. William Walker. I preached, and administered the Holy Communion, assisted by the Rev. James B. Avirett, Rector-elect. In the afternoon I had service in the same church for the colored people. Evening Prayer was said by the Rev. Mr. Avirett and the Rev. Henry B. Delany. I preached, and confirmed one person. In the evening, at the second service for the white congregation, Mr. Avirett said Evening Prayer and I preached.

The church for the colored congregation in Louisburg is now completed and ready, I believe, for consecration. Heretofore special services for them have been held in St. Paul's Church. I cannot refrain from suggesting in this connection that in many of our parishes much might be done for the enlightenment and elevation of the negro population, by special services for them in the parish church, where no other suitable building is available. This was the regular practice in my father's parishes, and generally, I believe, in those parts of the State where lived the largest slave-owners, both before and after the emancipation of the negroes, until such time as they had separate churches provided for them. The circumstances and feelings of both races have undergone very great changes, but this may still be practicable and useful in some places.

Monday, April 2d, in St. James' Church, Kittrell, the Rev. Mr. Avirett, Rector-elect, said Morning Prayer; I confirmed two persons, preached, and administered the Holy Communion. After the service I had the pleasure of meeting and dining with the members of the Vestry at the residence of the Rector.

I was much gratified to find that both at Louisburg and at Kittrell the Rev. James B. Avirett, who has recently assumed charge of these two parishes, has been received with great cordiality by the people, and feels much encouraged by the prospects of the work. He comes with additional satisfaction to take up his work among us from the fact that he had his birth and education in North Carolina.

Tuesday and Wednesday I spent in Henderson, closely occupied in endeavoring to attend to arrears of correspondence and other official business.

Thursday, April 5th, I attended the regular meeting of the Executive Missionary Committee in the vestry-room of Christ Church, Raleigh.

Friday, in the chapel of Christ Church, at the request of Dr. Marshall, I conducted the monthly Missionary service, being assisted by Dr. Marshall, and made an address.

The second Sunday after Easter, April 8th, after Morning Prayer by the Rev. Dr. Sutton and the Rev. A. B. Hunter, I confirmed twenty persons, preached, and administered the Holy Communion, assisted by the Rev. Dr. Marshall, Rector.

In the afternoon, in the chapel of St. Mary's School, after Evening Prayer by the Rev. Bennett Smedes, D.D., Principal, I confirmed five girls, pupils of the school, and made an address.

In the evening, in St. Augustine's Church, for colored people, after Evening Prayer by the Rev. Henry B. Delany and the Rev. A. B. Hunter, I preached, confirmed fifteen persons, presented by Mr. Delany, and addressed them.

Monday, April 9th, Pittsboro, in St. James' Chapel, for colored people, the Rev. William Walker read Evening Prayer; I preached, and confirmed four persons. The next day, in St. Bartholomew's Church, the Rev. Charles T. Bland, Rector, Morning Prayer was said by the Rector and Mr. Walker. I confirmed one person, preached, and administered the Holy Communion.

At this point I felt obliged to break off from my appointed scheme of visitations, and, having cancelled the appointments at Sanford and Laurinburg, proceeded to Tryon, in Polk county.

Thursday, April 12th, in the Church of the Holy Cross, Tryon, after Evening Prayer by the Rev. Charles Ferris, Priest in charge, assisted by the Rev. William S. Barrows, I preached. After the service I had a meeting with the members of the congregation, to whom I made a brief address. The next day, acting upon a petition previously presented to me, I organized the congregation as a "Mission," under our Diocesan Canon.

The third Sunday after Easter, April 15th, in the Presbyterian Church in Rockingham, kindly offered for the service, I said Morning Prayer, preached, and administered the Holy Communion. In the afternoon I said Evening Prayer, and baptized an infant.

Monday, April 16th, in the church at Ansonville, after Evening Prayer by the Rev. Charles C. Quin and the Rev. Dr. Murdoch, I preached, confirmed three persons and addressed them. The next forenoon I spent in visiting the members of the church in the neighborhood in company with the Rev. Dr. Murdoch and our hospitable entertainer, Mr. William A. Smith.

In the evening I said Evening Prayer, assisted by the Rev. Robert Bruce Owens, and Dr. Murdoch preached.

Wednesday, April 18th, had been appointed for the consecration of the new parish church of Calvary Parish, Wadesboro. The Convocation of Charlotte had also been called to meet at the same time and place, so that I found present for this interesting service the Rev. Drs. Murdoch and Wetmore, the Rev. James A. Weston, Francis W. Hilliard, Edwin A. Osborne, Charles C. Quin, Scott B. Rathbun, Priests, and Robert Bruce Owens and Thomas C. Wetmore, Deacons, of this Diocese, and the Rev. Anthony A. McDonough, of South Carolina.

The Petition for Consecration was read by Mr. Julius A. Little, Senior Warden, and the Sentence of Consecration by the Rev. Charles C. Quin, Rector. Morning Prayer was said by the Rev. Messrs. Weston and McDonough. The Rev. Dr. Murdoch preached, and the Rev. Dr. Wetmore assisted in the administration of the Holy Communion. The services were solemn and impressive, attended by a large congregation. The Rector and people of this parish have reason to feel deeply gratified at the completion and consecration of this beautiful church, which, for the situation and necessities of the parish, has not its superior in the Diocese for beauty and fitness.

In the afternoon I attended a business meeting of the Convocation, and in the evening took part in the services in the church. The next morning, in the church, I confirmed one person, delivered an address in connection with the subject before the Convocation, and took part in the service.

Thursday evening, in St. Paul's Church, Monroe, after Evening Prayer by the Rev. Francis W. Hilliard, Priest in charge, I preached, confirmed nine persons and addressed them. The next morning Mr. Hilliard said the Litany and I preached, and administered the Holy Communion. This congregation shows signs of progress, and it is much to be hoped that we shall be able to keep a resident Minister here.

The same afternoon I returned home, after a long and somewhat trying visitation. The importance of getting over the whole or the greater part of the Diocese before the Convention caused me to crowd the visitations into a shorter space of time than I should otherwise have done. I trust hereafter to be able to give more time to the several points, and to acquire that personal knowledge of the people which is necessary to the proper administration of this pastoral office.

The fourth Sunday after Easter, April 22d, being disengaged, I had the pleasure of being present morning and evening in my old parish church of St. Peter's, Charlotte, where I preached, and administered the Holy Communion in the morning, and took part in the service with Mr. Stickney in the evening, Mr. Stickney preaching at the latter service.

Wednesday, April 25th, St. Mark's Day, I buried an old friend and parishioner in the same parish, being assisted in the service by Messrs. Stickney and Osborne.

The fifth Sunday after Easter, April 29th, in Trinity Church, Statesville, after Morning Prayer by the Rev. Edwin A. Osborne, Rector, I preached, and administered the Holy Communion. In the same church, in the afternoon, Mr. Osborne said Evening Prayer; I preached, and confirmed two persons.

Monday, April 30th, in the Church of the Ascension, Hickory, the Rev. James A. Weston, Rector, said Evening Prayer; I preached, confirmed seven persons and addressed them. The next morning I was pleased to meet the members of the congregation, who had been invited to meet me at the house of my kind host. Mr. Oliver S. Royster.

Tuesday, May 1st, in a hall in the college building, at Rutherford College, Burke county, the Rev. James A. Weston read Evening Prayer; I preached, confirmed six persons presented by Mr. Weston and addressed them.

Much interest seems to be felt in the services which Mr. Weston maintains at this point. A large and attentive congregation took part in the service, and it seems not unlikely that we may build up a good congregation in this neighborhood.

Though this service was held on the first of May I have included it in this year's report because it was part of my visitation to Mr. Weston's parish, and the candidates were to have been confirmed at Hickory the evening of the preceding day, but found it impracticable to go down.

This, therefore, ends my report of services for the past year. Those after May 1st, following the analogy of the canonical provision as to the date of the parochial reports, will go over for next year's address.

The following is a summary of my work since my Conse-.cration: I have visited one hundred parishes, missions and other places, and have officiated one hundred and fifty-eight times in public services, not including funerals, baptisms, and the like. I have preached one hundred and nineteen times, and made forty-eight addresses; have confirmed three hundred and thirty-two persons, baptized six adults and nine infants, married one couple and officiated at three funerals. I have consecrated three churches, ordained three Deacons, and advanced one Deacon to the Priesthood.

Besides the Bishop, we have lost from our Clergy list by death one of the most devout and godly men who has ever served God at our altars, the Rev. Franklin L. Bush. He had been among us fifteen years, and had served in different capacities and in various parts of the Diocese. Everywhere and among all classes he was recognized as one whose life was a faithful presentation of the truth which he professed and taught. He commanded universal respect and affection as a pure, self-sacrificing, and devout soldier and servant of Jesus Christ. Would that we had many like him as fellow-laborers in our great work!

Besides these two lost by death, Bishop Lyman transferred the Rev. St. Clair Hester to the Diocese of Long Island and the Rev. Mynn T. Turner to the Diocese of Alabama.

We have received since last Convention by letters dimissory the Rev. Francis W. Hilliard, from Maryland; the Rev. Hardy H. Phelps and the Rev. Charles L. Hoffmann, from East Carolina; the Rev. John F. Milbank, from Indiana, and the Rev. John F. George, from Maine. Bishop Lyman ordained one Deacon, the Rev. James D. Miller, and the Rev. St. Clair Hester was ordained for him by the Bishop of New York. He also admitted to Priest's Orders the Rev. Alvin J. Vanderbogart, Deacon. I have ordained three Deacons, as heretofore mentioned, the Rev. Frederick A. Fetter, Charles Fetter and Thomas C. Wetmore. Our net gain in the Clergy list is therefore six, reckoning from May 1, 1893, and the present number is sixty-seven, one Bishop, fifty-three Priests and thirteen Deacons.

The postulants at present are John C. Seagle, John H. Gilreath, Isaac N. Neal, Charles S. Burgess and Thomas C. Brown; also a young colored man, Alfred J. Griffin. The candidates for Deacon's Orders are Samuel A. B. Trott, Thomas B. Bailey, James E. King and Eugene L. Henderson, all colored. The candidates for Priest's Orders are the. Rev. James D. Miller, John W. Barker, Thomas C. Wetmore, Gaston Battle, Frederick A. Fetter and Charles Fetter, Deacons, and Messrs. Nathan A. Seagle, George V. Gilreath and William B. Crittenden, the last a colored man.

The fields of labor of our Diocesan Clergy are the same as last year except as noted below: The Rev. Mr. Hilliard is Priest in charge of the church in Monroe, and also has occasional services in Rockingham and Laurinburg. The Rev. Hardy H. Phelps is Rector of Calvary Church, Henderson county; the Rev. Charles L. Hoffmann has become Rector of Calvary Church, Tarboro; the Rev. John F. Milbank, of Emmanuel Church, Warrenton, and the Rev. John F. George, of St. Paul's, Winston. The Rev. James B. Avirett has been called to the Rectorship of St. Paul's, Louisburg, and of St. James', Kittrell, and has entered upon his work with great acceptance with all the people, but I have not as yet received his letters dimissory from the Bishop of Central New York. The Rev. James D. Miller is in charge of the parish of St. Andrew's, Greensboro; the Rev. Frederick A. Fetter is serving the congregations at High Point and Lexington; the Rev. Charles Fetter ministers and labors in the congregations at Milton, Cuningham's, Madison, and Walnut Cove, and the Rev. Thomas C. Wetmore is acting as Missionary under his father's direction in Gaston and Lincoln counties.

The Rev. Fenner S. Stickney has become Rector of St. Peter's Church, Charlotte. The Rev. Samuel Rhodes has been assisting Mr. Barrows in the Missions served by him.

I do not feel able at this time to go into any important matters affecting our Diocesan interests except in a tentative way. A few years' experience may enable me to make more valuable suggestions to the Convention. At present I will only call attention to one or two matters of minor detail.

In the first place, I would remind members of parish Vestries of the canonical requirement that when they call a Minister to the parish they should at once notify the Bishop of their action.

I have been sorry to find that in many parts of the Diocese there has been the greatest carelessness, and in some cases gross negligence, in keeping the parochial records required by the canons. I would urge upon both Clergy and Laity the importance of having their records carefully and neatly kept in substantial, well-bound volumes. No man of business would employ for one week a clerk who should keep his books as some of our parish registers are kept. I feel it to be a part of the visitorial function of the Bishop to examine the parish records; and if his powers as Ordinary have any value whatever it seems to me that Rectors and Vestrymen should feel themselves bound to regard his suggestions as to what constitutes a proper register and the proper method of keeping it.

I would also call attention to the canon regarding lay readers, which allows no license to run more than one year.

I shall issue all licenses to extend until the Easter Monday following their date; consequently all should be renewed every Easter Monday. There are no properly licensed lay readers in any parish whose licenses have not been either issued or renewed within the past twelve months.

I would like to say many things with reference to our Church Institutions, did time and space permit. In my judgment we need in this Diocese, more than anything else, to realize our common bond of union in the Diocese. The only way we can come to this is by becoming interested in common Diocesan work. The unit in the Church is not the parish; it is the Diocese. Our Diocesan enterprises and institutions should stand first with all of us. They are valuable not only for their direct results in the accomplishment of their specific work; they are quite as valuable as being manifestations and exercises of corporate action, and as developing the life of the body. I ask this Convention to listen to all that may be presented in regard to these works of general interest and obligation. The Thompson Orphanage makes its annual report of its works and of its needs; we shall have reports from our hospitals; our schools and colleges should have their part of our time and consideration. First of all, the University of the South, at Sewanee, claims from us, by the highest and most sacred title, much more than we have ever given to it. I wish to say here to the Convention that I have the privi-

lege of naming two students, who, by virtue of my nomination, receive all the benefits of the University without
charge. I have applications from those who desire these
benefits. Now, can I with any propriety continue to exercise
this privilege if this Diocese and this Convention continue
to do so little for that institution which we took part in
founding, and to which we pledged our support?

And then we have our Church schools here in the Diocese—St. Mary's, at Raleigh, for girls, and the Ravenscroft
School, at Asheville, under Mr. McDonald. And at Raleigh
we have that most excellent institution for the colored people, St. Augustine's. So far as we can do so we should
support and encourage all these; and in pursuing these
common ends we shall find a growing unity and mutual
sympathy which shall draw us closer together, and make
our Diocese something more than a string of independent
congregations.

But chiefest of all we have the Missionary work of our
Diocese. By the term *Missionary work* many different kinds
of work may be meant. In its first significance it is the
work of carrying the knowledge of the Gospel to those who
have it not. In this sense we have no Missionary work in
this Diocese. I have a wide acquaintance with the people
in different parts of the Diocese, and have been in close
personal contact with the most ignorant class in some of its
darkest corners. In my judgment there is nowhere an
absence of the knowledge of the Gospel in the popular
sense of the words. I have seen statements to the contrary,
but in my judgment all such statements are wholly erro-
neous. But there are vast multitudes of people in all parts
of the Diocese who do not accept and follow the Gospel,
and there are a vast number who accept and follow it in a
very imperfect fashion, and many who possess a very
defective form of Christianity. To all these the Church
has a mission. She must awaken the careless, the impeni-
tent, the degraded, and bring to bear upon their lives the
power of the Truth given to us. That is what we are here
for. That is our only business as an organization. It is
to bring men to the knowledge of God, and to hold up
before all the true form and model of the Church of God,
the Tabernacle which the Lord hath pitched and not man.

We live in an age agitated with religious curiosity more

than any which has preceded it in our country. No one can foretell what a few years may bring forth in the extension and development of our forms of ecclesiastical organization. We have reason to know that no Christian body to-day has such a position of influence as our own in connection with this promise of the future. We believe that we have preserved from the past an heritage with which our whole American life may be enriched. We stand for the idea of authority and continuity in the Church, which so many of our Protestant brethren have long cast aside, but which they are, perhaps, coming to feel the value of. The services of the Church have long commanded the admiration of all devout and discerning men. There are not wanting indications that the Catholic doctrine and organization of the Church are beginning to command a like regard. How shall we here in North Carolina be true to the destiny of the Church, and respond to this great opportunity? It must be simply by doing the work set before us. We need to maintain the Church where it is now already established, and to put it wherever, in the Providence of our Lord and Master, a way is opened for us, and men need and desire our ministrations. To maintain our present work and to respond to the demands for its extension, we need for this current year at least five thousand dollars. I appeal to every member of the Executive Missionary Committee to confirm what I say. This is the greatest work before you at present, my dear brethren of the Clergy and Laity, so to realize your responsibility to God that you shall offer yourselves, your souls and bodies and possessions, to Him for His service.

In this connection it is eminently proper that I should call the attention of the whole Diocese in this, its representative assembly, to one recommendation of my brief Lenten Pastoral before spoken of. The last notable work of our late Bishop for the benefit of the Church was the resolution passed at his instance by the Missionary Council at Chicago, recommending that a Missionary service be held in each congregation of the Church in the United States, and in all its Missionary jurisdictions on Friday after the first Sunday of each month. Let me, with whatever weight my recommendation can carry, urge you all to observe this monthly service of prayer for Missions. We busy ourselves in vain in speaking and working for Missions as long as we do not *pray* for Missions.   The Clergy, I believe, are ready enough to have the services; the devout women are ready to attend them.   Let me say to the men of this Diocese that as long as they are not found adding their hearts and voices to the cry which the Church thus sends up to the Lord of the Harvest, we cannot expect success and prosperity in our Church at large or in our narrower field at home.

It is with much pleasure that I announce to the Convention that the Assistant Bishop of South Carolina, the Rt. Rev. Ellison Capers, D.D., has kindly consented to be with us on Sunday to preach a Memorial Sermon upon the life and character of our late Bishop.   I endeavored to have the sermon preached at the opening of the Convention, but found it impossible; therefore I had to arrange to have this memorial on Sunday.   I felt authorized to invite Bishop Capers in the name of this Diocese.   He is here as our guest.   I trust, therefore, that the Convention will remain in session through Sunday, and be present as the Convention at this solemn and interesting service.

May God both teach us what things we ought to do, and also give us grace and power faithfully to fulfil the same.

JOS. BLOUNT CHESHIRE, JR.

APPENDIX B.

PAROCHIAL, MISSIONARY AND OTHER REPORTS.

Ansonville, Ansonville Church; the Rev. CHARLES C. QUIN, Minister in Charge.

Families 12. Whole number of persons 34. Baptism: adult 1. Confirmed 3. Communicants: added by admission 2; present number 18. Burials 2. Public services: on Sundays 26; other days 3. Holy Communion: public 6; private 4. Sunday-school teachers 4; scholars 20. Church sittings 160. Value of church $1,500.

Offerings—Parochial: Communion alms, $4.89. Minister's salary $70—total $74.89. *Diocesan:* Episcopal and Contingent Fund $5.50. Diocesan Missions $20—total $25.50. *Aggregate* $100.39.

Asheville, Ravenscroft Mission and Training School; the Rev. WM. STANLEY BARROWS, S.T.B., Acting Principal; the Rev. Samuel Rhodes, Deacon. Messrs. Thomas A. Cox, Nathan A. Seagle, Frank L. Frost, M.D., Dillard L. Love and Reginald Heber Dykers, Lay Readers.

Cullowhee, St. David's Church.

Families 4. Whole number of persons 16. Baptisms: infant 2. Confirmed 1. Communicants: added by transfer 1; by admission 1; whole number added 2; removed 4; present number 11. Public services: on Sundays 48. Holy Communion 12. Sunday-school teachers 3; scholars 12. Church sittings 300. Value of church $3,000. Insurance $700.

Offerings—Parochial: Salary of Clergyman $68.90. Current expenses $12.50. Other parish expenses $2. Insurance $9—total $92.40. *Diocesan:* Diocesan Missions $9.60. Church Building Fund $1. Education Fund $1. Relief Fund $1—total $12.60. *General:* General Missions $3.50. Storm sufferers in South Carolina $5—total $8.50. *Aggregate* $113.50.

Henderson and Polk Counties, St. Paul's Church and other Stations.

Families, white 34; colored 1. Whole number of persons 166. Baptisms: infant 8; adult 1—total 9. Communicants: withdrawn 1; present

13

number 81. Marriage 1. Burial 1. Public services: on Sundays 24; other days 7. Holy Communion: public 5; private 1. Sunday-school teachers 2; scholars 30. Church sittings 300. Value of church $300; school-house $200—total $500.

Offerings—Parochial: $15.

Hot Springs, St. John's Church.

Families 5. Whole number of persons 12. Communicants: added by transfer 5; present number 9. Public services: on Sundays 47; other days 7. Holy Communion 14. Church sittings 175. Value of church $2,000; other church property $125—total $2,125. Insurance $1,000.

Offerings — Parochial: Salary of Priest in charge $56.95. To others officiating $93.67. Other parish expenses $15. Insurance premiums $37.50. Rectory Fund $14.40. Repairs and improvements $167.12—total $384.64. *Diocesan:* Episcopal and Contingent Fund $5. Diocesan Missions $3. Relief Fund $10. For rectory at Beaver Dam $10.92—total $28.92. *General:* General Missions $1. *Aggregate* $414.56.

During the past year the roof of the church has been re-covered with cypress shingles, a cross has been placed on the steeple, cushions have been purchased for the seats, and an insurance policy of $1,000, paid for five years, taken out on the building and furniture. We wish to express our appreciation of the kindness of Mr. Ebbs, merchant of Hot Springs, for generously donating all the nails and hardware used. The Rectory Fund, now amounting to $103.27, has, together with cash in hand, been invested in a deed of trust bearing eight per cent. interest.

Micadale, St. Mary's Church.

Families 10. Whole number of persons 60. Baptisms: infant 2. Communicants: added by transfer 1; present number 19. Public services: on Sundays 30. Holy Communion 1. Sunday-school teachers 5; scholars 50. Church sittings 200. Value of church $1,000; other church property $1,000—total $2,000. Insurance $400.

Offerings—Parochial: Parish expenses $6. *Diocesan:* Diocesan Missions 46 cents. *Aggregate* $6.46.

The Woman's Auxiliary has during the year made two excellent quilts, which have been given to Missionaries in our own Convocation. There is $31.41 in the fund to purchase the farm of thirty acres opposite the chapel and held at $500. Mr. T. C. Skinner is treasurer, and sums put in his hands will bear six per cent. interest till used. Through the liberality of Mr. John Nicholas Brown, of Providence, I have been able to take out a policy of insurance paid for five years.

Saluda, Church of the Transfiguration.

Families 4. Whole number of persons 11. Baptism: infant 1. Confirmed 1. Communicants: added by admission 1; present number 7.

Burial 1. Public services: on Sundays 30; other days 6. Holy Communion: public 13; private 5. Sunday-school teachers 5; scholars 25. Church sittings 110. Value of church $1,700. Amount of fire insurance $750; tornado insurance $600.

Offerings—Parochial: Expenses of Clergyman $9.90. Current expenses $30 65. Other parish expenses $18 22. Insurance premiums $14.67—total $73.44. *Diocesan:* Episcopal and Contingent Fund $5. Diocesan Missions $10.05. Church Building Fund $2. Education Fund $2. Relief Fund $2—total $21.05. *General:* General Missions $1.21. *Aggregate* $95.70

This church was built and is supported by Churchmen from South Carolina. It is open during the summer months only. A handsome stone font has been presented by Dr. F. L. Frost, of Charleston, in memory of his son, Mr. Pringle Frost. Other gifts have been a copy of the Standard Prayer-Book from Bishop Howe; a pair of vases through Sister Julia, of New York, and a pair of alms basins through Miss Howe.

[NOTE —Parochial offerings which should have been reported last year are as follows: To Clergymen, $10.31; other parish expenses, $22.55; insurance premiums, $22.50; Sunday-school Library, $30.75—total, $86.11.]

The Clergy House Association, of which all the Bishops of North and South Carolina are Honorary Trustees, has during the past year been incorporated and secured a remarkably fine site just out of Saluda, and containing over eleven acres. Here the Association hopes to erect cottages, furnish them inexpensively, and offer them, rent free, in summer and winter to those of our Reverend Brethren who have the need, far more than the means, to take refuge for health or rest. Contributions to the Building Fund are solicited. The Legal Trustees are: *President*, F. L. FROST, M.D., Charleston, S. C.; *Vice-President*, the Rev. EDMUND N. JOYNER, Columbia, S. C.; *Treasurer*, the Rev. WM. S. BARROWS, Asheville, N. C.; *Secretary*, EDWARD B. GOELET, M.D., Saluda, N. C. The members of the Woman's Auxiliary Board are Miss Howe, Charleston, S. C.; Mrs. Thomas W. Patton, Asheville, N. C.; Miss C. D. Dawson, Greenville, S. C.; Miss S. P. Carroll, Columbia, S. C.

Sylva, Jackson County.

Families 4. Whole number of persons 12. Communicants: died 1; present number 4. Burial 1. Public services: on Sundays 46. Holy Communion: private 1. Chapel sittings 150. Value of chapel $450.

Offerings—Parochial: Expenses of Clergymen $1.01. Repairs and improvements $78.51—total 79.52. *Diocesan:* Diocesan Missions $2.97. *Aggregate* $82.49.

Of the amount spent for repairs and improvements, $55 was a donation from Mr. Dillard L. Love.

Waynesville, Grace Church in the Mountains.

Families 19. Whole number of persons, white 66; colored 1. Baptism: infant 1. Confirmed 3. Communicants: added by admission 2; removed 1; present number, white 38; colored 1. Public services: on Sundays 82; other days 18. Holy Communion 14. Sunday-school teachers 5; scholars 50. Other Parochial Institutions: Woman's Auxiliary; Little Gleaners. Church sittings 200. Value of church $4,000. Insurance $300.

Offerings—Parochial: Parish Missions $17. Clerical service otherwise than by Priest in charge $71.73. Other parish expenses $28.50. For the poor $6.30. Sunday-school $10. Repairs $57 36—total $190.89. *Diocesan:* Episcopal and Contingent Fund $10. Diocesan Missions $2. Relief Fund $1.30. Thompson Orphanage $1.50. Permanent Episcopal Fund $10.20. Miscellaneous 40 cents—total, $25.40. *General:* General Missions $3.01. Foreign Missions 50 cents. Indian Missions $1.75—total $5.26. *Aggregate* $221.55.

Funds are in hand with which to purchase an Altar Cross as a memorial to the late Rev. D. Hillhouse Buel, D.D., who is most affectionately remembered in this Mission.

In addition to the work above reported the Rev. Mr. Barrows has officiated in the course of the past year at Govanstown, Md., Short Hills, N. J., at Flat Rock and Hendersonville; has baptized 5 infants and 1 adult, beside celebrating the Holy Communion and preaching frequently in the Mission fields of Henderson, Polk and Buncombe counties, assisting the Clergy of Asheville on many occasions and participating in the services of Convocation. He was editor of the *Dawn of Day,* the Convocational paper, till it was united with the *Messenger of Hope,* the Diocesan organ. He has, throughout the year, assisted the Rev. William F. Rice, the Rev. Samuel Rhodes, and Messrs. John H. Gilreath and John C. Seagle in their studies.

Asheville, St. Matthias' Church (colored); the Rev. HENRY S. McDUFFEY, Minister in Charge.

Families 32. Whole number of persons 170. Baptisms: infant 7; adult 2—total 9. Confirmed 22. Communicants: added by transfer 2; by admission 22; whole number added 24; died 1; present number 68. Marriage 1. Burials 3. Public services: on Sundays 144; other days 157. Holy Communion: public 52; private 2. Sunday-school teachers, white 3; colored 5; scholars 67. Parish school teachers 2; scholars 78. Other Parochial Institutions 2. Church sittings 200. Value of church $1,000; rectory $500; other church property $3,000—total $4,500. Insurance $1,300.

Offerings—Parochial: Communion alms $8.62. Salary of Clergyman $125.67. Current expenses $254.94. Miscellaneous $22.50—total $411.73. *Diocesan:* Episcopal and Contingent Fund $5—total $5. *Aggregate* $416.73.

Since my last report the work here in Asheville has been doing well. Twenty-two persons have been confirmed, and we have a class now waiting to be confirmed. On the 22d day of February Bishop Cheshire laid the corner-stone of our new church. The work has been suspended until summer. We have now in bank $458.68 as a building fund I am pleased to say the work is in a flourishing condition.

Asheville, Trinity Church; the Rev. McNeely DuBose, Rector.

Families 110. Whole number of persons 500. Baptisms: infant 37; adult 11—total 48. Confirmed 25. Communicants: added by transfer 11; whole number added 36; removed 8; died 4; whole number lost 12; present number 313. Marriage 1. Burials 12. Public services: on Sundays 144; other days 194. Holy Communion: public 86; private 18. Sunday-school teachers 10; scholars 110. Church sittings 400; chapel sittings 150. Value of church $20,000; value of chapel $3,000; value of rectory $10,000—total $33,000. Amount of indebtedness on church property $4,250. Insurance $10,000.

Offerings — Parochial: Communion alms $364.21. Parish Missions $453.05. Salary of Clergyman $1,625. Current expenses $2,220.99. Repairs $129.13. Sunday-school $98.72. Chancel Society $102.03. Paving $238.50— total $5,231.63. *Diocesan:* Episcopal and Contingent Fund $137.50. Diocesan Missions $200. Church in Cashier's Valley $37.50. Church at Chunn's Cove $20. To two Diocesan Missionaries $80. Thompson Orphanage $124.28. To education of Missionaries' daughters $150. Permanent Episcopal Fund $385. Convocation $5—total $1,139.28. *General:* General Missions $35.82. Domestic Missions $29.92. Foreign Missions $43.50. Colored Missions $17.12. Indian Missions $19. Jewish Missions $17.12. Sewanee $53.50. Central Fund Woman's Auxiliary $6. Church at Beaufort, S. C., $16. Yellow fever sufferers in Georgia $10 Scholarships in China $65—total $312.98. *Aggregate* $6,683.89.

Services out of parish: At Sewanee, Tenn., Union, S. C., and Old Fort, N. C. All parish institutions in good condition. Special Missionary services on Fridays after first Sundays, and also on afternoon of third Sundays. Funerals with interment elsewhere 4. Expended on the parish, $4,778.58; on parish Missions in parish, $453.05; outside of parish, $1,452.26; whole amount raised and expended, $6,683.89.

Battleboro, St. John's Church; the Rev. Gaston Battle, Minister in Charge.

Families 9. Whole number of persons 34. Baptisms: infant 1; adult 1— total 2. Confirmed 2. Communicants: added by transfer 5; by admission 2; whole number added 7; present number 20. Marriage 1. Public services: on Sundays 54; other days 18. Sunday-school teachers 3; scholars 21. Other Parochial Institutions: Church Aid Society; Junior

Aid Society. Church sittings 200. Value of church $1,500; land $500—total $2,000. Amount of indebtedness on church property $65.

Offerings — Parochial: Salary of Clergyman $124. Current expenses $15. Other parish expenses $7.50. Building Fund $105—total $251.50. *Diocesan:* Episcopal and Contingent Fund $2.32. Diocesan Missions 78 cents—total $3.10. *Aggregate* $254.60.

Bowman's Bluff, Gethsemane Church; the Rev. RICHARD WAINWRIGHT, Minister in Charge.

Families 4. Whole number of persons 23. Baptism: infant 1. Confirmed 2. Communicants: removed 4; present number 16. Public services: on Sundays 50; other days 2. Sunday-school teachers 2; scholars 12. Church sittings 80. Value of church $1,400; other church property $50—total $1,450

Offerings—Parochial: Communion alms $20. Salary of Clergyman $40—total $60. *Diocesan:* Diocesan Missions $7.75. *General:* Domestic Missions $10. Jewish Missions $6.25. Endowment Fund $5. Sewanee $5. Widows and Orphans' Fund $4.10—total $30 35. *Aggregate* $98.10.

Since November last the Rev. George H. Bell has officiated monthly.

Brevard, St. Philip's Church; the Rev. SCOTT B. RATHBUN, Minister in Charge.

Families 10. Whole number of persons 30. Communicants 16. . Public services: one each Sunday by a Lay Reader. Holy Communion 4. Church sittings 120. Value of church $3,000. Insurance $1,500.

Buncombe County, St. Andrew's Chapel; the Rev. JAMES H. PosTELL, Deacon in Charge.

Families 6. Communicants 7. Public services: on Sundays 2. Sunday-school teachers 2; scholars 34. Chapel sittings 125. Value of chapel $500; other church property $60—total $560.

Offerings—General: Domestic Missions $1.50.

Buncombe County, St. Paul's Chapel; the Rev. JAMES H. POSTELL, Deacon in Charge.

Families 6. Baptisms: infant 3. Communicants: died 2; present number 8. Burials 2. Public services: on Sundays 2. Chapel sittings 125. Value of chapel $1,000; other church property $85—total $1,085.

Offerings—General: Domestic Missions $1.75.

Burlington, St. Athanasius' Church; the Rev. ROBERT J. WALKER, Rector.

Families, white 56; colored 7. Whole number of persons, white 196; colored 14. Baptisms: infant 8; adult 3—total 11. Confirmed, white 3; colored 3. Communicants: added by transfer 5; by admission 10; whole number added 15; present number, white 104; colored 6. Marriage, 1. Burials 3. Public services: on Sundays 149; other days 187. Holy Communion: public 70; private 12. Sunday-school teachers, white 5; colored 3; scholars, white 83; colored 21. Other Parochial Institutions: Ladies' Guild; St. Andrew's Brotherhood. Church sittings 200. Value of church $4,000; value of rectory $2,500; other church property $600— total $7,100.

Offerings—Parochial: Communion alms $61. Parish Missions $15.22. Minister's salary $1,083.33. Current expenses $191.07. Other parish expenses $35.64. Miscellaneous $12.90—total $1,399.16. *Diocesan:* Episcopal and Contingent Fund $42. Diocesan Missions $134.83. Church Building Fund $2. Relief Fund $7.40. Thompson Orphanage $14.35. Miscellaneous $13.01—total $213.59. *General:* General Missions $14.43. Domestic Missions $2.50. Foreign Missions $8. Colored Missions $3.10. Indian Missions $1.50. Jewish Missions 50 cents. American Church Building Fund $2. Miscellaneous $300—total $332.03. *Aggregate* $1,944.78.

The Missions of this growing parish are in a healthful condition. The employees of the great factories of Alamance county ask for the services of the Church. St. Mary's Mission, for colored people, looks forward to a chapel. They now worship in an uncomfortable schoolhouse. St. John's and St. Paul's Missions much need *one* chapel at least. Money given for these chapels, through our Bishop, would bring God's blessings upon the donors. What a great field for some Priest to go in and live in the midst of these thousands of poor laborers of our Diocese, and gradually lead them up into the ways of our Holy Mother, the Church of the Living God!

Candler's, St. Clement's Church; the Rev. GEORGE H. BELL, Minister in Charge.

Families 8. Whole number of persons 42. Baptisms: infant 3. Confirmed 4. Communicants: added by admission 2; present number 12. Public services: on Sundays 18; other days 2. Holy Communion 4. Sunday-school teachers 3; scholars 38. Value of church $800.

Offerings—Parochial: Communion alms, $3.08.

Chapel Hill, Chapel of the Cross; the Rev. FREDERICK TOWERS, Rector.

Families 8. Whole number of person 49. Baptism: infant 1. Confirmed 3. Communicants: added by transfer 8; by admission 5; whole number added 13; removed 6; present number 30. Public services: on Sundays 130; other days 94. Holy Communion 38. Sunday-school teachers 4; scholars 20. Other Parochial Institution: Ladies' Altar Guild. Church sittings 200. Value of church $5,000; rectory $1,500— total $6,500.

Offerings—Parochial: Minister's salary $424.71. Current expenses $97.43—total $522.14. *Diocesan:* Episcopal and Contingent Fund $55. Diocesan Missions $23.25. Thompson Orphanage $18.32—total $96.57. *General:* General Missions $5.50. *Aggregate* $624.21.

The Rector has celebrated the Holy Communion three times in public and twice in private in St. Matthew's Parish, Hillsboro.

Charlotte, St. Michael and All Angels' Church (colored); the Rev. P. P. Alston, Minister in Charge.

Families 21. Whole number of persons 105. Baptisms: infant 7; adult 2—total 9. Confirmed 10. Communicants: added by transfer 1; by admission 10; whole number added 11; removed 3; died 2; suspended 2; whole number lost 7; present number 68. Marriage 1. Burials 3. Public services: on Sundays 101; other days 109. Holy Communion: public 19; private 3. Sunday-school teachers 8; scholars 175. Parish school teachers 2. Church sittings 250. Value of church $1,500; other church property $1,000—total $2,500.

Offerings—Parochial: Communion alms $7.31. Minister's salary $95.17. Current expenses $12.37. Other parish expenses $26. Miscellaneous $9—total $149.85. *Diocesan:* Episcopal and Contingent Fund $10. Diocesan Missions $2.19—total $12.19. *General:* Foreign Missions $2. Colored Missions $3—total $5. *Aggregate* $167.04.

I am proud to say that during the past year our work has been progressing nicely. The attendance at our services and Sunday-school has been larger than ever before. Our parish school has been well attended also, and we feel that much good is being done. We have an industrial department connected with our work, and it is proving to be of very great benefit to our girls. We need more financial help in order to carry this work on successfully, and we hope we shall get it.

Charlotte, St. Peter's Church; the Rev. Fenner S. Stickney, Rector.

Families 100. Whole number of persons 551. Baptisms: infant 14; adult 1—total 15. Confirmed 15. Communicants: added by transfer 21; by admission 15; whole number added 36; removed 9; died, 4; whole number lost 13; present number 286. Marriages 2. Burials 11. Public services: on Sundays twice every Sunday; other days, Saints' days, great festivals and fasts. Holy Communion: twice a month and great festivals; private, 2. Sunday-school teachers 13; scholars, 104. Other Parochial Institutions: Woman's Guild; Thompson Orphanage Guild; Chancel Committee; Daughters of the King; Woman's Auxiliary; Home and Hospital; Good Samaritan Hospital. Value of church $25,000; value of chapel $1,500; Home and Hospital $3,500—total $30,000. Insurance $10,000.

Offerings — Parochial: Communion alms $27.53. Minister's salary $1,500. Current expenses $200.50. Other parish expenses $87.59—total $1,815.62. *Diocesan:* Episcopal and Contingent Fund $75. Diocesan Missions $58 88. Church Building Fund $8.51. Education Fund $17.73. Relief Fund $9 90. Thompson Orphanage $126 25—total, $296.27. *General:* General Missions $64. Domestic Missions, $7.64. Foreign Missions $6.24. Colored Missions $7.09. Indian Missions $8.54. Sewanee $27. American Church Building Fund $9.73—total $130.24. *Aggregate* $2,242.13.

Young Ladies' Bible Class, about twenty members; St. Andrew's Bible Class, about fifteen members.

Charlotte, Chapel of the Virgin Mary, Thompson Orphanage; the Rev. EDWIN A. OSBORNE, Chaplain.

Families 1. Whole number of persons 56 Baptisms: Infant 8; adult 1— total 9. Communicants: removed 1; present number 23. Public services: on Sundays 14; other days 200. Holy Communion 13. Total value of church property, $2,200.

Offerings—Parochial: Communion alms $3.

The Sundays not accounted for in this and my other reports have been spent in other parishes while working in the interest of the Orphanage.

Chunn's Cove Mission, Buncombe County; the Rev. WILLIAM F. RICE, Deacon in Charge; William T. Owen, Lay Reader.

Families 4. Whole number of persons 13. Baptism: adult 1. Communicants 8. Public services: on Sundays 65; other days 38. Holy Communion: private 2. Sunday-school teachers 7; scholars 50. Building Fund $144.50

The Sunday-school is chiefly sustained by the efforts of the Faithful Endeavor Society of Trinity Church, Asheville. I am under many obligations to the Rev. Samuel Rhodes for frequent and very acceptable assistance here and elsewhere.

Concord, All Saints' Church; the Rev. J. C. DAVIS, Rector.

Families 12. Baptism: infant 1. Confirmed 8. Communicants: added by transfer 4; whole number added 12; removed 2; died 1; present number 24. Marriage 1. Burials 2. Public services: on Sundays 98; other days 78. Holy Communion 38. Church sittings 200. Value of church $3,000; other church property $700—total $3,700. Indebtedness $1,200.

Offerings—Parochial: Communion alms $44.18. Minister's salary $603. Current expenses $60. Other parish expenses $74. Sunday-school books $20. Special charities $40.50—total $841.68. *Diocesan:* Episcopal and Contingent Fund $20. Diocesan Missions $9.27. Thompson Orphanage

14

$37.27—total $66.54. *General:* Jewish Missions $1.50. *Aggregate* $909.72. Under the commission of our láte Diocesan, Bishop Lyman, given last October, I held several services at Greensboro, and administered Holy Communion twice; and also held several services at Lexington, and administered Holy Communion four times. Two things will be observed in the above report in comparison with all previous ones; (1) the remarkable increase of receipts and disbursements of this small parish, and (2) the increase of the debt to the amount of $700 in the purchase of the ground around the church, which became a necessity, and which calls for consideration when making out assessments. It still continues, as in years past, a struggle for existence in the face of a pronounced opposition, but we still pray, and trust, and work.

Cuningham's Chapel, Person County; the Rev. CHARLES FETTER, Deacon in Charge.

Families 3. Whole number of persons 11. Communicants 11. Public services: on Sundays 15; other days 2. Holy Communion 1. Sunday-school teachers 3; scholars 26. Chapel sittings 250. Value of chapel $1,000.

Offerings—Parochial: Salary of Clergyman $150. *Diocesan:* Thompson Orphanage $15. *General:* Domestic Missions $3.35. Foreign Missions $10. Jewish Missions $1. Miscellaneous $121.89—total $136 24. *Aggregate* $301.24.

This chapel is sustained by Colonel John S. Cuningham, the son of J. W. Cuningham, deceased, who built it. It is the only place in Person county where Episcopal services are regularly held The interest in this chapel is growing rapidly. There is a large Sunday-school five miles from Cuningham Depot, at the house of Colonel Cuningham, under the auspices of himself and his wife It is doing a noble work.

Durham, St. Philip's Church; the Rev. STEWART McQUEEN, Rector.

Families 40. Whole number of persons 200. Baptisms: infant 9; adult 3—total 12. Confirmed 5. Communicants: added by transfer 4; by admission 5; whole number added 9; removed 17; died 1; whole number lost 18; present number 95. Marriage 1. Burial 1. Public services: on Sundays 101; other days 99; sermons and addresses 152. Holy Communion 37. Sunday-school teachers 9; scholars 75. Church sittings 250. Value of church $3,000; rectory $2,700—total $5,700. Insurance $3,200.

Offerings—Parochial: Communion alms $74.95. Salary of Clergyman $866.67. Current expenses $135.60. Church debt $608.01. Miscellaneous $202—total $1,887.23. *Diocesan:* Episcopal and Contingent Fund $80; Diocesan Missions $35.30. Thompson Orphanage $14.75—total $130.05. *General:* Domestic Missions $27.35. Indian Missions $2. Jewish Missions $3.85. Sewanee $9.50. Clergy Retiring Fund $16.40. American

Church Building Fund $2. Society for Increase of the Ministry $8.30—total $69.40. *Aggregate* $2,086 68.

The Colored Mission in Durham has had a day-school of twenty-two scholars and a Sunday-school of twenty. There are about eight communicants connected with the work.

Enfield, Church of the Advent; the Rev. GASTON BATTLE, Deacon in Charge.

Families 13. Whole number of persons 53. Baptism: infant 1. Communicants: added by transfer 2; removed 1; present number 19. Marriage 1. Public services: on Sundays 18. Holy Communion 4. Sunday-school teachers 3; scholars 12. Other Parochial Institution: Ladies' Parish Guild. Church sittings 125. Value of church $1,500.

Offerings—Parochial: Communion alms $2.18 Salary of Clergyman $125. Current expenses $25—total $152.18.

Flat Rock, St. John's Church; the Rev. SCOTT B. RATHBUN, Rector.

Families 44. Baptisms: infant 4. Confirmed 5. Communicants 80. Burials 3. Public services: twice each Sunday; other days, Saints' Day Eucharists. Holy Communion 15. Sunday-school teachers 4; scholars 30. Parish school teacher 1; scholars 25. Church sittings 200. Value of church $8,000; rectory $6,000; other church property $300—total $14,500.

Offerings—Parochial: Communion alms $58. Minister's salary $800. Current expenses $130. Parish school $165—total $1,153. *Diocesan:* Episcopal and Contingent Fund $50. Diocesan Missions $14.10—total $64.10. *Aggregate* $1,217.10.

Franklin Mission; the Rev. JOHN A DEAL, Priest in Charge; the Rev. J. W. BARKER and the Rev. JAMES T. KENNEDY, Assistant Ministers.

Franklin, St. Agnes' Church.

Families 10. Whole number of persons 49. Baptisms: infant 2; adult 1—total 3. Confirmed 3. Communicants: added by transfer 4; by admission 2; whole number added 6; removed 3; present number 23. Public services: on Sundays 35; other days 6. Holy Communion 13. Sunday-school teachers 2; scholars 10. Other Institution: St. Agnes' Female School. Church sittings 150. Value of church $4,000; school $2,000—total $6,000.

Offerings—Parochial: Current expenses $23.81. *Diocesan:* Episcopal and Contingent Fund $10.78. Diocesan Missions $11.16. Church Building Fund 80 cents. Education Fund 80 cents. Relief Fund 75 cents. Thompson Orphanage $6.85. Convocation Fund $3.52—total $34.66. *General:* Domestic Missions $5.80. Foreign Missions $15.70. Jewish Missions $2. Sewanee $2.75—total $26.25. *Aggregate* $84.72.

Franklin, *St. Cyprian's Chapel* (*colored*).

Families 25. Whole number of persons 125. Baptisms: infant 1; adult 1—total 2. Confirmed 1. Communicants: added by admission 1; present number 14. Marriage 1. Burial 1. Public services: on Sundays 119; other days 4. Holy Communion 5. Sunday-school teachers 4; scholars 75. Parish school teachers 2; scholars 40. Other Parochial Institution: Industrial School. Chapel sittings 125. Value of chapel $1,000; rectory $1,200; other church property $1,000—total $3,200. Insurance $1,200.

Offerings—Parochial: Current expenses $19.11. *General:* Foreign Missions $8.05. *Aggregate* $27.16.

Bryson City, *St. Stephen's Church.*

Families 5. Whole number of persons 22. Baptism: infant 1. Communicants: removed 2; present number 7. Public services: on Sundays 13; other days 2. Holy Communion 1. Church sittings 150. Value of church $1,000; other church property (one lot) $100—total $1,100. Indebtedness on lot $75.

Offerings—Parochial: Minister's salary $5.50. Current expenses $336.68—total $342.18. *Diocesan:* Diocesan Missions 55 cents. *Aggregate* $342.73.

Since January 1st the relation of the Rev. Mr. Barker to St. Stephen's has been that of Deacon in Charge. The item of current expenses—large for a small Mission—comes from the adding up of local contributions and offerings for building St. Stephen's Church.

Cashier's Valley, *Church of the Good Shepherd.*

Families 7. Whole number of persons 80. Communicants 18. Public services: on Sundays 8; other days 4. Holy Communion 4. Sunday-school teachers 2; scholars 35. Parish school teacher 1; scholars 36. Church sittings 200. Value of church $2,500; other church property $1,000—total $3,500. Insurance $1,900.

Offerings — Parochial: Salary of Clergyman $25. Current expenses $12.98—total $37.98.

The church has been rebuilt and is now ready for consecration. The parish school was quite successful last year, and will be re-opened in July.

Highlands Mission.

Families 4. Whole number of persons 24. Marriage 1. Burial 1. Public services: on Sundays 8; other days 4. Holy Communion 1.

Offerings—Parochial: Current expenses $10.34.

Rev. Mr. Barker held one or two services at this place and Rev. Mr. Rhodes officiated several times. A few of the natives are very favorably disposed to the Church, and a goodly percentage of the large number of summer visitors are of our communion. Large congregations always greet the Missionary.

Nonah, St. John's Church.

Families 7. Whole number of persons 32. Baptism: infant 1. Confirmed 3. Communicants: added by admission 3; present number 17. Public services: on Sundays 23; other days 11. Holy Communion 8. Sunday-school teachers 3; scholars 20. Church sittings 200. Value of church $2,000.

Offerings—Parochial: Communion alms $5.63. Salary of Clergyman $25 47—total $31.10. *Diocesan:* Episcopal and Contingent Fund $2.25. Thompson Orphanage $7.95—total $10.20. *General:* Domestic Missions $2. *Aggregate* $43.30.

Since January last the relation of the Rev. Mr. Barker to St. John's has been that of Deacon in Charge.

Mr. Barker reports the following services in other places:

I have attended two Convocations, preaching once and assisting in the services. I have held one service and preached in St. David's, Cullowhee, and baptized one child there. Held service and preached in Cashier's and Highlands—once in each place. I have made fifty visits, conducted three funerals, baptized five children; held service and preached thirty-three times in St. Agnes, and officiated on ten other occasions; traveled 859 miles.

The Priest in Charge reports as follows:

During the fiscal year past I have built an addition to St. Agnes' School, Franklin, supplied some school furniture, and paid for the same. The church at Cashier's Valley has been rebuilt and paid for, and the church at Bryson City is now about complete. The hope is that both these may be consecrated this year At Highlands we only have a few people, and growth is impossible until we can have a building of our own. When at home I visit our schools here weekly, or oftener if necessary. Both St. Cyprian's and St. Agnes have done good work during the past year. The stringency in money matters has hurt the latter, and we have been compelled to ask aid to enable us to get through the present school year, and the same course may be necessary for the next year.

I have raised the money for colored school and Deacon until January 1st next, also for white assistant for the same time, also money to pay off the original contract for St. Stephen's.

In addition to work above reported I have held twenty-eight services and administered the Holy Communion ten times. Part of this work was in this Convocation and part outside the Diocese.

Gaston, St. Luke's Chapel.

Families 5. Whole number of persons 15. Baptism: adult 1. Confirmed 1. Communicants: added by admission 1; present number 15. Holy Communion 2. Sunday-school teachers 3; scholars 32. Church sittings 300. Value of church $1,500; other church property $150—total $1,650.

Offerings—Diocesan: Diocesan Missions $2.36.

There being no Rector nor Minister in charge, the above report is made by Mr. A. Wilkins, who, with some noble and self-sacrificing ladies, has been conducting a Sunday-school at St. Luke's for the past year. We are thankful to say that we believe St. Luke's Sunday-school is now on a stable foundation.

Germanton, St. Philip's Church.

Families 9. Whole number of persons 29. Baptisms: infant 1; adult 1— total 2. Confirmed 1. Communicants: died 1; present number 20. Burial 1. Public services: on Sundays 6. Holy Communion 3. Sunday-school teachers 3; scholars 10. Value of church $1,500.

Offerings—Parochial: Communion alms $3.

We have no Minister at present, and there is no prospect of our getting one. For the past two years we have had monthly services only about two or three months at a time.

Goshen, St. Paul's Church; the Rev. J. M. Horner, Minister in Charge.

Families 5. Whole number of persons 13. Baptisms: infant 2. Communicants 5. Public services: on Sundays 10; other days 1. Holy Communion 4. Church sittings 150. Value of church $500.

Offerings—Parochial: Communion alms $2. Minister's salary $40. Current expenses $1—total $43. *Diocesan:* Diocesan Missions $4.76. *General:* General Missions $1.40. *Aggregate* $49.16.

Grace, Beaver Dam Mission; the Rev. William F. Rice, Deacon in Charge.

Families 16 Whole number of persons 63. Baptisms: infant 6. Confirmed 5. Communicants: added by admission 4; removed 3; present number 39. Marriage 1. Public services: on Sundays 89; other days 14. Holy Communion 5. Sunday-school teachers 4; scholars 35. Chapel sittings 125. Value of chapel $750; rectory $1,800; other church property $200—total $2,750. Insurance $500.

Offerings—Parochial: Communion alms $1.05. Parish Missions $2.35. Minister's salary $22.25. Other parish expenses $11.23. Convocation 42 cents. Rectory debt $203.55. For new chapel at Upper Beaver Dam $70—total $310.85. *Diocesan:* Episcopal and Contingent Fund $6.60. Diocesan Missions $6.91—total $13.51 *General:* General Missions $5.87. *Aggregate* $330.23.

In accordance with the Canon I report that during the year I have officiated once at Calvary Church, Fletcher, twice at Waynesville and frequently at Hot Springs, and thrice at St. Paul's, Henderson county. Provision has been made for paying off the entire debt upon the rectory. We hope soon to build a chapel on the lot last year bought for the upper Mission. Among our benefactors of the past year we are particularly under obligations to Mr. George W. Pack, of Asheville, for $50, and Mr. John Nicholas Brown, of Providence, R. I., for $100. Besides the salary noted above I have received numerous contributions in kind from my parishioners.

Greensboro, St. Andrew's Church; the Rev. J. D. MILLER, Deacon in Charge.

Families, white 33; colored 2. Whole number of persons, white 121; colored 16. Baptisms: infant, white 12; colored 1; adult 7—total 20. Confirmed 32. Communicants, white 78; colored 2. Marriage 1. Burial 1. Public services: on Sundays 59; other days 60. Holy Communion 2. Sunday-school teachers 14; scholars 150. Parish school teachers 5; scholars 25. Other Parochial Institutions: Brotherhood of St. Andrew 27; Daughters of the King 22; Faithful Endeavor and Ladies' Aid Societies.

Offerings—Parochial: Salary of Clergyman $287.64. Current expenses $246.60. Other parish expenses $260.83—total $795.07. *Diocesan:* Episcopal and Contingent Fund $10. Diocesan Missions $5. Thompson Orphanage $7.60—total $22.60. *General:* Foreign Missions $5.50. *Aggregate* $823.17.

The services reported include only those since October 15th, at which time the present incumbent took charge. Services were held regularly at Blowing Rock, Boone and Valle Crucis from July 15th to October 15th. Services twice almost every Sunday at Blowing Rock by the aid of visiting Clergy, and at Boone in morning and Valle Crucis in afternoon each alternate Sunday.

Greensboro, St. Barnabas' Church; the Rev. ALFRED H. STUBBS, Rector.

Families, white ⁻0; colored 2. Whole number of persons, white 180; colored 10. Baptisms: infant 8; adult 2—total 10. Confirmed 8. Communicants: added by transfer 7; by admission 8; whole number added 15; removed 11; died 1; whole number lost 12; present number, white 101; colored 3. Marriages 4. Burials 3. Public services: on Sundays 114; other days 205. Holy Communion 77. Sunday-school teachers 8; scholars 40. Church sittings 300. Value of church $4,500. Insurance $3,000.

Offerings—Parochial: Communion alms $39. Salary of Clergyman $355. Current expenses $164.33. Miscellaneous $30—total $588 33. *Diocesan:* Episcopal and Contingent Fund $40. Diocesan Missions $20. Thomp-

son Orphanage $5—total $65. *General:* General Missions $8. Domestic
Missions $5.11. Foreign Missions $3. Colored Missions $2 07. Indian
Missions $3. Jewish Missions $1.05—total $22.23. *Aggregate* $675.56.

Halifax, St. Mark's Church; the Rev. WALTER J. SMITH, Rector.

Families 8. Whole number of persons 60. Baptism: adult 1. Confirmed 1. Communicants: added by admission 1; removed 1; present
number 28. Marriages, white 1; colored 1. Burial, white 1; colored 1.
Public services: on Sundays 9; other days 8. Holy Communion 7. Sunday-school teachers 6; scholars 17. Other Parochial Institution: St.
Mark's Guild. Church sittings 150. Value of church $1,500; cemetery
$50—total $1,550.

Offerings — Parochial: Salary of Clergyman $34.50. Current expenses
$5.93. Other parish expenses $1.57—total $42. *Diocesan:* Diocesan Mis-
sions $5.21. Relief Fund $1.95. Thompson Orphanage $3. Memorial to
Dr. Smith $1.75 - total $11.91. *General:* General Missions $6.83. For-
eign Missions $2.28. Sewanee $3.47. N. Y. Bible and Prayer-Book
Society $2.15—total $14.73. *Aggregate* $68.64.

I accepted the charge of this parish October 1, 1893. The above report
does not include services held by Lay Readers. Owing to sickness and
bad weather I have missed several appointments.

Haw Creek, Trinity Chapel; the Rev. GEORGE H. BELL, Minister in Charge.

Families 8. Whole number of persons 36. Baptisms: infant 6. Confirmed 6. Communicants: added by admission 4; present number 10.
Marriages 2. Burials 2. Public services: on Sundays 15; other days 15.
Holy Communion 4. Sunday-school teachers 4; scholars 38. Value of
church $500.

Offerings—Parochial: Current expenses $2.80.

Henderson, Holy Innocents' Church; the Rev. JULIAN E. INGLE, Rector.

Families 65. Whole number of persons 300. Baptisms: infant 16.
Confirmed, white 9; colored 1. Communicants: added by transfer 1; by
admission 21; whole number added 22; removed 14; died 3; withdrawn 1;
whole number lost 18; present number 154. Marriages 2. Burials 5.
Public services: twice or thrice on all Sundays and other Holy Days;
daily Evening Prayer throughout the year. Holy Communion: public,
every Sunday, and occasionally at other times; private 4. Sunday-
school teachers 12; scholars 62. Other Parochial Institution: Parish
Guild and Auxiliaries. Church sittings 350. Value of church $11,350;
rectory $3,000; other church property $1,200—total $15,550. Insurance
$7,500.

Offerings — Parochial: Communion alms $25.25. Minister's salary $891.24. Current expenses $201 51. Endowment $80—total $1,198. *Diocesan:* Episcopal and Contingent Fund $83. Diocesan Missions $75. Church Building Fund $3 Education Fund $3. Relief Fund $3. · Orphanages $80. Permanent Episcopal Fund $225. Aged Clergy $22—total $269. *General:* General Missions $33. Domestic Missions $16. Foreign Missions $6. Colored Missions $2. Indian Missions $2. Jewish Missions $7. Sewanee $5. Clergy Retiring Fund $35. Widows and Orphans' Fund $5. American Church Building Fund $4—total $155. *Aggregate* $1,582.

Since the beginning of Lent 1893, a daily evening service has been maintained, and it is hoped that this will henceforth be the rule of the parish.

Henderson County, Calvary Church; the Rev. H. H. PHELPS, Rector.

Families, white 34; colored 1. Whole number of persons, white 187; colored 6. Baptisms: infant, white 8; colored 2; adult, colored 1—total, white 8; colored 3 Communicants 44. Marriage 1. Burials, white 8; colored 1. Public services: on Sundays 72; other days 108. Holy Communion: public 55; private 1. Sunday-school teachers 7; scholars 54. Parish school teacher 1; scholars 33. Church sittings 200. Value of church $6,000; two rectories $2,000—total $8,000. Insurance $3,000.

Offerings — Parochial: Minister's salary $553.50. Current expenses $49.07—total $602.57. *Diocesan:* Episcopal and Contingent Fund $55. Diocesan Missions $43.94. Thompson Orphanage $5—total $103.94. *General:* General Missions $6.73. Jewish Missions $1.20. Sewanee $4.85. General Clergy Relief $6.43. Prayer-Book Society $4.37. Sea Island sufferers $25 16—total $48.74. *Aggregate* $755.25.

The Rector took charge of this parish June 1, 1893. The report, therefore, covers only eleven months.

Henderson County, Mt. Calvary Chapel; the Rev. H. H. PHELPS, Minister in Charge.

Families 10. Whole number of persons 45. Baptisms: infant 7. Communicants 13. Public services: on Sundays 25; other days 20. Holy Communion 6. Sunday-school teachers 7; scholars 40. Church sittings 125. Value of church $600.

Offerings—Parochial: Communion alms $2. Minister's salary $5. Current expenses $5—total $12.

The above report includes the Mission at Reid's, in Buncombe county. I hold a Sunday afternoon service at each of these points once a month, and services on week days from time to time. At three other places I have held services. At Fairview I baptized five children, included in this report. Whole number of extra services at different places 22. Whole number of Mission services for the past eleven months 67.

Hendersonville, St. James' Church; the Rev. Scott B. Rathbun,
Minister in Charge.

Families 12. Baptisms: infant 2; adult 1—total 3. Confirmed 2. Communicants: added by admission 2; removed 5; present number 25.
Burial 1. Public services: once each Sunday. Holy Communion 9. Value
of church $5,000; rectory $3,000—total $8,000.

Offerings—Parochial: Communion alms $8.50. Salary of Clergyman
$34—total $42 50. *Diocesan:* Diocesan Missions $5.36 Thompson Or-
phanage $1—total $6.36. *Aggregate* $48.86

Hickory, Ascension Church; the Rev. James A. Weston, Rector.

Families, white 27; colored 1. Whole number of persons, white 106;
colored 1. Baptisms: infant 5. Confirmed 13. Communicants: added
by admission 13; removed, white 2; colored 1; died 4; whole number
lost, white 6; colored 1; present number, white 67; colored 1. Burials 4.
Public services: on Sundays 76; other days 40. Holy Communion: public
12; private 1. Sunday-school teachers 4; scholars 32. Other Parochial
Institutions: Woman's Guild and St. Agnes' Guild. Church sittings 176.
Value of church $1,500; other church property $500—total $2,000. Insur-
ance $1,000.

Offerings—Parochial: Communion alms $14.50. Parish Missions $9.
Salary of Clergyman $300. Current expenses $86. Other parish expenses
$32—total $441.50. *Diocesan:* Episcopal and Contingent Fund $22. Dioce-
san Missions $12.80. Thompson Orphanage $32—total $66.80. *General:*
Domestic Missions $2. Foreign Missions $2. Jewish Missions $1. Sewa-
nee $2. Clergy Retiring Fund $4. Widows and Orphans' Fund $6—total
$17. *Aggregate* $525.30.

Of the confirmations reported above six were at Rutherford College.
This is an important Mission. During the past year I have visited it
once a month with most encouraging results.

High Point, St. Mary's Church; the Rev. Frederick A. Fetter,
Deacon in Charge.

Families 15. Whole number of persons 32. Baptisms: infant 3;
adult 3—total 6. Confirmed 9. Communicants 32. Public services:
twice on two Sundays in each month; other days 8 Holy Communion 2.
Sunday-school teachers 6; scholars 41. Church sittings 300. Value of
church $2,640. Amount of indebtedness on church property $1,104.

Offerings—Parochial: Salary of Clergyman $200. *Diocesan:* Thompson
Orphanage $3.79. *Aggregate* $203.79.

High Shoals, St. John's Chapel; the Rev. W. R. WETMORE, D.D., Minister in Charge; the Rev. THOS. C. WETMORE, Assistant.

Families, white 10; colored 2. Whole number of persons 45. Baptisms: infant 2. Confirmed 3. Communicants: added by transfer 2; by admission 3; whole number added 5; died, colored 1; withdrawn 1; present number, white 23; colored 3. Burial 1. Public services 27. Holy Communion: public 10; private 3. Sunday-school teachers 3; scholars 25. Chapel sittings 150. Value of chapel $400; rectory $150—total $550.

Offerings—Parochial: Salary of Clergyman $155.

Hillsboro, St. Matthew's Church; the Rev. BENJ. S. McKENZIE, Rector.

Families 28. Whole number of persons 145. Baptism: infant 1. Confirmed, colored 1. Communicants: added by transfer 2; by admission 1; whole number added 3; removed 2; died 3; present number 80. Marriages, white 2; colored 1. Burials 2. Public services: on Sundays 116; other days 120. Holy Communion: public 11; private 4. Sunday-school teachers 7; scholars 30. Other Parochial Institutions: Woman's Auxiliary; Parish Aid Society; Church-yard Society. Church sittings 250; chapel sittings 75. Value of church $7,000; value of chapel $400; rectory $1,200—total $8,600. Insurance $2,500.

Offerings — Parochial: Communion alms $27.75. Minister's salary $541.75. Current expenses $59.14. Other parish expenses $155.09. Miscellaneous $89.40—total $873.13. *Diocesan:* Episcopal and Contingent Fund $139. · Diocesan Missions $30.62 Church Building Fund $1. Relief Fund $3.50. Thompson Orphanage $48.78. Miscellaneous $3—total $22͵.90. *General:* General Missions $7.60. Domestic Missions $17.82. Foreign Missions $8.40. Jewish Missions $4.55. Miscellaneous $34—total $72 37. *Aggregate* $1,171 40.

Iredell County, St. James' Church; the Rev. F. J. MURDOCH, D.D., Priest in Charge; the Rev. R. B. OWENS, Minister.

Whole number of persons 101. Baptisms: infant 5. Confirmed 5. Communicants 41. Marriages 3. Burials 2. Public services: on Sundays 12; other days 2. Holy Communion 2. Sunday-school teachers 4; scholars 40. Church sittings 250. Value of church $500.

Offerings — Parochial: Salary of Clergyman $37.50. Miscellaneous $12.50—total $50.

Jackson, Church of the Saviour; the Rev. W. T. PICARD, Deacon in Charge.

Families 18. Whole number of persons 86. Baptisms: infant 1; adult 3—total 4. Confirmed 5. Communicants: added by admission 5; removed 1;

present number 38. Burials 3. Public services: on Sundays 98; other days 75. Holy Communion: public 10; private 1. Sunday-school teachers 3; scholars 22. Other Parochial Institution: Ladies' Aid Society. Church sittings 250. Value of church $3,000; rectory fund $450; schoolhouse $500—total $3,950. Insurance $1,200.

Offerings — Parochial: Salary of Clergyman $67. Current expenses $106.76. Other parish expenses $30 50—total $204.26. *Diocesan:* Episcopal and Contingent Fund $50. Diocesan Missions $61.68. Education Fund $2. Thompson Orphanage $26.31—total $139.99. *General:* General Missions $44 89. Jewish Missions $3.79—total $48.68. *Aggregate* $392.93.

I have held regular services once a month at Rich Square, and have made two visits to Margarettsville. From these places I have baptized three adults and one infant, and presented three candidates for confirmation. Mr. J. A. Burgwyn continues his very efficient work as Lay Reader. Everything in the parish is doing as well as we could expect, considering we have no regular services from a Priest.

Kittrell, St. James' Church; the Rev. JAMES B. AVIRETT, Rector-elect.

Families 15. Whole number of persons 45. Baptism: infant 1. Confirmed 2. Communicants: removed 4; present number 30. Marriage 1. Public services: second and fifth Sundays, also Wednesdays and Fridays. Holy Communion: every Sunday morning service. Sunday-school teachers 2; scholars 10. Value of church $1,200; rectory $800—total $2,000. Amount of indebtedness on church property $80. Insurance $1,200.

Offerings—Parochial: Salary of Clergyman $280.12. Debt·on rectory $132.35. Miscellaneous $43.80—total $506.27. *Diocesan:* Diocesan Missions $4. *General:* Foreign Missions $4.50. *Aggregate* $514.77.

In the upper part of the parish there has been established a Mission Station, where a Sunday-school of about 30 scholars and a good congregation have been brought together through the untiring energy and self-sacrifice of one of God's noble women. Services are held there in the afternoons of the first and fifth Sundays by the Clergyman officiating at St. James in the morning. By the aid of the Rev. Julian E. Ingle, a former Rector, notwithstanding the breaks in the rectorate, the work has been pushed on with energy and devotion to the Church's best interests, responded to by a small but devoted band of the Laity.

Leaksville, Epiphany Church.

Families 8. Whole number of persons 42. Baptisms: infant 2; adult 4—total 6. Confirmed 3. Communicants: added by transfer 2; by admission 3; whole number added 5; removed 2; present number 26. Burial 1. Public services: on Sundays 4; other days 4. Holy Communion 1. Sunday-school teachers 4; scholars 25. Other Parochial Institution: Woman's

Auxiliary. Church sittings 300. Value of church $1,000; other church property $1,000 – total $2,000. Insurance $1,750.

Offerings—Parochial: Communion alms $5. Parish Missions $11. Salary of Clergyman $50 Current expenses $19.21. Other parish expenses $15. Miscellaneous $7 50—total $107.77. *Diocesan:* Episcopal and Contingent Fund $15. Thompson Orphanage $8—total $23. *General:* General Missions $7.75. Domestic Missions $2.50. Foreign Missions $3—total $13.25. *Aggregate* $144 02.

No regular services have been held since last July.

Lenoir, St. James' Church; the Rev. J. BUXTON, D.D., Rector.

Families 18. Whole number of persons 75. Baptisms: infant 4; adult 1— total 5. Confirmed 4. Communicants: added by transfer 1; by admission 4; whole number added 5; present number 59. Marriage 1. Burials 2. Public services: on Sundays, morning and afternoon, Wednesday and Friday, Festival Days. Holy Communion: public, monthly and occasional; private 2. Sunday-school teachers 5; scholars 25. Parish school teacher 1. Scholars, 35. Other Parochial Institution: Woman's Parochial Guild. Church sittings 150. Chapel sittings 200. Value of church $1,200. Value of chapels $1,000; rectory $1,200—total $3,400. Amount of indebtedness on church property $100.

Offerings — Parochial: Communion alms $20.72. Current expenses $34.93—total $55.65. *Diocesan:* Episcopal and Contingent Fund $50. Diocesan Missions $15.27. Church Building Fund $1. Education Fund $1. Relief Fund $1. Thompson Orphanage $5.25—total $73.52. *General:* Domestic Missions $5. Foreign Missions $5. Jewish Missions $3. Sewanee $2—total $15. *Aggregate* $144.17.

The Chapel of Rest, in the valley of the Yadkin, is included in this parish, and is visited monthly. The Chapel of Peace, two miles from Lenoir, is a part of the parish. At Riverside, fifteen miles from Lenoir, in the valley, there are five communicants. All are included in the report above. The Woman's Guild is a useful assistant in parish work and charity. The colored parish school, under the charge of Miss Caison, pursues diligently its proper work. The school building is soon to be enlarged. Last summer I visited the Watauga Missions. It is a most interesting field of labor, though destitute at this time of a resident Missionary.

Lexington, Church of the Redemption; the Rev. FREDERICK A. FETTER, Deacon in Charge.

Families 7. Whole number of persons 14. Communicants 11. Public services: twice on two Sundays in each month; other days 6. Holy Communion 3. Church sittings 300. Value of church $1,500.

Offerings — Parochial: Communion alms $9.15. Minister's salary $166.66—total $175.81.

Lincoln County, Church of Our Saviour; the Rev. W. R. Wetmore, D D., Minister in Charge; the Rev. T. C. Wetmore, Assistant.

Families 6. Whole number of persons 25. Baptism: infant 1. Communicants 10. Public services: on Sundays 12; other days 1. Holy
Communion 2. Sunday-school teachers 4; scholars 60. Church sittings
200. Value of church $500.

Offerings: Diocesan Missions 88 cents.

Since the ordination of my son, Mr. T. C. Wetmore, to the Diaconate
in February last, he has been placed by the Bishop to assist me in the
Mission field. He gives one Sunday in each month to Gastonia, Maiden
and McPaul's, and one Sunday to St. Stephen's and to the Church of Our
Saviour. When a fifth Sunday occurs he gives that day to St. John's
and Rush Mountain.

Lincoln County, St. Paul's Chapel; the Rev. W..R. Wetmore, D.D.,
Minister in Charge; the Rev. T. C. Wetmore, Assistant.

Families 12. Whole number of persons 65. Baptisms: Infant 9;
adult 1—total 10. Communicants: added by admission 5; suspended 1;
present number 19. Public services: on Sundays 14; other days 2.
Holy Communion 4. Sunday-school teachers 8; scholars 50. Chapel
sittings 125. Value of chapel $175.

Offerings—Parochial: Salary of Clergyman $6. Current expenses $3—
total $9.

Lincoln County, St. Stephen's Chapel; the Rev. W. R Wetmore,
D.D., Minister in Charge; the Rev. T. C. Wetmore, Assistant.

Families 8. Whole number of persons 36. Baptisms: infant 7. Communicants: added by transfer 2; removed 1; withdrawn 1; whole number lost 2; present number 15 Burials 5. Public services 13. Holy
Communion 4. Sunday-school teachers 3; scholars 25. Chapel sittings
100. Value of chapel $150.

Lincoln and Other Missions; the Rev. W. R. Wetmore, D.D., Minister in Charge; the Rev. T. C Wetmore, Assistant.

Families 8. Whole number of persons 45. Baptisms: infant 4. Confirmed 4. Communicants: added by transfer 2; by admission 2; whole
number added 4; present number 18. Public services: on Sundays 4;
other days 5. Holy Communion: public 7; private 1.

Offerings—Parochial: Salary of Clergyman $10.50. *Diocesan:* Diocesan
Missions $6.70. *Aggregate* $17.20.

Lincolnton, St. Cyprian's Chapel (colored); the Rev. W. R. WET-
MORE, D D., Minister in Charge; the Rev. P. P. ALSTON, Assistant.

Familes 7. Whole number of persons 40. Communicants: removed
1; died 1; whole number lost 2; present number 18. Burial 1. Holy
Communion 1. Sunday-school teachers 6; scholars 40. Chapel sittings
80. Value of chapel $200.
  Offerings—Diocesan: Episcopal and Contingent Fund $2.73.
Rev. P. P. Alston visits this Mission one Sunday in each month.

Lincolnton, St. Luke's Church; the Rev. W. R. WETMORE, D.D.,
Rector.

Families 28. Whole number of persons 114. Baptisms: infant 10;
adult 1—total 11. Confirmed 11. Communicants: added by transfer 2;
by admission 10; whole number added 1z; removed 3; present number
77. Marriages 3. Burial 1. Public services: on Sundays 92; other days
93. Holy Communion: public 28; private 6. Sunday-school teachers 4;
scholars 18. Church sittings 250. Value of church $3,600. Insurance
$2,000.
  Offerings—Parochial: Communion alms $2. Minister's salary $438.08.
Current expenses $85.93. Other parish expenses $90.23—total $616.24.
Diocesan: Episcopal and Contingent Fund $65.50. Diocesan Missions
$37.60. Thompson Orphanage $20 10—total $123.20. *General:* Domestic
Missions $16.39. Foreign Missions $16.39. Jewish Missions $3.75.
Sewanee $21.50—total $58.03. *Aggregate* $797.47.
  The above report includes statistics for Beattie's Ford.

Littleton, Chapel of the Cross.

Families, white 6; colored 2. Whole number of persons, white 28;
colored 3. Baptism: adult 1. Confirmed 2. Communicants: added by
transfer 1; by admission 2; whole number added 3; died 1; withdrawn
1; whole number lost 2; present number 29. Burial 1. Public services:
on Sundays 5; other days 7. Holy Communion: public 10; private 2.
Sunday-school teachers, white 4; colored 6; scholars, white 24; colored
47. Parish school teachers, white 1; colored 1; scholars, white 20; colored 35. Chapel sittings 250 Value of chapel $750. Amount of in-
debtedness on church property $20.
  Offerings—Parochial: Communion alms $10. *Diocesan:* Diocesan Mis-
sions $5. *General:* Foreign Missions $11.25. *Aggregate* $26.25.
  We have had no minister in charge during the past year. The Rev.
William Walker has given us services about once a month and the Rev.
Mr. Milbank has also visited us.

Louisburg, St. Matthias' Chapel (colored); the Rev. WM. WALKER,
Minister in Charge; the Rev. H. B. DELANY, Assistant.

Families 4. Whole number of persons 50. Baptisms: adult 9. Confirmed 28. Communicants: removed 2; suspended 2; present number
24. Public services: on Sundays 35; other days 4. Holy Communion
12. Sunday-school teachers, white 2; colored 3; scholars 90. Chapel
sittings 200. Value of chapel $2,000

Offerings—Parochial: Communion alms $8.61. Current expenses $9.11.
Other parish expenses $30—total $47.72. *Diocesan:* Diocesan Missions
$5.66. *Aggregate* $53.38.

This report does not include the amounts collected and expended in
the construction of the chapel, nor the amount of indebtedness. We
have just completed the chapel and will have the first service in it on
Whitsunday.

Louisburg, St. Paul's Church; the Rev. JAMES BATTLE AVIRETT,
Rector-elect.

Families 18. Whole number of persons, white 58; colored 1. Bap-
ism: infant 1. Confirmed 1. Communicants: added by transfer 1; whole
number added 2; removed 17; died 2; whole number lost 19; present
number, white 47; colored 1. Marriage 1. Burial 1. Public services:
on Sundays 16; other days 10 Holy Communion 8. Sunday-school
teachers 5; scholars 22. Church sittings 200. Value of church $1,000;
rectory fund $1,000; one lot $100—total $2,100.

Offerings—Parochial: Communion alms $7.98. Salary of Clergyman
$100. Current expenses $7.96. Repairs $90. Sunday-school $7.12 Vest-
ments $25—total $238.06. *Diocesan:* Episcopal and Contingent Fund $16.
Diocesan Missions $27.58. Thompson Orphanage $5—total $48.58. *Gen-
eral:* General Missions $2.79. Domestic Missions $5. Foreign Missions
$5—total $12.79. *Aggregate* $299.43.

The Rector-elect entered upon his duties in this parish February 1,
1894, and the above offerings represent the contributions since the beginning of his Rectorate. The number of services and celebrations of the
Holy Communion reported refer only to those given by the Rector since
February 1st. On the part of the Wardens, Vestry and congregation
there has been a blessed response to every suggestion, both to dignify
and elevate the tone of the services. Never were a people kinder than
here and at St. James, Kittrell.

Madison, St. John's Church; the Rev. CHARLES FETTER, Deacon in
Charge.

Baptisms: infant 4; adult 1—total 5. Confirmed 1. Communicants:
added by transfer 2; by admission 1; whole number added 3; removed

3; present number 11. Public services: on Sundays 20; other days 5. Holy Communion 4. Sunday-school teachers 4; scholars 20. Church sittings 250. Value of church $1,300; other church property $200—total $1,500.

Offerings—Parochial: Communion alms $20. Minister's salary $150. Current expenses $20—total $170. *Diocesan:* Diocesan Missions $3. *General:* General Missions $2.75. *Aggregate* $175.75.

I took charge of this church last February. I have baptized one adult and two infants. Much praise is due Mrs. John M. Galloway for her noble efforts in keeping alive the Sunday-school and church interest during the absence of ministerial work.

Marion, St. John's Church; the Rev. G. W. PHELPS, Minister in Charge.

Families 8. Whole number of persons 25. Baptism: infant 1. Confirmed 5. Communicants: added by admission 5; present number 14. Public services: on Sundays 18; other days 12. Holy Communion 8. Sunday-school teachers 2; scholars 12. Church sittings 80. Value of church $1,000.

Offerings—Parochial: Salary of Clergyman $63.51. *Diocesan:* Diocesan Missions $2.78. *Aggregate* $66.29.

At this place there is a growing interest in the services of our Church. Old prejudices seem to be breaking away. We have a small Sunday-school here that is zealously kept up by the ladies, and if their success could equal their efforts to promote the good of the Mission, we should soon have a large Sunday-school and many added to the Church.

Mecklenburg County, St. Mark's Church; the Rev. E. A. OSBORNE, Minister in Charge.

Families 16. Whole number of persons 100. Baptisms: infant 2. Confirmed 6. Communicants: added by admission 6; died 1; present number 55. Marriage 1. Burials 2. Public services: on Sundays, once a month; other days 3. Holy Communion: public, monthly; private 1. Sunday-school teachers 4; scholars 40. Value of church $2,500. Amount of indebtedness on church property $175. Insurance $350.

Offerings—Parochial: Salary of Clergyman $27. Other parish expenses $13—total $40. *Diocesan:* Episcopal and Contingent Fund $5.50. Diocesan Missions $5. Thompson Orphanage $1.95—total $12.45. *Aggregate* $52.45.

Owing to the urgent claims upon my time in connection with the care of the Thompson Orphanage and the congregation at Statesville, I have not been able to do any pastoral work at St. Mark's. There is a most inviting field here for an active and efficient Missionary.

16

Middleburg, Chapel of the Heavenly Rest; the Rev. WILLIAM S. PETTIGREW, Minister in Charge.

Families 6. Whole number of persons 30. Confirmed 5. Communicants 20. Burials 5. Public services 30. Holy Communion 4. Chapel sittings 100. Value of chapel $400.
Offerings—Parochial: Salary of Clergyman $66.84. Current expenses $5—total $71 84. *Diocesan:* Episcopal and Contingent Fund $10. Diocesan Missions $11 86—total $21.86. *General:* Foreign Missions $4.43. *Aggregate* $98.13.

Milton, Christ Church; the Rev. CHARLES FETTER, Deacon in Charge.

Families 5. Whole number of persons 13. Baptisms: adult 3. Confirmed 1. Communicants: added by admission 1; removed 1; present number 5. Public services: on Sundays 27; other days 2. Holy Communion: public 1; private 1. Sunday-school teachers 4; scholars 21. Church sittings 200. Value of church $1,800. Amount of indebtedness on church property $350. Insurance $1,000.
Offerings — Parochial: Parish Missions $6.24. Salary of Clergyman $150. Current expenses $7. Other parish expenses $1.60—total $164.84. *Diocesan:* Diocesan Missions $5.38. *Aggregate* $170.22.
This is the only Episcopal Church in Caswell county. Its work and influence are very encouraging. There is such a kindly feeling towards the Church. Our work is purely Missionary in its character. We have a Sunday-school of about 25 members, while there are others besides these dependent on us. We have been able to give bodily and spiritual comfort to many poor creatures in destitute circumstances.

Monroe, St. Paul's Church; the Rev. FRANCIS W. HILLIARD, Minister in Charge.

Families 17. Whole number of persons 65. Baptisms: infant 3; adult 3—total 6. Confirmed 9 Communicants: added by transfer 2; by admission 3; whole number added 5; removed 2; died 1; whole number lost 3; present number 35. Burial 1. Public services: on Sundays 119; other days 95. Holy Communion 65. Sunday-school teachers 6; scholars 32. Other Parochial Institution: Woman's Auxiliary. Church sittings 150. Value of church $1,500; rectory $1,200—total $2,700.
Offerings — Parochial: Salary of Clergyman $231. Current expenses $60.63. Other parish expenses $91.76—total $383.39. *Diocesan:* Episcopal and Contingent Fund $16.50. Diocesan Missions $4. Church Building Fund $1.20. Education Fund $1.39. Relief Fund $2. Thompson Orphanage $4 06—total $29.14. *General:* General Missions $4.50. Jewish Missions $1.05. American Church Building Fund $2.83—total $8.38. *Aggregate* $420.91.

The present incumbent took charge July 1, 1893. There is much to stimulate in the interest and importance of the field, and much to encourage in the results already achieved, though without, a resident Minister, and the ready and loving co-operation of the people. The excess in the number of confirmations over that of admissions to the Communion is accounted for by the Bishop's visit, about ten days before the date of this report I am holding monthly services at two or three points in Richmond county, where there are about twelve communicants. At Laurel Hill I have baptized one adult.

Morganton, Grace Church; the Rev. E. P. GREEN, late Rector.

Baptisms: infant 7. Communicants 89. Burials 2. Public services 126 Holy Communion 12. Sunday-school teachers 8; scholars 40. Other Parochial Institutions: King's Daughters, Bishop Atkinson Memorial Society.

Offerings—Parochial: Communion alms $14.49. Salary of Clergyman $388.85. Other parish expenses $146.46—total $549.80. *Diocesan:* Episcopal and Contingent Fund $36.65. Diocesan Missions $4.69. Thompson Orphanage $13.40—total $54.74. *General:* Domestic Missions $2.40. Jewish Missions $4.60. Sewanee $2 59. General Clergy Relief $4.95—total $14.54. *Aggregate* $619.08.

Morganton, St. Stephen's Church (colored); the Rev. HENRY S. McDUFFEY, Minister in Charge.

Families 8. Whole number of persons 39. Baptisms: infant 2. Confirmed 4. Communicants: added by admission 4; died 2; suspended 1; present number 20. Burials 2. Public services: on Sundays 10; other days 5. Holy Communion 4. Sunday-school teachers, white 4; colored 3; scholars 40. Parish school teacher 1; scholars 80. Chapel sittings 250. Value of chapel $1,200; rectory $400—total $1,600. Insurance $800.

Offerings—Parochial: Communion alms $3.52. Minister's salary $10. Current expenses $32—total $45.52. *Diocesan:* Diocesan Missions $5.50. *General:* Colored Missions $5.50. *Aggregate* $56.52.

I am sorry to say I have been unable to give the attention to St. Stephen's that it should have had. The Rev. E. P. Green, Rector of Grace Church, Morganton, has been very kind in holding services for that congregation. I believe the church would do well at Morganton if the congregation had a resident Minister. The parochial school is in a good condition, and our teacher, Mrs. F. Wilson, is doing a good work.

Noise, Moore County, St. Philip's Chapel (colored); the Rev. WILLIAM WALKER, Minister in Charge.

Families 20. Whole number of persons 128. Baptisms: infant 9. Communicants 16. Public services: every Sunday lay service; also daily.

Holy Communion: public 5; private 1.   Sunday-s chool teachers 6; scholars 109.   Parish school teachers 3; scholars 43.   Chapel sittings 100. Value of chapel and parsonage $500; other church property $76—total $576.

Offerings—Parochial: Minister's salary $20.44.   *General:* General Missions $1.26.   *Aggregate* $21.70.

Mr. S. A. B. Trott has been discharging his duties zealously during the past year as Lay Reader and School-master at this Mission.   Through the kindness of friends we have purchased thirty acres of land about five miles from St. Philip's, where a new Station has been established.   There are several families connected with this venture.   The statistics are included in this report.   Six of the baptisms were at this new parish.   We are about to build a school chapel at this Station, which will be called St. Monica.

Old Fort Mission; the Rev. G. W. Phelps, Minister in Charge.

Families 5.   Whole number of persons 23.   Confirmed 2.   Communicants: added by admission 2; removed 5; died 2; whole number lost 7; present number 7.   Burial 1.   Public services: on Sundays 16; other days 11.   Holy Communion: public 7; private 2.   Sunday-school teachers 3; scholars 15.   Church sittings 80.   Value of church $800.

Offerings—Parochial: Salary of Clergyman $38.63.   *Diocesan:* Diocesan Missions $1.36.   *General:* Domestic Missions $1.93.   *Aggregate* $41.92.

The work at this place has, in the past year, been favored, and though we have suffered much from the death of two members, and the moving away of others, yet, by the merciful help of our Heavenly Father, the church has been nearly completed.   The ladies have been, from the very start, full of zeal and love for their work, and have neglected no opportunity of promoting it.   And now success crowns their efforts with a nice, comfortable little church, an organ, the gift of a merchant of the place, and a communion service from friends abroad.

Orange County, St. Mary's Chapel; the Rev. Benjamin S. McKenzie, Minister in Charge.

Families, white 12; colored 1.   Whole number of persons 75.   Baptisms: infant 2; adult, colored 1—total 3.   Communicants: added by admission 2; present number 35.   Public services: on Sundays 10; other days 6. Holy Communion 1.   Sunday-school teachers 4; scholars 30.   Church sittings 200.   Value of church $1,000.

Oxford, St. Stephen's Church; the Rev. Edward Benedict, Rector.

Families 36.   Whole number of persons 200.   Baptisms: infant 9; adult 1—total 10.   Confirmed 16.   Communicants: added by admission

16; removed 4; died, white 3; colored 1; whole number lost 8; present
number 115. Burials 5. Public services: on Sundays 153; other days
97. Holy Communion: public 91; private 1. Sunday-school teachers
8; scholars 75. Other Parochial Institutions: Ladies' Aid Society;
Woman's Auxiliary; Junior Auxiliary. Church sittings 300. Value of
church $2,500; rectory $4,000 – total $6,500. Insurance $2,500.

Offerings—Parochial: Communion alms $17. Salary of Clergyman
$800. Current expenses $259.87. Other parish expenses $19.23—total
$1,096.10. *Diocesan:* Episcopal and Contingent Fund $96.58. Diocesan
Missions $84.02. Thompson Orphanage $27.90—total $208.50. *General:*
Domestic Missions $40.68. Foreign Missions $7.25. Indian Missions
$2. Jewish Missions $3.35. Sewanee $5. Clergy Retiring Fund $24—
total $82.28. *Aggregate* $1,386.88.

Pittsboro, St. Bartholomew's Church; the Rev. C. T. BLAND, Rector.

Families 12. Whole number of persons 56. Baptisms: infant 2. Confirmed 1. Communicants: removed 2; withdrawn 3; whole number lost 5;
present number 31. Burials 2. Public services: on Sundays 85; other
days 97. Holy Communion 13. Sunday-school teachers 4; scholars 16.
Other Parochial Institution: Thompson Orphanage Guild.

Offerings—Parochial: Communion alms $55.12. Salary of Clergyman
$346. Current expenses $59.70—total $460.82. *Diocesan:* Episcopal and
Contingent Fund $55. Diocesan Missions $53.60. Thompson Orphanage
$14.50. Miscellaneous $12 80—total $135.90. *General:* Domestic Mis-
sions $3.68. Foreign Missions $5.40. Colored Missions $3.50. Indian
Missions $4. Jewish Missions $3.60. Sewanee $8.65. General Clergy
Relief $19.55—total $48.38. *Aggregate* $645.10.

I have visited St. Mark's, Gulf, twice, administered the Holy Communion each time, and baptized one infant.

Pittsboro, St. James' Chapel (colored); the Rev. WILLIAM WALKER,
Minister in Charge.

Families 30. Whole number of persons 125. Baptisms: Infant 3. Confirmed 4. Communicants: added by admission 2; present number 40.
Public services: on Sundays, twice a month (two services). Holy Communion: at every Sunday morning service. Sunday-school teachers 2;
scholars 20. Chapel sittings 150. Value of church property $1,280.

Offerings—Parochial: Minister's salary $1.15. Current expenses $12.24—
total $13.39. *Diocesan:* Episcopal and Contingent Fund $3.80. Diocesan
Missions $2.93—total $6.73. *General:* General Missions 63 cents. Jewish
Missions 64 cents—total $1.27. *Aggregate* $21.39.

I have visited this Mission as often as I have had opportunity. At
Haywood we have begun a work which has been beneficial, and I hope
will develop into a Mission. A day-school has been carried on with good
results, and the Sunday-school is increasing.

Raleigh, Christ Church and Chapels; the Rev. M. M. MARSHALL, D.D., Rector.

Families 145. Whole number of persons 650. Baptisms: infant 14; adult 2—total 16. Confirmed 21. Communicants: added by admission 21; removed 5; died 13; whole number lost 18; present number 275. Marriages 4. Burials 20. Public services: on Sundays 124; other days 204. Holy Communion: public 58; private 10. Sunday-school teachers 17; scholars 154. Other Parochial Institutions: St. Agnes' Guild and St. Timothy's Guild for Thompson Orphanage; Relief Society for the Poor; Altar Guild; St. Thomas' Guild; Woman's Auxiliary to Board of Missions; Chapter of the Brotherhood of St. Andrew, and Chapter of the Daughters of the King.. Church sittings 600. Chapel sittings 350. Value of church $30,000. Value of chapels $4,000; rectory $10,000—total $44,000. Amount of indebtedness on church property $3,000. Insurance $22,800.

Offerings—Parochial: Communion alms $189.45. New Mission chapel $654.50. Salary of Clergyman $2,000. Current expenses $1,055. Other parish expenses $240.95. For the poor $183. Church furnishings $76.50 —total $4,399.40. *Diocesan:* Episcopal and Contingent Fund $362.50. Diocesan Missions $227.54. Church Building Fund $3.73. Education Fund $16.23. Relief Fund $14 73. Thompson Orphanage $286.50. Special Mission work $139.53. Miscellaneous $11—total $1,061.76. *General:* General Missions $229.07. Jewish Missions $30.67. Sewanee $21.31. Clergy Retiring Fund $40—total $321.05. *Aggregate* $5,782.21.

Of the amount above reported for Diocesan Missions, $19.43 was collected at our late Bishop's Jubilee Service and $37.71 at the first regular visitation of the present Bishop to the parish. As required by Canon, the Rector reports the burial of an adult in the parish of Grace Church, Weldon He has also administered the Holy Communion and preached twice in Emmanuel Church, Warrenton, and performed the same services in St. Clement's Church, Ringwood, during vacancies in the rectorships of those parishes. Regular monthly Sunday afternoon services have been kept up at the Soldier's Home, the Penitentiary, and the Asylum for the Insane. Vigorous chapters of the Brotherhood of St. Andrew and of the Daughters of the King have been organized, and our beautiful new Mission Chapel—St. Saviour's—has been completed at a cost of about $1,500, although it is at present unfurnished and so not yet in use.

Raleigh, Church of the Good Shepherd; the Rev. I. McK. PITTENGER, D.D., Rector.

Baptisms: infant 17; adult 6—total 23. Confirmed 16. Communicants: added by transfer 19; by admission 18; whole number added 37; removed 6; died 1; whole number lost 7; present number 264. Burials 9.

Public services: on Sundays 136; other days 168. Holy Communion: public 74; private 1. Sunday-school teachers 13; scholars 130. Other Parochial Institutions: St. Mary's Guild; Altar Guild; Woman's Auxiliary; Brotherhood of St. Andrew; Thompson Orphanage Guild. Church sittings 400. Insurance $4,900.

Offerings—Parochial: Communion alms $99.13. Salary of Clergyman $1,625. Current expenses $596.87. Other parish expenses $149.47. Payment of debt $638.65. Repairs and improvements $484.64. Miscellaneous $125.20—total $3,718.96. *Diocesan:* Episcopal and Contingent Fund $143.75. Diocesan Missions $181.56. Thompson Orphanage $98. Miscellaneous $25.05—total $448.36. *General:* General Missions $34.16. Domestic Missions $21.42. Foreign Missions $12.08—total $67.66. *Aggregate* $4,234.98.

The Church of the Good Shepherd was made the recipient of some benefactions through the will of the late Bishop Lyman, but these bequests are of indefinite value, and have not yet come into the possession of the church. A handsome brass lectern has been placed in the church as a memorial to Mrs. Anna Godman Pittenger, the deceased wife of the Rector. The lectern was consecrated on All Saints' Day, 1893. A beautiful altar-cloth for Easter, with appropriate belongings, was presented to the church on Easter Day, 1894. An organization within the parish has been discontinued, viz., the Hospital Chapter, because the object for which it was organized—St. John's Hospital—has ceased to exist.

Raleigh, St. Augustine's Church (colored); the Rev. A. B. HUNTER, Rector; the Rev. R. B. SUTTON, D.D., and the Rev. H. B. DELANY, Assistant Ministers.

Families 27. Whole number of persons 175. Baptisms: infant 7. Confirmed 23. Communicants: added by admission 23; removed 3; present number 103. Marriages 2. Burials 4. Public services: on Sundays 128; other days 422. Holy Communion: public 17; private 12. Sunday-school teachers, white 2; colored 10; scholars 222. Church sittings 200. Value of church $2,000.

Offerings—Parochial: Communion alms $19.85. Salary of Clergyman $28.85. Current expenses $49.90. Other parish expenses $5.40—total $104. *Diocesan:* Episcopal and Contingent Fund $25. Diocesan Missions $9.76. Good Samaritan Hospital $3—total $37.76. *General:* Foreign Missions $25.52. Jewish Missions $3. Clergy Retiring Fund $12—total $40.52. *Aggregate* $182 28.

The three Clergy of this parish have also duties as teachers in St. Augustine's school. The Rev. H. B. Delany has held monthly services at Louisburg and Warrenton.

Raleigh, St. Mary's School Chapel; the Rev. BENNETT SMEDES, D.D.,
Rector.

Baptism: adult 1. Confirmed 6. Public services: on all Sundays and
other days. Holy Communion 17.

Offerings—Parochial: Communion alms $30. Miscellaneous $20—total
$50. *Diocesan:* Episcopal and Contingent Fund $60. Miscellaneous
$77.60—total $137.60. *General:* Foreign Missions $40. Miscellaneous $50
—total $90. *Aggregate* $277.60.

Reidsville, St. Thomas' Church.

Families 12. Whole number of persons 39. Baptisms: infant 5; adult 1—
total 6. Confirmed 5. Communicants: added by transfer 2; by admission 5; whole number added 7; removed 2; present number 40. Burial 1.
Public services: on Sundays 5; other days 11. Holy Communion 2. Sunday-school teachers 5; scholars 46. Value of church $1,500; other church
property $300—total $1,800.

Offerings—Parochial: Salary of Clergyman $50. *Diocesan:* Thompson
Orphanage $3. *General:* Foreign Missions $5. *Aggregate* $58.

The Church and work are not in a flourishing condition, with no Rector
for the past ten months, and the church poorly situated, with a luke-
warmness of the members, there has been a backward tendency. We
cannot accomplish much without a Minister. Our Sunday-school is a
success and is conducted regularly every Sunday morning, and much
interest is manifested. However, we still pray that we may soon have a
shepherd and accomplish much to the glory of God and our own spiritual
welfare.

Ridgeway, Chapel of the Good Shepherd; the Rev. WILLIAM S.
PETTIGREW, Rector.

Families 20. Whole number of persons 60. Baptisms: infant 4. Communicants 21. Marriage 1. Burials 3. Public services: on Sundays 37;
other days 20. Holy Communion 6. Sunday-school teachers 4; scholars 20.
Church sittings 150. Value of church $3,000; rectory $3,000—total $6,000.
Amount of indebtedness on church property $1,000.

Offerings—Parochial: Salary of Clergyman $174.85. Current expenses
$18.35—total $193.20. *Diocesan:* Episcopal and Contingent Fund $24.
Diocesan Missions $4. Thompson Orphanage $9—total $37. *General:*
Foreign Missions $3. *Aggregate* $233.20.

Ringwood, St. Clement's Church.

Families 8. Whole number of persons 46. Baptism: infant 1. Confirmed 1. Communicants: added by transfer 2; by admission 1; whole

number added 3; removed 2; present number 19. Burial 1. Sunday-school teachers 6; scholars 30. Church sittings 200. Value of church $2,000. Amount of indebtedness on church property $24.

Offerings—Parochial: Salary of Clergyman $150. *Diocesan:* Episcopal and Contingent Fund $10. Thompson Orphanage $10—total $20. *General:* Domestic Missions $26. *Aggregate* $196

This church has been without a Rector since last November. The Rev. Gaston Battle took charge of it in April, 1893, but resigned in November. Since then there has been no regular service. During the past year our church has been greatly improved. A handsome recess chancel has been added by Miss Lucy W. Garrett as a memorial of her father and mother. In this chancel three memorial windows have been placed, one being to the memory of our late beloved Rector, the Rev. Aristides S. Smith, D.D., who for eighteen years served this church faithfully. Besides these mentioned, several other handsome gifts have been made to our church as memorials of departed friends.

Rockwood, Buncombe County, Church of the Redeemer; the Rev.

WILLIAM F. RICE, Deacon in Charge; John C. Seagle, Lay Reader.

Families 3. Whole number of persons 18. Baptisms: infant 1; adult 1 —total 2. Confirmed 3. Communicants: added by admission 3; present number 10. Public services: on Sundays 24; other days 2. Holy Communion 8. Sunday-school teachers 3; scholars 20. Value of church $3,500.

Offerings—Parochial $20. *Diocesan:* Diocesan Missions 90 cents. *Aggregate* $20.90.

This church, one of the most beautiful and substantial in this end of the State, was opened by Bishop Lyman, who preached in it on the afternoon of Lord's Day, September 17, 1893.

The existence of this Mission is due to the indefatigable efforts of Dr. Francis Willis.

Rocky Mount, Church of the Good Shepherd; the Rev. ALVIN

JONES VANDERBOGART, Rector.

Families 31. Whole number of persons, white 150; colored 2. Baptisms: infant 3; adult 1—total 4. Confirmed 8. Communicants: added by transfer 14; by admission 6; whole number added 28; removed 4; died 3; whole number lost 7; present number, white 90; colored 2. Marriages 3. Burials 4 Public services: on Sundays 134; other days 95. Holy Communion: public 55; private 3. Sunday-school teachers, white 6; colored 1; scholars, white 42; colored 5. Other Parochial Institutions: Church Aid Society; Altar Guild; Junior Auxiliary. Church sittings 300; chapel sittings 75. Value of church $4,000; value of chapel $250; other church property $900—total $5,150.

17

Offerings—Parochial: Minister's salary $600. Current expenses $109.05. Other parish expenses $50. Paid on rectory debt $128 76.—total $887.81. *Diocesan:* Diocesan Missions $12.17. Thompson Orphanage $6.25—total $18.42. *Aggregate* $906.23.

Rowan County, Christ Church; the Rev. F. J. MURDOCH, D.D., Priest in Charge; the Rev. S. S. BOST, Minister.

Whole number of persons 92. Baptisms: infant 4. Confirmed 3. Communicants 38. Marriage 1. Burials 2. Public services: on Sundays 24; other days 2. Holy Communion 4. Sunday-school teachers 6; scholars 30. Church sittings 300. Value of church $900; two-thirds rectory $800—total $1,700.

Offerings—Parochial: Salary of Clergyman $75. Other parish expenses $15—total $90. *Diocesan:* Thompson Orphanage $7.28. *Aggregate* $97.28.

For many years the report for Christ Church was made out by adding and subtracting names from the last report. This report is made out from an actual census, and the names of all those who have died and moved away have been stricken from the list.

Rowan County, St. Andrew's Church and St. George's Chapel: the Rev. F. J. MURDOCH, D.D., Priest in Charge; the Rev. S. S. BOST, Minister.

Whole number of persons 60 Baptisms: infant 8. Confirmed 2. Communicants 29. Burial 1. Public services: on Sundays 30; other days 4. Holy Communion 4. Sunday-school teachers 5; scholars 35. Church sittings 200. Chapel sittings 200. Value of church $750. Value of chapel $500; one-third rectory $400—total $1,650. Amount of indebtedness on church property $60.

Offerings—Parochial: Salary of Clergyman $30.50. Miscellaneous $19.50 —total $50.

Rowan County, St. Jude's Chapel; the Rev. F. J. MURDOCH, D.D., Minister; the Rev. S. S. BOST, Assistant.

Whole number of persons 22. Baptisms: infant 2; adult 1—total 3. Confirmed 1. Communicants 10. Public services: on Sundays 24; other days 2. Holy Communion 2. Sunday-school teachers 3; scholars 15. Chapel sittings 80. Value of chapel $325.

Offerings—Parochial: Salary of Clergyman $5. Other parish expenses $75. Miscellaneous $5—total $85.

The chapel has been improved at a cost of $75.

Rowan County, St. Mary's Church; the Rev. F. J. MURDOCH, D.D., Rector; the Rev. R. B. OWENS, Assistant Minister.

Whole number of persons 37. Baptism: infant 1. Confirmed 1. Communicants: added by removal 1; present number 22. Burials 2. Public services: on Sundays 24; other days 4. Holy Communion 4. Sunday-school teachers 2; scholars 9. Church sittings 120. Value of church $1,000; endowment $550—total $1,550.

Offerings—Parochial: Salary of Clergyman $53.76. Other parish expenses $10—total $63.76. *Diocesan:* Episcopal and Contingent Fund $5.50. *Aggregate* $69.26.

Rowan County, St. Matthew's Chapel; the Rev. F. J. MURDOCH, D.D., Minister; the Rev. S. S. BOST, Assistant.

Whole number of persons 52. Baptisms: infant 7. Confirmed 14. Communicants 30. Burial 1. Public services: on Sundays 24; other days 4. Holy Communion 4. Sunday-school teachers 9; scholars 45. Chapel sittings 80. Value of chapel $250.

Offerings—Parochial: Salary of Clergyman $20. Miscellaneous $10—total $30.

Rowan County, St. Paul's Church; the Rev. F. J. MURDOCH, D.D., Minister; the Rev. R. B. OWENS, Assistant.

Whole number of persons 40. Baptism: adult 1. Confirmed 7. Communicants 32. Marriage 1. Public services: on Sundays 52; other days 10. Holy Communion 52. Sunday-school teachers 13; scholars 125. Chapel sittings 120. Value of chapel $600. Insurance $400.

Offerings—Parochial: Salary of Clergyman $46.75. Miscellaneous $43.25 —total $90.

Rutherfordton, St. John's Church and Henrietta Mills Mission; G. W. PHELPS, Minister in Charge.

Families 8. Whole number of persons 33. Baptism: adult 1. Communicants: added by transfer 3; removed 3; present number 14. Burial 1. Public services: on Sundays 23; other days 2. Holy Communion 5. Church sittings 100. Value of church $1,000.

Offerings—Parochial: Minister's salary $44.16. Other parish expenses $38.25—total $82.41.

At Rutherfordton the congregations are generally good. During the last year, and through the enterprise and zeal of the ladies of the church here, we have secured a new roof on the church and have made some other needful repairs.

At Henrietta Mission our work has been much hindered by the moving away of the few members we had there; but I hope others will come in so that the work will move on in a little while, for Henrietta is growing to be quite a place of importance in numbers.

Salisbury, St. Luke's Church; the Rev. F. J. MURDOCH, D.D., Rector.

Whole number of persons, white 207; colored 1. Baptisms: infant 7; adult 1—total 8. Confirmed 10. Communicants, white 103; colored 1.

Marriage 1. Public services: on Sundays 104; other days 84. Holy Communion: public 52; private 2. Sunday-school teachers 8; scholars 65. Church sittings 300. Value of church $7,000; rectory $3,500; other church property $1,000—total $11,500. Amount of indebtedness on church property $300. Insurance $1,200.

Offerings—Parochial: Communion alms $48. Missions in Rowan $455. Other parish expenses $149.95. Improvements $969.69—total $1,622.64. *Diocesan:* Episcopal and Contingent Fund $100. Diocesan Missions $25.95. Thompson Orphanage $80—total $205.95. *General:* Domestic Missions $37.80. Foreign Missions $2.07. Sewanee $1 70—total $41.57. *Aggregate* $1,870.16.

Salisbury, St. John's Church; the Rev. F. J. Murdoch, D.D., Minister in Charge.

Whole number of persons 25. Baptisms: infant 9. Confirmed 2. Communicants 7. Public services: on Sundays 50; other days 20. Holy Communion 2. Sunday-school teachers 3; scholars 60. Value of chapel $500; rectory $1,000—total $1,500. Insurance $400.

Offerings—Parochial: Salary of Clergyman $2.50. Other parish expenses $12.50—total $15.

Salisbury, St. Peter's Chapel; the Rev. F. J. Murdoch, D.D., Minister; the Rev. R. B. Owens, Assistant.

Whole number of persons 36. Baptisms: infant 15; adult 5—total 20. Confirmed 6. Communicants: present number 15. Public services: on Sundays 52; other days 20. Holy Communion 12. Sunday-school teachers 5; scholars 35. Chapel sittings 120. Value of chapel $700. Amount of indebtedness on church property $340. Insurance $400.

Offerings—Parochial: Salary of Clergyman $5. Miscellaneous $25—total $30.

Report of Salisbury Associate Mission; the Rev. F. J. Murdoch, D.D., the Rev. S. S. Bost, the Rev. R. B. Owens, Clergy.

The work of these Clergy is so intermingled that we deem it proper to give a summary of the whole as contained in our ten Parochial reports. We have 11 churches and chapels under our care, 573 baptized people, 328 communicants; attendants on worship 1,000. There have been 51 confirmations within our charge during the year.

	Baptisms.	Burials.	Marriages.
Rev. Dr. Murdoch	37	6	3
Rev. S. S. Bost	23	4	1
Rev. R. B. Owens	7	2	5
	67	12	9

There are 60 teachers and 457 pupils in our Sunday-schools. We have in our field ten Bible classes, with an average attendance of about 150.

Sanford Mission; the Rev. C. T. Bland, Minister in Charge.

Families 5. Whole number of persons 15. Baptism: infant 1. Communicants: added by admission 1; removed 1; present number 10. Public services 22. Holy Communion: public 4; private 1. Value of church lot $100. Building Fund $50—total $150.

Offerings—Parochial: Salary of Clergyman $18.18.

The ladies have raised funds to pay for a lot upon which to build a church. The deed is in the hands of Trustees of the Diocese. They have about $50 more towards erecting a church building.

Scotland Neck, Trinity Church; the Rev. Walter J. Smith, Rector.

Families 38. Whole number of persons, white 160; colored 2. Baptisms: infant 6; adult 2—total 8. Confirmed 11. Communicants: added by transfer 3; by admission 10; whole number added 13; removed 6; died 8; whole number lost 14; present number, white 121; colored 2. Marriages, white 1; colored 1. Burials, white 13; colored 1. Public services: on Sundays 53; other days 95. Holy Communion: public 32; private 3. Sunday-school teachers 8; scholars 55. Other Parochial Institutions: Ladies' Sewing Society; Trinity Parish Guild; Boys' Guild; St. Andrew's Brotherhood; Altar Society. Church sittings 500. Value of two churches $6,800; rectory $2,000—total $8,800.

Offerings—Parochial: Communion alms $4.38. Minister's salary $442.16. Current expenses $53.27. Other parish expenses $108.83—total $608.64. *Diocesan:* Episcopal and Contingent Fund $33.30. Diocesan Missions $32.35. Education Fund $1.06. Relief Fund $1.22. Thompson Orphanage $71.14. Memorial to Dr. Smith $8.26—total $147.33. *General:* General Missions $39.06. Domestic Missions $32.50. Foreign Missions $2.29. Jewish Missions $2.15. Sewanee $4.53. Deaf mutes $3.98. Charleston sufferers $3.90. Brunswick sufferers $4.76—total $93.17. *Aggregate* $849.14.

This report does not include the services held by the Lay Reader. Services have been held monthly at Tillery and Spring Hill, and occasionally at Hobgood. Work done at these points is included in the above report. The parish has suffered heavily by removals and deaths, but notwithstanding this fact and the hard times the offerings are more than a hundred dollars in excess of the amount reported last year. Services other than the above have been as follows: Morganton, Hickory, Littleton and Warrenton, each twice; Gaston, Rocky Mount, Weldon and Jackson, each once, and Ringwood three times, with five celebrations of the Holy Communion at different points. The various aid societies of the parish have done much towards increasing the offerings.

Shelby, Church of the Redeemer; the Rev. G. W. PHELPS, Minister in Charge.

Families 5. Whole number of persons 15. Baptism: infant 1. Communicants: removed 1; present number 7. Public services: on Sundays 28; other days 3. Holy Communion 8. Church sittings 300. Value of church $800.

Offerings—Parochial: Salary of Clergyman $24.95. Other parish expenses $6—total $30.95.

I am sorry to say that I have not been able to do much towards the repairs of the church building at this place. It greatly needs a new roof, and some money has been secured for the repairs, but not enough to begin that part of the work, and our church members here are not able to do the work without help from others more favored with wealth.

Statesville, Trinity Church; the Rev. EDWIN A. OSBORNE, Rector.

Families 11. Whole number of persons 60. Baptism: infant 1. Confirmed 2. Communicants: added by transfer 3; died 2; present number 32. Marriage 1. Burials 2. Public services: on Sundays 12; other days 3. Holy Communion 12. Sunday-school teachers 4; scholars 25. Other Parochial Institution: Woman's Guild. Value of church property $3,000.

Offerings—Parochial: Communion alms $13.14. Salary of Clergyman $175. Current expenses $24. Other parish expenses $100—total $312.14. *Diocesan:* Episcopal and Contingent Fund $27.50. Diocesan Missions $15. Thompson Orphanage $10.55—total $53.05. *General:* General Missions $3.30. *Aggregate* $368.49.

Stovall, St. Peter's Church; the Rev. J. M. HORNER, Minister in Charge.

Families 7. Whole number of persons 23. Baptisms: infant 1; adult 1 —total 2. Confirmed 1. Communicants: added by admission 1; present number 10. Marriage 1. Public services: on Sundays 10; other days 1. Holy Communion 4. Church sittings 150. Value of church $500; other church property $100—total $600.

Offerings—Parochial: Communion alms $2.50. Salary of Clergyman $31.84. Other parish expenses $12.10—total $46.44. *Diocesan:* Diocesan Missions $7.45. *General:* Domestic Missions $2.02. *Aggregate* $55.91.

Tarborough, Calvary Church; the Rev. CHARLES L. HOFFMANN, Rector.

Families 74. Baptisms: infant 6; adult 13—total 19. Confirmed 16. Communicants: added by admission 7; removed 3; died 3; whole number lost 6; present number 208. Marriages 3. Burials 10. Public services: on Sundays 64; other days 92. Holy Communion 49. Sunday-school teachers 20; scholars 197. Other Parochial Institutions 7. Church sittings 500. Chapel sittings 250. Value of church $25,000; value of chapels $2,000; rectory lot $1,800—total $28,800. Insurance $7,000.

Offerings—Parochial: Communion alms $63.08. Salary of Clergyman $1,019.19. Current expenses $189.50. Other parish expenses $57.89. New furnace $326 26—total $1,655.92. *Diocesan:* Episcopal and Contingent Fund $26.76. Diocesan Missions $144.28. Thompson Orphanage $50. Permanent Episcopal Fund $100.02. Miscellaneous $30—total $351.06. *General:* Jewish Missions $8.27. *Aggregate* $2,015.25.

In this report are included St. Mary's and Lawrence Missions, both in Edgecombe county. The present Rectorate began September 1, 1893, and this report only dates back that far.

Tarborough, St. Luke's Church (colored); the .Rev. JOHN W. PERRY, Rector.

Families 20. Whole number of persons 120. Baptisms: infant 11; adult 7—total 18. Confirmed 15. Communicants: added by transfer 2; by admission 14; whole number added 16; removed 1; withdrawn 1; whole number lost 2; present number 70. Marriages 2. Public services: on Sundays 72; other days 62. Holy Communion 14. Sunday-school teachers 9; scholars 72. Parish school teachers 3; scholars 73. Other Parochial Institutions 3. Value of church $1,900. Insurance $1,250.

Offerings—Parochial: Communion alms $15.61. Salary of Clergyman $50.10. Current expenses $41.09. Other parish expenses $550—total $656.80. *Diocesan:* Episcopal and Contingent Fund $16.50. Diocesan Missions $13 58—total $30.08. *General:* Domestic Missions $1. Colored Missions $2—total $3. *Aggregate* $689.88.

The new church is not finished, but we have been holding services in it over a year. All the outside work is completed, except the steeple. We hope to be able to begin work on this in a few days. Our work here has gone on very prosperously since my last report.

Tryon, Holy Cross Church; the Rev. CHARLES FERRIS, Minister in Charge.

Families 28. Baptisms: infant 3. Communicants: added by transfer 5; by admission 1; whole number added 6; removed 4; present number 40. Marriage 1. Burials 5. Public services: on Sundays 49; other days 60. Holy Communion: public 15; private 2. Sunday-school teachers 7; scholars 40. Church sittings 140. Value of church $300; church lot $200—total $500.

Offerings—Parochial: Salary of Clergyman $156; other parish expenses $70—total $226. *Diocesan:* Diocesan Missions $11.23. *General:* Foreign Missions $1.89. Jewish Missions $2.05. General Clergy Relief $2.35— total $6.29. *Aggregate* $243.52.

The colored Mission at this place has a Sunday-school with an average attendance of 40 pupils. Religious services are held every Sunday afternoon, and instruction is given as well to adults as to children.

Wadesboro, Calvary Church; the Rev. CHARLES C. QUIN, Rector.

Families 21. Whole number of persons 98. Baptisms: infant 5. Confirmed 2. Communicants: added by transfer 2; by admission 1; whole number added 3; died 2; present number 42. Marriage 1. Burials 4. Public services: twice every Sunday and twice in each week. Holy Communion: public, monthly, High Festivals and Saints' Days; private 1. Sunday-school teachers 4; scholars 15. Church sittings 300. Value of church $5,000; rectory $1,000; other church property $75—total $6,075.

Offerings—Parochial: Communion alms $17.33. Salary of Clergyman $313 50. Current expenses $31.07. Other parish expenses $34.41—total $396.31. *Diocesan:* Episcopal and Contingent Fund $45. Thompson Orphanage $16.11. Convocation $9.06—total $70.17. *General:* Jewish Missions $1.25. *Aggregate* $467.73.

The new church was consecrated on the 18th day of April, 1894, ten of the Clergy present. In the death of Mrs. Caroline Burgwin Ashe, who was taken from us March 6th, this parish has sustained a great loss.

Walnut Cove, Christ Church; the Rev. CHARLES FETTER, Deacon in Charge.

I took charge of this church last February. I am not able to make an accurate statement of the work done by my predecessors, there being no record of any, nor to get a statement of the statistics. There is an awakening of interest in Church work. The number of Sunday-school teachers and scholars has doubled. This is a fine field for the Church.

Warren County, St. Luke's Chapel (colored); the Rev. WILLIAM WALKER, Minister in Charge.

Families 7. Whole number of persons 26. Baptism, infant 1. Communicants 15. Marriage 1. Public services: on Sundays, monthly. Holy Communion: public, at every Sunday morning service; private 1. Sunday-school teachers 2; scholars 20. Chapel sittings 150. Value of church property $200.

*Offerings—*Total $2.21.

I visit St. Luke's Chapel one Sunday in each month.

Warrenton, All Saints' Chapel (colored); the Rev. JOHN F. MIL-
BANK, Minister in Charge; the Rev. H. B. DELANY, Assistant Minister.

Families 7. Whole number of persons 45. Baptism: infant 1. Confirmed 4. Communicants: added by transfer 1; whole number added 5;
present number 14. Burial 1. Public services: on Sundays 31; other
days 1. Holy Communion 13. Sunday-school teachers, white 6; scholars 37. Value of chapel $400.

Offerings — Parochial: Communion alms $7.84. Current expenses
$22.01—total $29.85. *General:* General Missions $16. *Aggregate* $45.85.

The·Mission at Warrenton is full of promise. The property has a
mortgage of $200 on it. The members of the Mission have subscribed
as much as $150 towards lifting the mortgage, and are gradually paying it.

Warrenton, Emmanuel Church; the Rev. JOHN F. MILBANK, Rector.

Families 40. Whole number of persons 120. Baptisms: infant 4. Confirmed 5. Communicants: added by transfer 3; by admission 5; whole
number added 8; died 3; present number 65. Marriage 1. Burials 2.
Public services: on Sundays 102; other days, every day in the week as
per Prayer-Book instructions. Holy Communion: public 70; private 6.
Sunday-school teachers 8; scholars 30. Value of church $3,000; rectory
$2,500—total $5,500. Insurance $3,475.

Offerings—Parochial: Communion alms $6. Salary of Clergyman $700.
Other parish expenses $85—total $791. *Diocesan:* Episcopal and Contin-
gent Fund $50. Thompson Orphanage $12.58—total $62.58. *General:*
General Missions $12. Colored Missións $16. Indian Missions 65 cents.
Jewish Missions $2.50. Clergy Retiring Fund $7.81—total $38.96. *Aggre-
gate* $892.54.

The Rector took charge of this parish in November last. Within the
past year several improvements have been made in the church. A very
handsome altar and reredos, pulpit, faldstool and Bishop's chair have
been presented as memorials by members of the parish. An anonymous
friend has given $250 and made an indefinite loan of $150 more with
which to make further additions in the way of furnishing and ornamen-
tation. When these shall have been provided we expect to have one of
the handsomest interiors in the Diocese.

Watauga Mission.

The items of a partial report from this Mission are included in the
Abstract given below.

Weldon, Grace Church.

Families 18. Whole number of persons, white 75; colored 1. Baptisms:
Infant 4; adult 5—total 9. Confirmed 5. Communicants: added by

18

removal 6; died 2; present number, white 33; colored 1. Burials 2. Public services: every Sunday; other days 65. Holy Communion 12. Sunday-school teachers 7; scholars 34. Church sittings 250. Value of church $4,100; rectory $850; other church property $300—total $5,250.

Offerings—Parochial: Current expenses $224.54. *Diocesan:* Episcopal and Contingent Fund $9.18. Thompson Orphanage $10.51—total $19.69. *General:* General Missions $15.35. *Aggregate* $259 58.

Wilkesboro, St. Paul's Church; the Rev. R. W. BARBER, Rector.

Families 7. Whole number of persons 31. Baptism: infant 1. Communicants 16 Burials 2. Public services: on Sundays 22; other days 3. Holy Communion 8. Sunday-school teachers 3; scholars 35. Church sittings 150 Value of church $1,600.

Offerings—Parochial: Current expenses $8. *Diocesan:* Episcopal and Contingent Fund $8. Thompson Orphanage $1.25—total $9 25. *General:* General Missions $1 35. *Aggregate* $18.60.

The church building has within the past year been much improved by putting in new windows, painting the interior, and refurnishing, to some extent, the chancel. This work was undertaken by a young layman, who, with the aid of the ladies, raised the necessary funds, superintended the work and had it completed. As it was undertaken with the express understanding that no debt was to be entailed on the parish, I have made no inquiry as to the cost; it must have cost nearly $200. By the aid of kind friends, many of whom were pupils of my school years ago, I have been able to place in the church a superior Mason & Hamlin organ.

Wilkes County, Gwyn's Chapel; the Rev. R. W. BARBER, Minister in Charge.

Families 1. Whole number of persons 7. Communicants 6. Public services: on Sundays 22; other days 3. Holy Communion: public 3; private 3.

Offerings—Parochial: Salary of Clergyman $50. *Diocesan:* Episcopal and Contingent Fund $14. Diocesan Missions $6.10. Miscellaneous $20— total $40.10. *Aggregate* $90.10.

Besides the work above reported, other services have been rendered by the Rev. Vardry McBee, who has given valuable aid to the Rector at all times, kindly officiating for him when, because of feebleness, he was unable to be present. There are six communicants residing at Elkin, Surry county. One service, on Sunday, has been given there during the year. I have services on fifth Sundays at an academy eight miles from Wilkesboro on the Jefferson road. Always have large and attentive congregations. The ladies at Gwyn's Chapel are members of the Elkin Mission branch of the Woman's Auxiliary, and are liberal contributors to the work reported by its Secretary.

Williamsboro, St. John's Church; the Rev. WILLIAM S. PETTIGREW, Rector.

Families 20. Whole number of persons, white 60, colored 2. Confirmed 2. Communicants, white 39; colored 2. Public services 20. Holy Communion 6. Church sittings 300. Value of church $2,000; rectory $1,000; other church property $100 —total $3,100.
Offerings—Parochial: Salary of Clergyman $74. Current expenses $9.43—to'al $83.43. *Diocesan:* Episcopal and Contingent Fund $7. Diocesan Missions $4.35—total $11 35. *General:* Foreign Missions $2 07. *Aggregate $96.85.*

Wilson, St. Mark's Church (colored); the Rev. JOHN W. PERRY, Minister in Charge.

Baptisms: infant 15. Communicants 13. Public services 32. Holy Communion 4. Sunday-school teachers 3; scholars 52. Parish school teacher 1; scholars 40. Value of church $1,500. Insurance $1,000.
Offerings—Parochial: Current expenses $2.40. Other parish expenses $28.14 — total $30.54. *Diocesan:* Diocesan Missions $2.80. *General:* Domestic Missions $2.08. Colored Missions $2.08—total $4.16. *Aggregate* $37.50.

Wilson, St. Timothy's Church; the Rev. C. J. WINGATE, Rector.

Families 37. Whole number of persons 185. Baptisms: infant 7; adult 1—total 8. Confirmed 5. Communicants: added by transfer 2; by admission 4; whole number added 6; present number 91. Marriages 2. Burials 4. Public services: on Sundays 100; other days 90. Holy Communion: public 20; private 4. Sunday-school teachers 10; scholars 55. Church sittings 150 Value of church $2,500; rectory $2,000; other church property $2,400—total $6,900.
Offerings—Parochial: Salary of Clergyman $821. Current expenses $110.90. Other parish expenses $138.97. Miscellaneous $73 25—total $1,144.12. *Diocesan:* Episcopal and Contingent Fund $66. Diocesan Missions $9. Thompson Orphanage $23—total $98. *General:* General Missions $17.70. *Aggregate $1,259 82*

Winston, St. Paul's Church; the Rev. JOHN FRANCIS GEORGE, Rector.

Families, white 60; colored 2. Whole number of persons 225. Baptisms: infant 3. Communicants: added by transfer 15; removed 5; died 1; withdrawn 1; whole number lost 7; present number 108. Marriage 1. Burial 1. Public services: on Sundays 96; other days 75. Holy Communion: public 27; private 1. Sunday-school teachers 6; scholars 60. Other Parochial Institutions: Ladies' Aid Society; Woman's Auxiliary;

Daughters of the King; Brotherhood of St. Andrew. Church sittings 225. Value of church $5,300; rectory $3,500; other church property $800—total $9,600. Amount of indebtedness on church property $2,000. Insurance $1,800.

Offerings—Parochial: Communion alms $24.42. Parish Missions $9.07. Salary of Clergyman $711.50. Current expenses $217.57. Other parish expenses $473.74. Miscellaneous $81—total $1,517.30. *Diocesan:* Episcopal and Contingent Fund $38.50. Diocesan Missions $26.21. Thompson Orphanage $38.65—total $103.36. *General:* Domestic Missions $12.76. Foreign Missions $5. Colored Missions $5. Indian Missions $4.30. Jewish Missions $4.45—total $31.51. *Aggregate* $1,652.17.

NO REPORTS have been received from the Missions at LEICESTER and SMITHFIELD, nor from the Rev. Messrs. A. H. BOYLE and HENRY M. JOSEPH.

The Rev. BENJAMIN S. BRONSON, of Warrenton, reports as follows:
I have been engaged in teaching for the last ecclesiastical year a small number of boys. The home school has always been limited to a small number, but the last year it did not reach the number desired. My ministerial work has been mostly confined to my own school.

The Rev. WILLIAM S. BYNUM, residing in Lincolnton, makes due and satisfactory report to the Bishop, though the report contains no matters necessary to be published here.

The Rev. JOSEPH W. MURPHY, residing in Washington, D. C., reports as follows:
In nineteen different places of worship, without responsibility of management of work anywhere and therefore able to do more, I have taken part in twenty-seven services, have held fifty-three services myself, have administered the Holy Communion thirteen times publicly and twice in private to the sick, have preached fifty-eight times, have married one couple, have baptized one infant, and have officiated once at a burial. Not fit for a regular charge, I do what I can, and am thankful to God for ability thus to be useful.

REPORTS OF THE DEANS OF CONVOCATIONS.

Dean of Asheville.

The Convocation met twice during the past year, first in St. Philip's, Brevard—a two days' session, and second in St. Clement's, Candler's, Buncombe county—a three days' session. In each case, after the transaction of the regular business, a series of interesting services was held; congregations generally large and attentive.

I have visited Murphy, held two services, administered the Holy Communion and visited quite a number of families, and find that we have ten or twelve communicants, all anxious for the service, and several of the citizens, not of our communion, express a desire for us to build a church and carry on regular work in the town.

At Andrews I called on some of our Church people and learned of others out in the country, but could not spare the time to look them up.

I also held a series of services in the Missions north of Asheville, under the charge of Rev. W. F. Rice; also one service each at Cullowhee, Sylva and Dillsboro.

The work demanded in this Convocation is far greater than the small number of men employed can perform.

The scattered efforts make poor results. The neglect of the past is avenging itself on us to-day, in rendering work more difficult and results meager, and we can only pray to the Lord of the harvest to give us more helpers, and to bless and make fruitful the seed sown in His name.

J. A. DEAL, *Dean.*

Dean of Charlotte.

There has been but one meeting of this Convocation since the Convention in May last year, viz., the one held at Wadesboro on April 18th and 19th, which was both well attended and profitable.

I have been unable to do any Missionary work beyond the limits of my charge.

The Church School for Boys at Salisbury has been kept up, with an attendance of over forty pupils. The property belonging to this institution is worth about $7,000, and encumbered with a debt of $3,000. We are unable as yet to open a boarding department.

F. J. MURDOCH, *Dean.*

Dean of Raleigh.

The Convocation met in the Church of St. Athanasius, Burlington, in October last, and in the Church of the Good Shepherd, Raleigh, in January. At the former of these meetings the Rev. Dr. Sutton, who had held the office of Dean since the organization of the Convocation in 1875, declined a re-election, and the present Dean was nominated to the Bishop of the Diocese as his successor. Resolutions in recognition of the faithful services of the retiring Dean were unanimously adopted.

A memorial was adopted, also, in regard to the saintly life and character of our departed brother—Franklin Leonard Bush.

At the meeting in Raleigh the attendance of the Clergy was unusually large, and on both occasions the public services and discussions were of a most helpful character.

I haye supplied services several times in the vacant parishes at Kittrell and Louisburg, and have presented the work of Diocesan Missions in these and other places as opportunity offered.

                                                    JULIAN E. INGLE, *Dean.*

Dean of Tarboro.

Since my last report I have visited the following points, viz : Gaston, Littleton, Warrenton, Weldon, Tarboro (Calvary Church and St. Luke's), and St. Mary's, Edgecombe county.

During the year meetings of the Convocation have been held at the following places, viz.: Rocky Mount, Weldon and Jackson. Another meeting was appointed to be held at Halifax, but owing to different causes no one was present except the Dean, who held services for three days, morning and night, with a very gratifying attendance. The Convocation is anxious to see a good, earnest man, unmarried if possible, placed at Jackson, and another at Weldon. With each of these points as a center the right kind of a man could do very effective work.

                                                    W. J. SMITH, *Dean.*

REPORT OF THE ARCHDEACON FOR COLORED WORK.

To the Rt. Rev. Joseph Blount Cheshire, Jr., D.D.,
                                    Bishop of North Carolina:

While sorrowing for the loss of our late Diocesan, it is with feelings of thankfulness that his mantle has fallen upon one who so thoroughly spmpathizes with this work, and who has at heart the responsibility of the Church to push it forward.

A detailed account of all duty performed during the year would make my report too lengthy, and I accordingly present a summary of it.

Since we last met in Convention we have lost from among us the holy life of the Reverend F. L. Bush. His life had been devoted to this work, and it was one of patient, noble self-sacrifice. He was a man of God, full of the Holy Ghost and faith. We mourn his loss here, but rejoice in the assurance of his intercessions in Paradise. A pure and gentle soul, but strong and unwavering in the performance of his duty as a Priest in the Church of God, he redeemed the time by incessant toil and study. His presence was a benediction, and this branch of the Church's work is blessed by his example He laid down his life in this cause, and his memory will be cherished in many an humble, sin-laden heart that he had helped and cheered to a better life.

The number of Clergy engaged wholly in this work, at the present time, in this Diocese is nine—three white and six colored. The only change from our staff of last year is the addition of one colored Deacon, the Rev. Dr. Morris, who is canonically connected with the Diocese of Connecticut, and doing temporary duty in this Diocese.

The number of Stations, chapels and schools will be seen by the accompanying table, and these have been visited during the year as need seemed to require. Of these several have been under my especial care, and have depended on me for all clerical ministrations. While steady progress has been made in the older Missions some new work has been undertaken which promises to bring good results; of this I shall have occasion to speak.

In Tarboro the new church has been further advanced towards completion, but the tower remains unfinished.

The church in Morganton, St. Stephen's, was consecrated on the 20th of November, and is a monument to the faith and patience of the Rev. H. S. McDuffey, the Priest in charge. Through his perseverance, by the help of generous friends, it was cleared of debt, and he has felt that he could no longer give it the attention he has done, owing to his increasing cares in Asheville. It is hoped that a way may be found to supply this point and Lincolnton with more frequent ministrations.

In Asheville the name of the Mission has been changed from Trinity Chapel to St. Matthias, and the corner-stone of a new church was laid on the 22d day of February. The new church is to be of brick and will be a substantial and imposing structure in its commanding situation. In Louisburg the chapel of St. Matthias, contemplated in my last report, has been built and is now occupied. This was effected largely through the perseverance of Mr. John Williamson, who superintended the work and has carried it to a successful completion. I was present at the first service held in the chapel on Whitsunday, and preached on the occasion. The work at this place is very promising and far-reaching in its influence and should receive more support.

At Littleton, through the exertions of Mr. Virgil Bond, an active and earnest colored man, and of the Hon. H. P. Cheatham, ex-member of Congress, a school was begun in October last, and the services of a graduate of St Augustine's School, Raleigh, were secured as teacher. A school chapel is now in course of erection on land given by Mr. Bond. This chapel will be a valuable center of work among a large population.

In Haywood a school has been begun by Mr. Albert J. Council with prospect of success

St. Philip's Mission, at Noise, under Mr. Trott, has done much and valuable work. He has persevered with a faith and patience beyond praise, and has taken into his family of four children five others whom he has rescued from want and crime. This in the face of poverty is unexampled in the history of our Missions. There are many more of these children who might be rescued but for the want of means. It is heart-rending to see these lives going to destruction when a few dollars would enable us to place them in a decent home. About five miles from St. Philip's we have been enabled by the kindness of friends to procure a tract of thirty acres of land, and here a new Mission has been begun, and we are struggling to build a school-house.   At this place, on the Feast of the Circumcision, I baptized six children and preached in the open air to a number of people.

There is a work to which I have called the attention of the Clergy and the Laity, and that is the instruction of the convicts on the State farms. About eighty per cent of them are colored, and no systematic attempt is made to secure religious instruction for them.   I have made two visits to one of the farms, but was unable to undertake regular ministrations.   It is a work that zealous, consecrated laymen might well undertake, and they would receive the co-operation of the authorities.   If this could be done, and occasional visits by the neighboring Clergy could be given, much good would undoubtedly be done to these unfortunate men and women.

I have appended to this report a tabulated statement of all the work in the Diocese, so far as it is known to me.

Respectfully submitted,

WILLIAM WALKER, *Archdeacon.*

STATISTICS OF COLORED WORK.

LOCATION	NAME	Families	Persons	Baptisms	Confirmed	Communicants	Marriages	Burials	Sunday Schools Teachers	Sunday Schools Scholars	Day Schools Teachers	Day Schools Scholars	Churches	Parsonages	School-houses	Contributions	Value of Property
Asheville	St. Matthias	32	170	9	22	68	1	3	8	67	2	78	1	1	—	$416 73	$4,500
Burlington		7	14	—	3	6	—	—	3	21	—	—	—	—	1	—	—
Charlotte	St. Michael's	21	105	—	10	68	1	3	8	175	2	122	1	—	1	167 04	2,500
Durham	St. Philip's	—	—	—	—	8	—	—	1	20	1	22	1	1	1	—	—
Franklin	St. Cyprian's	25	125	2	1	14	—	1	4	75	2	40	1	1	1	27 16	3,200
Lenoir		—	—	—	—	—	—	—	—	—	1	35	—	—	—	—	—
Littleton		6	40	2	—	4	—	—	6	47	1	35	—	—	—	132 67	—
Lincolnton	St. Cyprian's	7	40	—	—	18	—	1	6	40	—	—	1	—	—	2 73	200
Louisburg	St. Matthias	4	50	9	6	24	—	—	5	90	—	—	1	—	—	53 38	2,000
Haywood		—	—	—	—	—	—	—	—	—	1	18	—	—	—	—	—
Morganton	St. Stephen's	8	39	2	4	20	—	2	7	40	3	80	1	1	—	56 62	1,600
Noise	St. Philip's	20	128	9	—	16	—	—	6	109	3	43	1	1	—	21 70	576
Pittsboro	St. James	30	125	4	4	40	2	—	2	20	—	—	1	—	—	21 39	1,280
Raleigh	St. Augustine's	27	175	7	23	103	2	—	12	222	—	—	1	—	—	182 28	2,000
Raleigh	St. Luke's	20	120	18	15	70	—	—	9	72	3	73	1	—	1	689 88	1,900
Tryon City		—	—	—	—	6	—	—	3	54	—	—	—	—	—	—	—
Warrenton	All Saints	7	45	1	4	14	1	1	6	37	—	—	1	—	—	45 85	400
Warren Cnty	St. Luke's	7	26	—	—	15	1	—	2	20	—	—	1	—	—	2 21	200
Wilson	St. Mark's	—	—	15	—	13	—	—	3	52	1	40	1	—	—	37 50	1,500
Reported in white con-gregations		11	43	5	2	21	3	4	1	5	—	—	—	—	—	—	—
Total		232	1,245	90	94	528	11	19	93	1,186	18	586	13	4	5	$1857 04	$21,856

TWELFTH ANNUAL REPORT OF WOMAN'S AUXILIARY, APRIL 1, 1894.

PARISH BRANCHES.	Members.	Central Fund.	United Offering.	Missions.			Boxes.	Value.	Total.
				Foreign.	Domestic.	Diocesan.			
Asheville, Trinity	60	$6 00	$	$ 70 66	$ 5 66	$ 295 00		$	$ 377 32
Brinkleyville	1			50	50	1 00			2 00
Bowman's Bluff, Gethsemane	2	20					1 to T. Orphanage	6 00	6 20
Chapel Hill, Chapel of the Cross	10	1 00			2 00	5 00			8 00
Charlotte, St. Peter's	31	3 10		28 33	20 00		1 Diocesan	15 00	66 43
Durham, St. Philip's	15	1 60					1 Diocesan	15 00	16 00
Elkin	5	50				12 00	1 T. Orphanage	28 00	40 50
Geno, St. Barnabas	19	1 25		5 00					6 25
Hillsboro, St. Matthew's	27	2 50		4 00		3 00	{1 Domestic / 1 T. Orphanage	30 00 / 14 00	53 50
Henderson, Holy Innocents	28	2 20					{1 Domestic / 2 T. Orp'ge	25 00 / 30 00	57 20
Leaksville, Epiphany	10	1 00		3 50	2 50	8 50	1 Diocesan	3 50	19 00
Lincolnton, St. Luke's	5	50	7 00				1 Domestic	22 50	30 00
Louisburg, St. Paul's	7	1 00	5 00	2 00	2 00	10 00			20 00
Lucia, White Haven	4	40		3 60			1 pkg. T. Orphanage	1 00	5 00
Oxford, St. Stephen's	20	1 50		10 61	4 35	40 50	1 T. Orphanage	26 00	82 96
Raleigh, Christ Church	38	3 80				15 00	{2 Diocesan / 3 Parcels Misc.	116 88 / 3 85	139 53
Raleigh, Good Shepherd	53	5 30		10 00	9 75	67 00	{1 Diocesan / 2 T. Orphanage	77 76 / 70 00	239 81
Raleigh, St. Augustine			3 74	Lately organiz ed.		5 85	No report		9 59
Salisbury, St. Luke's					1 02	1 25	1 T. Orphanage		
Scotland Neck, Trinity	23	2 30						19 35	23 92

Statesville, Trinity	2	20			40	6 00			7 00
Tarborough, Calvary	20	2 00		10 00		25 00	{1 Domestic	20 00	82 00
Warrenton, Emmanuel	20	2 00				12 57	1 T. Orphanage	25 00	64 57
Waynesville, Grace	10	40		50	1 75	8 55		50 00	11 20
Winston, St. Paul's	5	50		1 13	1 13	5 00	1 T. Orphanage	20 00	27 76
25 Branches	415	$39 25	$15 74	$150 23	$51 06	$521 22	26 boxes	$618 84	$1396 34

FIRST ANNUAL REPORT OF JUNIOR DEPARTMENT.

Asheville, Faithful Endeavor Soc'y	36	$	$	$5 00	$1 00	$135 18		$	$141 18
Asheville, Ministering Children's League	34			5 00	6 00	87 00			98 00
Hillsboro, Junior Auxiliary							1 T. Orphanage	8 00	8 00
High Point, St. Mary's Guild	15	50				50			50
Henderson, Junior Auxiliary					1 00		1 pkg. T. Orphanage	2 00	3 50
Louisburg, Sunday-school Class					2 79	1 13			3 92
Oxford, Junior aux	21	50		1 00	2 00	12 00			15 50
Raleigh, St. Mary's School	75			40 00	3 50	23 10	3 T. Orphanage	30 50	97 10
Raleigh, St. Agnes' Guild	146					166 50	1 T. Orphanage	25 00	191 50
Raleigh, Girls' Friendly Guild	14		1 49		5 00				6 49
Sand Neck, Junior auxiliary	13	25			1 00		1 Diocesan	3 00	4 25
Tarboro, Ministering Children's League	18						1 Diocesan	10 00	10 00
Warrenton, Junior Auxiliary	36	50			2 00	50	1 Diocesan	10 00	13 00
Waynesville, Missionary Gleaners	6	15			2 00	1 39			3 54
Wan, Junior Auxiliary	2					2 00			2 00
15 Branches	416	$1 90	$1 49	$51 00	$26 29	$429 30	9 boxes.	$88 50	$598 48

Ridgeway, Junior Auxiliary, and Rocky Mount, Junior Auxiliary, recently organized—no report.

In the Diocesan work of the Junior Department certain local charities are included, as follows: Asheville, Endeavor Society $75.18, Children's League $7, and Raleigh, St. Mary's $7.

JANE R. WILKES, *Diocesan Secretary.*

MARY E. HORNER, *Secretary for Junior Auxiliary.*

EIGHTEENTH ANNUAL REPORT OF ST. PETER'S HOSPITAL, CHARLOTTE, N. C., DECEMBER 31, 1893.

During 1893 forty-seven patients have been cared for for a total number of 990 days. Males 25; females 22; adults 41; children 6. Of this number 3 were Episcopalians; 11 Baptists; 10 Methodists; 7 Presbyterians; 2 Roman Catholics; 2 Friends; 1 Reformed Presbyterian; 1 Lutheran; 1 Greek. Fifteen belonged to Charlotte; 11 to Mecklenburg county; 13 to other parts of North Carolina, and 1 each to Sweden, England, Syria, Texas, Ohio, Georgia, Virginia and South Carolina One death occurred during the year—an old Confederate soldier, who was laid to rest in the Hospital lot in Elmwood Cemetery.

At the close of the year Mrs. Fox, who has been President of the Board for many years, resigned the office, and Mrs. T. R. Robertson was elected in her place.

Doctors Meisenheimer and R. L. Gibbon are physicians in charge. Several other physicians have had patients in the Hospital, and all the doctors have been most kind in responding to any calls the Hospital has made upon them.

Balance cash from 1892		$ 8 52
Received in 1893		1,027 30
Total cash		$1,035 82
Current expenses paid	$1,005 04	
Bills due	85 80	
Total expenses		1,090 84
Balance due December 31		$ 55 02

At the close of the eighteenth year of the work of this Hospital the managers are encouraged by the knowledge of the great good done and the suffering relieved. And also by the fact that "the cruse of oil has not failed, nor the barrel of meal wasted," but that God's mercy has ever been shown in the steady support given to it by our people. So they look forward hopefully to the coming year, trusting that "to-morrow shall be as this day and much more abundant."

Respectfully submitted by the

BOARD OF MANAGERS—Mrs. T. R. Robertson, President; Mrs. John Wilkes, Secretary and Treasurer; Mrs. W. R. Taliaferro, Mrs. Julia Fox, Mrs. H. C. Jones, Mrs. R. J. Brevard, Mrs. T. S. Clarkson, Mrs. J. S. Myers, Mrs. W. C. Maxwell.

SECOND ANNUAL REPORT OF THE GOOD SAMARITAN HOS-
PITAL FOR COLORED PEOPLE, DECEMBER 31, 1893.

The Hospital has had 54 patients during 1893. Males 30; females 24.
Total number of days 1,402. Thirty-five patients belonged to Charlotte;
three to Mecklenburg county; seven to other parts of North Carolina;
eight to South Carolina; one to Virginia.

Ten deaths occurred. Most of the interments were made in the Hospital lot in Pinewood cemetery, at the expense of the Hospital.

Several valuable boxes of clothing, sheets, towels and other useful
articles have been received from Woman's Auxiliaries and Church Societies North, and from North Carolina friends. A donation of books was
given by the Bible Society, and some necessaries by Charlotte merchants
and friends.

There is an impression abroad that this Hospital has añ endowment,
or some assured support. This is an entire mistake. It is purely a
Charity Hospital, organized by charity to aid the poorest and most help-
less class of our people. This is shown by the fact that not one of the
fifty-four patients paid for the care they received, although the Richmond & Danville Railroad and the Charlotte Oil and Fertilizer Company
paid partial board for their employees. The Hospital is entirely dependent upon charitable gifts.

Cash receipts in 1893		$825 52
Balance from 1892		26 74
Total cash		$852 26
Paid to debt on building	$140 00	
Current expenses paid	712 22	
Total paid		852 22
Balance to 1894		$ 04
Still due on building		202 51
Current expenses due December 31		186 45

Respectfully submitted by the

BOARD OF MANAGERS—Mrs. John Wilkes, Mrs. R. P. Lardner, Mrs.
Julia Fox, Mrs. R. Lockwood Jones, Mrs. T. S. Clarkson.

REPORT OF THE PRINCIPAL OF ST. AUGUSTINE'S SCHOOL.

During the past year there have been 11 teachers and 174 students.
Every effort has been made to strengthen the influences under which the
school is carried on. The principle of self-help is continually insisted
on. The students are received for $7 per month, $2 of which is paid in

work and $5 in money. If students are received for a less amount of money a larger amount of work is rendered. A number of the young men have been working as carpenters and several improvements have been undertaken. Happily, also, the order and discipline have been very satisfactory and have shown marked progress. "I have been much struck," says Bishop Cheshire, "at every visit for the last year or two with the improvement in the appearance, bearing and tone of the whole student body, with the admirable condition of the buildings and premises, with the faithfulness and zeal of the teachers, and with the many other evidences that the school is admirably performing its function in educating and teaching the youth committed to its care."

At the last meeting of the Board of Trustees a new charter, obtained from the last Legislature of North Carolina, was adopted, requiring that the trustees should consist of the Bishop of North Carolina and of clerical and lay members of the Protestant Episcopal Church; thus making the school in name what it has always been in fact, a Church school. Morning and Evening Prayer are said every day of the school year. The resident teachers are all communicants of the Church and every effort is used to keep the students in constant personal contact with the teachers.

The School Library has been greatly enriched by two hundred volumes of theological books left it by the last will and testament of our late Bishop, whose interest in our work was constant.

It is earnestly desired that the Clergy and Laity of the Diocese would make an earnest effort to direct the minds of young colored men and women, seeking an education, towards this school.

Respectfully submitted,   A. B. HUNTER,
May 16, 1894.   *Principal.*

ABSTRACT OF PAROCHIAL AND MISSIONARY REPORTS.

CHURCHES AND MISSIONS.	CLERGY IN CHARGE.	Families.	Persons.	Baptisms. Infant.	Adult.	Total.	Confirmed.	Communicants.	Marriages.	Burials.	Sunday Schools Teachers.	Scholars.	Parish Schools Teachers.	Scholars.	Church Edifices.	Parsonages.	Contributions.	Value of Property.
Anville, Mission	Has C. Quin	12	34	—	1	1	3	18	—	2	4	20	—	—	1	1	$ 100 39	$ 1,500
Mille, St. Ms (ol.)	Henry S. McDuffey	32	170	7	2	9	22	68	1	3	8	67	2	78	1	1	416 73	4,500
Trinity	McNeely DuBose	110	500	37	11	48	25	313	1	112	10	110	—	—	2	1	6,683 89	33,000
Ral oo, St. John's — fle	Richard Wht	9	34	1	1	2	2	20	1	—	3	21	—	—	1	—	254 60	2,000
Bowman's Bluff,		4	23	1	—	1	2	16	—	—	2	12	—	—	1	—	98 10	1,450
Brevard, St. Philip's	cStt B. Rathbun	10	30	—	—	—	—	16	—	—	—	—	—	—	2	—	—	3,000
Buncombe G., St. Andrew's	Ins H. Postell	6	14	3	—	3	—	7	—	2	2	34	—	—	1	—	1 50	560
St. Paul's	James H. Postell	6	50	8	—	11	—	8	1	3	—	—	—	—	1	—	1 75	1,085
Burlington, St. ins	Rol art J. Var	63	210	8	3	11	6	110	1	3	8	104	—	—	1	1	1,944 78	7,100
fts, St. Gfnt's	nge H. Bell	8	42	3	—	3	4	12	—	—	3	38	—	—	1	—	3 08	800
fiel Hill, fiel of he Cross	Wers	8	49	1	—	1	—	30	1	—	4	20	—	—	1	1	624 21	6,500
Charl ot, St. Mai's (ol.)	P. P. lston	21	105	7	2	9	10	68	1	3	8	175	2	122	1	1	167 04	2,500
S. Peter's, with Chapel	Fenner S. Stickney	100	551	14	1	15	15	286	2	11	13	104	—	—	2	2	2,242 13	30,000
fiel of the Virgin Mary	E. A. nOe	1	56	8	1	9	—	23	1	—	—	—	—	—	i	1	3 00	2,200
Chunn's Cove fth	Wm. F. Rce	4	13	—	—	1	—	8	1	—	7	50	—	—	—	—	—	145
Concord, All Saints	J. C. Davis	12	50	—	1	1	8	24	1	2	4	20	—	—	1	1	909 72	3,700
Cuningham's fl fl	Hs Fetter	3	11	—	—	—	—	11	i	—	3	26	—	—	1	—	301 24	D00
Durham, St. Philip's fh	Stewart McQueen	40	200	9	3	12	5	95	1	1	9	75	—	—	1	1	2,086 68	5,700
St. Philip's Mission (col.)	Stewart M	—	—	—	—	—	—	8	—	—	—	20	1	22	—	—	—	—
Enfield, flnt	Gn Battle	13	53	1	—	1	—	19	1	—	3	12	—	—	1	1	152 18	1,500
Flat fdk, St. Jfn's	Scott B. Rathbun	44	—	4	—	4	5	80	—	3	4	30	1	25	1	1	1,217 10	11,500

Churches and Missions.	Clergy in Charge.	Families.	Persons.	Baptisms: Infant.	Baptisms: Adult.	Baptisms: Total.	Confirmed.	Communicants.	Marriages.	Burials.	Sunday Schools: Teachers.	Sunday Schools: Scholars.	Parish Schools: Teachers.	Parish Schools: Scholars.	Church Edifices.	Parsonages.	Contributions.	Value of Property.
Franklin Mission:																		
St. Agnes	John A. Deal	10	49	2	1	3	3	23	—	—	2	10	—	—	1	1	84 72	6,000
St. Cyprian's (col.)		25	125	1	1	2	1	14	1	1	4	75	2	40	1	1	27 16	3,200
Bryson City, St. Stephen's	John W. Barker	5	22	—	—	—	—	7	—	—	—	—	1	—	1	—	342 73	1,100
Cashier's Valley, Good Shepherd	J. T. Kennedy	7	80	—	—	—	—	18	1	1	2	35	1	36	1	—	37 98	3,500
Highlands Mission		4	24	1	—	1	—	—	—	—	—	—	—	—	—	—	10 34	—
Nonah, St. John's		7	32	1	—	1	3	17	1	—	3	20	—	—	1	—	43 30	2,000
Gaston, St. Luke's		5	15	1	1	2	1	15	1	—	3	32	—	—	1	—	2 36	1,650
Germanton, St. Philip's		9	29	2	—	2	1	20	—	—	3	10	—	—	1	—	3 00	1,500
Goshen, St. Paul's	Junius M. Horner	5	13	6	—	6	5	5	—	3	4	35	—	—	1	—	49 16	500
Grace, Beaver Dam Missions	Wm. F. Rice	16	63	8	2	10	5	39	1	1	8	40	—	—	1	—	330 23	2,750
Greensboro, St. Barnabas	Alfred H. Stubbs	52	190	13	7	20	8	104	4	2	14	150	5	25	1	—	675 56	4,500
Greensboro (South), St. Andrew's	J. D Miller	35	137	1	—	1	32	80	1	2	—	—	—	—	1	—	823 17	—
Gulf, St. Mark's	Charles T. Bland	6	18	—	—	—	1	9	2	5	6	17	—	—	1	—	68 64	300
Halifax, St. Mark's	Walter J. Smith	8	60	6	—	6	6	28	2	9	4	38	—	—	1	—	2 80	1,550
Haw Creek, Trinity	George H. Bell	8	36	—	—	—	6	10	2	—	12	62	—	—	1	—	—	500
Henderson, Holy Innocents	Julian E. Ingle	65	300	16	—	16	10	154	1	—	7	54	1	33	1	—	1,582 00	15,550
Henderson Co., Calvary	H. H. Phelps	35	193	10	1	11	—	44	—	—	—	—	—	—	1	2	755 25	8,000
Henderson Co., Mt. Calvary, Chapel and Mission	H. H. Phelps	10	45	7	—	7	2	13	—	1	7	40	—	—	1	—	12 00	600
Hendersonville, St. James	Scott B. Rathbun	12	—	2	1	3	—	25	1	—	—	—	—	—	1	1	48 86	8,000
Hickory, Ascension	James A. Weston	28	107	5	—	5	13	68	—	4	4	32	—	—	1	1	525 30	2,000

Parish and Church	Rector															Amount
High Point, St. Mary's	Frederick A. Fetter	15	32	3	3	—	32	9	6	—	41	—	1	—	203 79	2,640
High Shoals, St. John's	W. R. Wetmore, D.D.	12	45	2	2	2	26	3	2	2	25	—	1	1	155 00	550
Hill ... St.	Benjamin S.	28	145	—	—	3	80	1	5	—	30	—	2	1	1,171 40	8,600
Iell Co., St.	F. J. Murdoch, D.D.	20	101	5	5	3	41	5	4	3	40	—	1	1	50 00	500
Kittrell, St.	W. T. Picar ...	18	86	1	1	3	38	4	1	—	22	—	1	1	392 93	3,950
...	F. W. Hilli ...	15	45	—	—	1	30	5	1	—	10	—	1	1	514 77	2,000
Leaksville,		8	42	2	2	1	12	—	6	4	—	—	—	—	—	—
Leicester, St.		5	27	—	4	—	26	3	—	1	25	—	1	—	144 02	2,000
L ..., St.	Jarvis Buxton, D.D.	18	75	4	1	1	7	—	5	—	—	—	1	—	—	600
Lexington	Frederick A. F ...	7	14	—	—	2	59	4	—	1	25	1	3	1	144 17	3,400
... Co., Church of		6	25	1	1	—	11	1	5	—	60	—	1	1	175 81	1,500
St. Paul's	W. R. Wetmore, D.D.	12	65	9	9	1	10	1	—	—	50	—	1	1	88	500
St. ...	Thos C. Wet ...	8	36	7	7	5	19	10	10	—	25	—	1	1	9 00	175
...	P. P. Alon ...	8	45	—	4	—	15	7	—	—	—	—	—	—	—	150
Lincoln ...		7	40	1	—	1	18	4	4	1	40	—	1	—	17 20	—
..., St. Cyprian's (col.)		2	114	—	10	1	18	4	—	1	18	—	1	1	2 73	200
... St.		28	114	11	—	1	77	3	11	1	71	2	1	1	77 47	3,600
... St. Paul's		8	31	—	—	1	29	2	2	—	90	—	1	1	26 25	750
... St. Paul's	Wm. ...	4	50	9	9	1	24	9	1	—	22	—	—	1	53 38	2,000
... St.	... Fetter	19	59	—	1	1	48	1	5	—	20	—	1	1	29 43	2,100
M... St. John's	Girard V. ...	3	8	—	4	—	11	1	—	—	12	—	—	—	75 75	1,500
... Co., St. Mark's	E. A. ...	16	100	1	—	1	14	5	2	—	40	—	2	1	(66 29)	1,000
...	Wm. S. Pettigrew	6	30	2	2	2	55	6	—	1	—	—	2	1	52 45	2,500
... fist Church	... Fetter	5	13	—	—	5	20	5	2	2	—	—	5	1	98 13	400
Mn, ...		17	65	3	3	—	5	—	5	—	21	—	—	1	70 22	1,800
Monroe, St.	F. W. Hill	41	180	6	3	3	35	3	1	1	32	—	1	1	40 91	2,700
...	E. P. Green	8	39	7	7	6	89	6	3	—	40	—	1	1	09 08	5,000
... Co., & ... (col.)	Henry S. McDuffey	20	128	2	2	7	20	9	6	—	40	1	2	1	56 52	1,600
...	Wm. ...	5	23	9	9	—	16	4	2	—	109	3	2	1	21 70	576
...	Girard W. Phelps	13	75	2	2	2	7	3	—	1	15	—	1	1	41 92	800
... Co., St.	B. S.	36	200	1	9	1	35	10	3	—	30	—	1	1	1 86 88	1,000
..., St.	Edward Benedict	12	56	2	2	2	115	16	8	5	75	80	1	1	45 10	6,500
... Mew's	Chs T. Bd ...			2	3	5	31	2	4	2	16	—	1	1		3,200
Pit ... wo, St. James (col.)	Wm. Wal dr ...	30	125	3	3	2	40	4	2	—	20	43	1	1	21 39	1,280

Churches and Missions	Clergy in Charge	Families	Persons	Baptisms			Confirmed	Communicants	Marriages	Burials	Sunday Schools		Parish Schools		Church Edifices	Parsonages	Contributions	Value of Property
				Infant	Adult	Total					Teachers	Scholars	Teachers	Scholars				
Polk and Henderson Cos., Mission		23	111	14	2	16	—	66	—	—	17	154	—	—	3	—	$ 5,782 21	$ 44,000
Raleigh, Christ Church	M. M. Marshall, D.D.	145	650	17	6	23	21	275	4	20	13	130	—	—	3	1	4,234 98	17,000
Good Shepherd	I. McK. Pittenger, D.D.	86	350	7	—	7	16	264	—	9	12	222	—	—	1	1	182 28	2,000
St. Augustine's (col.)	A. B. Hunter	27	175	—	1	1	23	103	2	4	—	—	—	—	1	—	277 60	
St. Mary's Chapel	Bennett Smedes, D.D.	—	—	—	—	—	6	—	—	—	—	—	—	—	1	—		
Ravenscroft Associate Mission:																		
Cullowhee, St. David's		4	16	2	—	2	1	11	—	—	3	12	—	—	1	—	113 50	3,000
Henderson Co., St. Paul's and other Missions		35	166	8	1	9	—	81	1	1	2	30	—	—	1	1	15 00	500
Hot Springs, St. John's	Wm. S. Barrows	5	12	—	—	—	—	9	—	—	3	30	—	—	1	—	414 56	2,125
Micadale, St. Mary's	Samuel Rhodes	10	60	2	—	2	—	19	—	—	5	50	—	—	1	1	6 46	2,000
Saluda, Transfiguration		4	11	1	—	1	1	7	—	—	5	25	—	—	1	—	95 70	1,700
Sylva, Jackson Co.		4	12	—	1	1	—	4	—	—	—	—	—	—	1	—	82 49	450
Waynesville, Grace		20	67	1	—	1	3	39	—	1	5	50	—	—	1	—	221 55	4,000
Reidsville, St. Thomas		12	39	5	1	6	3	40	—	3	5	46	—	—	1	—	58 00	1,800
Ridgeway, Good Shepherd	Wm. S. Pettigrew	20	60	4	—	4	5	21	1	—	4	20	—	—	1	1	233 20	6,000
Ringwood, St. Clement's		8	46	1	—	1	—	19	—	—	6	30	—	—	1	—	196 00	2,000
Rockwood, Buncombe Co.	Wm. F. Rice	3	18	1	1	2	1	10	—	—	3	20	—	—	—	—	20 90	3,500
Rocky Mt., Good Shepherd and Chapel	Alvin J. Vanderbogart	33	152	3	1	4	3	92	3	4	7	47	—	—	2	1	900 23	5,150
Rowan Co., Christ Church		—	92	4	—	4	8	38	1	2	6	30	—	—	1	1	97 28	1,700
St. Andrew's, St. George's	F. J. Murdoch, D.D.	—	60	8	—	8	3	29	1	1	5	35	—	—	2	—	50 00	1,650
St. Jude's	S. S. Bost	—	22	2	1	3	1	10	—	—	3	15	—	—	1	1	85 00	325
St. Mary's	R. B. Owens	—	37	—	—	—	—	21	—	—	2	9	—	—	1	—	69 26	1,550
St. Matthew's		—	52	7	—	7	14	30	—	1	9	45	—	—	1	—	30 00	250
St. Paul's		—	40	—	1	1	7	32	1	—	13	125	—	—	1	—	90 00	600

Parish and Church	Clergyman																		Contributions	Value of Property
Rutherfordton, St. John's and Mission,	Girard W. Phelps	8	33	--	1	1	1	14	--	1	1	3	--	1	--				82 41	1,000
Salisbury, St. John's	F. J. Murdoch, D.D.	--	25	9	1	9	2	7	2	9	3	60	--	1					15 00	1,500
St. Luke's		--	208	7	1	8	10	104	10	7	8	65	--	1					1,870 16	11,500
St. Peter's		--	36	15	5	20	6	15	6	15	5	35	--	1					30 00	700
Sanford, Moore Co., Mission	Charles T. Bland	5	15	1	--	1	--	10	--	--	--	--	--	1					18 18	150
Scotland Neck, Trinity	Walter J. Smith	38	162	6	2	8	2 14	123	11	8	8	55	--	2 1					849 14	8,800
Shelby, Redeemer	Girard W. Phelps	5	15	1	--	1	--	7	--	1	--	--	--	1					30 95	800
Smithfield, Mission		--	--	--	--	--	--	10	--	1	1	--	--	--						
Statesville, Trinity	E. A. Osborne	11	60	1	--	1	2	32	2	1	4	25	--	1					368 49	3,000
Stovall, St. Peter's	Junius M. Horner	7	23	1	1	2	1	10	1	2	--	--	--	1					55 91	600
Tarboro, Calvary, with Chapel and two Missions	Charles L. Hoffmann	74	--	6	13	19	16	208	14	3 10	20	197	--	3					2,015 25	28,800
St. Luke's (col.)	John W. Perry	20	120	11	7	18	15	70	2 1	2	9	72	3	1					689 88	1,900
Tryon, Holy Cross	Charles Ferris	28	--	3	--	3	--	40	1 5	1	7	40	--	1					243 52	500
Colored Mission	Wm. Walker	10	27	--	1	1	--	6	--	--	3	54	--	--						
Wadesboro, Calvary	Charles C. Quin	21	98	5	--	5	2	42	1	4	4	15	--	1					467 73	6,075
Walnut Cove, Christ Church	Charles Fetter	30	125	--	--	--	--	33	--	--	6	60	--	1						1,500
Warren Co., St. Luke's (col.)	Wm. Walker	7	26	1	--	1	1	15	1	--	2	20	--	1					2 21	200
Warrenton, All Saints' Chapel (col.),	Henry B. Delany	7	45	1	--	1	1	14	4	1 2	6	37	--	1					45 85	400
Emmanuel	John F. Milbank	40	120	4	--	4	2	65	5	1	8	30	--	1					892 54	5,500
Watauga, Mitchell and Ashe Cos.:																				
Boone, St Luke's		10	60	--	--	--	--	18	--	--	9	35	--	3						2,600
Blowing Rock	R. W. Barber																			
Valle Crucis, St. John's																				
Bakersville, Cranberry, Linville																				
Weldon, Grace	R. W. Barker	18	76	4	5	9	2	34	5	--	7	34	--	1					259 58	5,250
Wilkesboro, St. Paul's		7	31	1	--	1	2	16	1	--	3	35	--	1					18 60	1,600
Wilkes Co., Gwyn's Chapel with Elkin Mission		1	7	--	--	--	--	6	--	--	--	--	--	1						
Williamsboro, St. John's	Wm. S. Pettigrew	20	60	--	--	--	2	41	2	--	3	52	1	1					90 10	3,100
Wilson, St. Mark's (col.)	John W. Perry	--	--	15	--	15	--	13	--	--	10	55	40	1					96 85	1,500
St. Timothy's	Charles J. Wingate	37	185	7	1	8	2 4	91	8	1 1	6	60	--	1					37 50	6,900
Winston, St. Paul's	John F. George	62	225	3	--	3	1 1	108	5	--				1					1,259 82	9,600
																			1,652 17	

SUMMARY OF DIOCESAN STATISTICS

AS GATHERED FROM THE ADDRESS OF THE BISHOP AND THE LATEST PAROCHIAL REPORTS.

Clergy belonging to the Diocese—

Bishop	1
Priests	53
Deacons	13
Total	67
Clergy Ordained—Deacons	5
Priests	2
Churches consecrated	3
Candidates for Priest's Orders (1 a Layman)	9
Candidates for Deacon's Orders	4
Postulants	7
Families	2,229
Persons	9,897
Baptisms—infant 470; adult 128	598
Confirmations reported by the Bishop	332
Communicants	5,418
Marriages	68
Burials	210

Sunday-school—

Teachers	579
Scholars	4,813

Parish School—

Teachers	26
Scholars	707
Churches and Chapels	133
Rectories	34
Total contributions	$54,915 29
Total value of Church property	$460,386 00

APPENDIX C.

TREASURER'S REPORT

FOR THE FISCAL YEAR 1893-'94.

TREASURER'S REPORT

FOR THE FISCAL YEAR ENDING MARCH 31, 1894.

To the Convention of the Diocese of North Carolina.

Your Treasurer presents herewith his accounts for the fiscal year ending March 31, 1894, showing balances as follows :

	DR.	CR.
Permanent Episcopal Fund		$ 273 51
Fund for Education of Children of Deceased Clergymen		1,063 35
Fund for Relief of Disabled Clergymen, &c		535 87
Current Episcopal and Contingent Fund	$ 1,333 59	
Fund for Diocesan Missions	89 02	
Relief Fund		371 58
Education Fund	48 55	
Church Building Fund		73 18
	$ 1,471 16	$ 2,317 49
	846 33	
	$ 2,317 49	$ 2,317 49

CHAS. E. JOHNSON, *Treasurer.*

LIST OF SECURITIES OF THE DIOCESE OF NORTH CAROLINA
IN HANDS OF TREASURER APRIL 1, 1894.

PERMANENT EPISCOPAL FUND.

	Par Value.
Bond of Trinity Church, Scotland Neck, 6 per cent _____ $	700 00
Bond of L. A. and V. C. Talton _____	500 00
1 North Carolina 4 per cent. bond, No. 1862_____	1,000 00
2 North Carolina 6 per cent. bonds, Nos. 45, 184 _____	2,000 00
9 shares Missouri Pacific Railroad stock _____	900 00
University of North Carolina scrip (nominal)_____	10 00
5 Western North Carolina Railroad bonds, 6 per cent_____	5,000 00
38 shares North Carolina Railroad stock _____	3,800 00
1 bond and mortgage, J. R. Pearce and wife_____	500 00
1 bond and mortgage, J. R. Pearce and wife _____	200 00
1 Raleigh Cotton Mill bond_____	1,000 00
20 shares Wilmington and Weldon Railroad stock _____	2,000 00
North Carolina 4 per cent. bonds_____	1,500 00

$ 19,110 00

FUND FOR EDUCATION OF CHILDREN OF DECEASED CLERGYMEN.

2 Craven County bonds, $500 each, 6 per cent., payable 1909,
  Nos. 218, 219 _____ $ 1,000 co

Dr.   *Permanent Episcopal Fund, in Account*

1894		
April 1	To amount paid N. C. 4 per cent. bonds	$ 1,500 00
	To credit balance carried down	273 51
		$ 1,773 51

Dr.   *Fund for the Education of Children of Deceased*

1894		
April 1	To Treasurer's commissions on receipts	$ 3 00
	To credit balance carried down	1,063 35
		$ 1,066 35

Dr.   *Fund for Relief of Disabled Clergymen and Widows*
Fund.''—in Account with

1894		
April 1	To amount loaned Ravenscroft Fund to pay estate of Dr. Buel	$ 870 71
	To credit balance carried down	535 87
		$ 1,406 58

Dr.   *Income of Permanent Episcopal Fund,*

1894		
April 1	To amount carried to credit of Current Episcopal and Contingent Fund	$ 742 77
		$ 742 77

with Chas. E. Johnson, Treasurer.   *Cr.*

1893 April	1	By credit balance ------- ------ ------------------------	$ 1,673 51
		By amount paid on notes Trinity Church, Scotland Neck ------- ------- ----- ------ ------- --------- ---	100 00
			$ 1,773 51
1894 April	1	By credit balance --- ------ --------- ----- ------	$ 273 51

Clergymen, in Account Chas. E. Johnson, Treasurer.   *Cr.*

1893 April	1	By credit balance ---- ------- ------- ------ ------ ----	$ 1,006 35
		By July coupons Craven County bonds ----- -----	60 00
			$ 1,066 35
1894 April	1	By credit balance ----- -------- ----- ------ ------- --	$ 1,063 35

and Orphans of Deceased Clergymen—"Clergy Relief   *Cr.*
Chas. E. Johnson, Treasurer.

1893 April	1	By credit balance ---- ---- ------ ------ -------- ------	$ 1,406 58
			$ 1,406 58
1894 April	1	By credit balance ------- --- ------ --- ---- -----	$ 535 87

in Account with Chas. E. Johnson, Treasurer.   *Cr.*

	By interest on J. R. Pearce notes ------ -- ---------	$ 56 00
	By dividends N. C. R. R. stock, 38 shares --- -----	114 00
	By interest collected on Trinity Church, Scotland Neck notes ------ ------ ------ --- ---- ---- ----	22 77
	By July and January coupons, 1 N. C. 4 per cent. bond --- ------ ----------- ------ --- ---- --- --	40 00
	By July and January coupons, 5 W. N. C. Railroad bonds ---- --------- . -- --------- ------ ----,. -	300 00
	By October and April coupons, 2 N. C. 6 per cent. bonds ------ --- ------ -------------------	120 00
	By September and March coupons, 1 Raleigh Cot- ton Mill bond----- ------ -- ---- ------ ----- --	60 00
	By January coupons, $1,500 N. C. 4 per cent. bonds	30 00
		$ 742 77

Dr.	*Current Episcopal and Contingent Fund*

To amount paid shipping Diocesan Library to Asheville -- $	9 26
To stationery, &c., Finance Committee and Treasurer-- .	11 50
To amount paid Christ Church Sexton by order of Convention---------------------------------------	10 00
To amount paid printing Treasurer's report--------	27 50
To amount paid printing and mailing Journal------	226 64
To amount paid circulars in connection with election of Bishop -----------------------------------	12 74
To amount paid expenses Standing Committee in connection with election of Bishop -------------	2 94
To amount paid Bishop Lyman's salary to January 1st, 1894--	1,875 00
To amount paid Bishop Cheshire, on salary account	1,250 00
To amount paid expenses Dr. R. B. Sutton, attending Missionary Committee -----------------------	4 75
To amount paid expenses Rev. J. A. Deal, attending Missionary Committee -----------------------	25 65
To amount paid expenses Rev. W. J. Smith, attending Missionary Committee ---------------------	14 00
To amount paid expenses Mr. John Wilkes, attending Missionary Committee ----------------------	30 35
To amount paid for case for Bishop Ravenscroft's robes--	12 50

To amount paid Clergymen's expenses to Convention, as follows :

W. J. Smith------	$ 6 15	J. W. Barker------	$18 00
J. C. Davis-------	8 00	J. H. Bell--------	14 90
J. A. Deal--------	17 65	A. H. Stubbs-----	4 00
C. T. Bland------	3 00	S. S. Bost--------	7 50
Ed. Benedict-----	2 80	E. A. Osborne----	8 30
Jarvis Buxton----	11 00	W. L. Reaney----	10 75
P. P. Alston------	7 30	A. J.Vanderbogart	4 65
Fred. Towers-----	2 50	R. B. Owens-----	7 50
J. B. Cheshire----	7 30	B. S. McKenzie --	2 00
H. S. McDuffey --	12 50	W. S. Barrows ---	12 50
J. W. Perry------	4 80	W. T. Picard-----	4 75
R. J. Walker-----	3 00	C. C. Quin -------	5 65
J. T. Kennedy----	22 50	McN. DuBose----	13 25
J. A. Weston-----	9 50	S. B. Rathburn---	15 50
S. McQueen------	1 50	M. T. Turner-----	2 00
W. F. Rice-------	14 00	R. W. Barber ----	1 00

265 75

In Account with Chas. E. Johnson, Treasurer.   Cr.

Dr.   *Current Episcopal and Contingent Fund*

Amount brought forward ------------------	$

To amount paid Clergymen's expenses to Convention, as follows :

W. S. Bynum ----$15 00	R. B. Owens------$ 7 50		
J. A. Deal--------- 17 80	S. B. Rathburn--- 15 50		
J. W. Barker----- 17 00	J. Buxton-------- 10 40		
A. H. Stubbs----- 5 25	F. Towers-------- 2 50		
G. H. Bell ------- 14 45	C. J. Wingate ---- 3 40		
McN. DuBose --- 13 50	W. F. Rice-------- 12 00		
W. J. Smith------ 7 80	S. McQueen------ 1 50		
S. Rhodes-------- 17 65	C. C. Quin------- 5 65		
G. W. Phelps ---- 12 05	E. A. Osborne --- 8 45		
G. W. Perry------ 4 50	W. S. Barrows --- 11 75		
Ed. Benedict----- 2 30	R. J. Walker ---- 3 90		
P. P. Alston------- 7 30	S. Bost ---------- 7 50		
J. M. Horner----- 3 00	J. A. Weston----- 9 00		
E. P. Green------ 8 40	M. T. Turner ---- 2 00		
A. J. Vanderbogart 3 40			

	$ 250 45

To amount paid Clergymen's expenses in attending funeral of Bishop Lyman :

S. Bost ----------$ 9 90	F. S. Stickney ---$12 50
Ad. Benedict----- 5 30	J. A. Weston------ 15 00
Fred. Towers ---- 2 05	E. A. Osborne----- 5 00
I. McK. Pettinger 10 00	W. J. Smith------ 8 15
C. C. Quin------- 7 90	J. D. Miller------ 3 20
A. H. Stubbs----- 4 95	P. P. Alston ----- 14 00
J. C. Davis------- 10 85	S. B. Rathburn--- 3 50
J. F. Wingate---- 3 50	S. McQueen------ 2 20
A. J. Vanderbogart 5 00	

	123 00
To amount paid expenses telegrams, printing, &c., Bishop Lyman's funeral -------------------------	40 42
To amount Secretary's salary--------------------	150 00
To amount Secretary's expenses Bishop Lyman's funeral ------------------------------------	6 60
To amount Secretary's account, stationery, &c----	17 22
To am't Treasurer's expenses printing, postage, &c	37 02
To Amount Treasurer's commissions--------------	157 96

	$ 4,561 26

1894	
April 1 To debit balance ---------------------------------	$ 1,333 59

In Account with Chas. E. Johnson, Treasurer.   Cr.

1893		
April 1	By credit balance ___ .___ ._____ _____ $	68 29
	By income from Permanent Episcopal Fund _____	742 77
1894		
April 1	By amount from Parishes and Congregations. (See tabular statement) ___ ____ ____ _____ ____ _____	2,416 61
	By debit balance carried down ____ _ ____ _____ ___	1,333 59
	$	4,561 26

Dr.   *Fund for Diocesan Mission, in Account*

1894			
April	1	To debit balance_____ $	13 03
		To amount paid missionary stipends, as follows :	
		Rev. W. J. Smith _____$100 00	
		Rev. J. H. Postell_____ 100 00	
		Rev. W. T. Picard _____ 100 00	
		Rev. W. R. Wetmore _____ 100 00	
		Rev. G. W. Phelps_____ 100 00	
		Rev. J. A. Deal _____ 200 00	
		Rev. W. F. Rice _____ 150 00	
		Rev. G. H. Bell_____ 150 00	
		Rev. S. B. Rathburn _____ 50 00	
			1,050 00
		To amount paid Rev. F. A. Fetter, order Bishop Lyman_____	75 00
		To amount paid Rev. Chas. Fetter, order Bishop Lyman_____	75 00
		To amount paid appropriation to Chapel Hill_____	479 16
		To amount paid Rev. S. B. Rathburn, on account salary _____	100 00
		To amount paid Rev. Mr. Stickney, on account expenses _____	11 50
		To amount paid Rev. Mr. Stickney, on account salary _____	50 44
		To amount paid stationery for Secretary of Missionary Committee_____	5 80
		To amount paid 1,000 copies " Messenger "_____	14 00
		To amount paid traveling expenses Secretary Missionary Committee_____	26 90
		To amount paid expenses Mr. Rathburn, attending meetings Missionary Committee_____	31 95
		To amount Treasurer's commissions on receipts___	97 03
			$ 2,029 81
1894			
April	1	To debit balance_____ $	89 02

with Chas. E. Johnson, Treasurer.   Cr.

By amount from Woman's Auxiliary, Warrenton, through Mrs. Wilkes _____ $	1 18
By amount from St. Mathew's Church, Oakland, Maryland _____	6 50
By amount from Sunday School at Ringwood _____	4 00
By amount collected at Consecration of Bishop Cheshire, in Calvary Church, Tarboro _____	93 66
By amount from St. Augustine's, Raleigh, balance of 1892-'93 _____	11 59
By amount from Woman's Auxiliary, |Leaksville, through Mrs. Wilkes _____	50
By amount from Woman's Auxiliary, Warrenton, through Mrs. Wilkes _____	4 00
By amount from Woman's Auxiliary, Warrenton, through Mrs. Wilkes _____	3 00
By amount from member of Missionary Committee.	12 35
By amount from Mrs. Speight _____	20 00
By amount from Miss Parker, Tarboro _____	5 00
By amount coll'ted by Mr. Stickney at High Point.	20 00
By amount collected by Mr. Stickney, at Charlotte.	22 14
By amount collected by Mr. Stickney at Durham __	9 80
By amount collected by Mr. Stickney at Wilson ___	10 00
By amount collected by Mr. Rathburn at Stoval ___	4 53
By amount collected by Mr. Rathburn at Goshen __	2 58
By amount collected by Mr. Rathburn at Bowman's Bluff _____	4 50
By amount collected by Mr. Rathburn at St. Mary's School, Raleigh _____	9 10
By amount collected by Mr. Rathburn at St. Agnes, Franklin _____	3 20
By amount collect'd by Mr. Rathburn at Warrenton	4 55
By amount collected by Mr. Rathburn at Warrenton, Junior Auxiliary _____	50
By amount collected by Mr. Rathburn at Weldon.	2 90
By amount from parishes and congregations (see tabular statement) _____	1,107 80
By amount from Bishop's collections (see tabular statement)_____	577 41
1894 April 1 By debit balance carried down _____	89 02
$	2,029 81

Dr.   *Relief Fund, in Account with*

1894		
April 1	To amount paid appropriation to Rev. R. W. Barber	$ 100 00
	To Treasurer's commissions on receipts	2 63
	To credit balance carried down	371 58
		$ 474 21

Dr.   *Education Fund, in Account with*

	To amount appropriated to Mr. Thos. Wetmore	$ 50 00
	To amount appropriated to Mr. E. S. Henderson	10 00
	To amount appropriated to Mr. John H. Gilreath	50 00
	To amount appropriated to Mr. John C. Seagle	25 00
	To Treasurer's commissions on receipts	2 26
		$ 137 26
1894 April 1	To debit balance	$ 48 55

Dr.   *Church Building Fund, in Account*

1894		
April 1	To Treasurer's commissions on receipts	$ 1 22
	To credit balance carried down	73 18
		$ 74 40

Chas. E. Johnson, Treasirer.　　　　　　　　　*Cr.*

1893		
April 1	By credit balance_____ $	421 49
	By amount from parishes and congregations. (See	
	tabular statement) _____	52 72
		$ 474 21
1894		
April 1	By credit balance_____ $	371 58

Chas. E. Johnson, Treasirer.　　　　　　　　　*Cr.*

1893		
Aptil 1	By credit balance _____ $	43 36
1894		
April 1	By amount from parishes and congregations. (See	
	tabular statement)_____	45 35
	By debit balance_____	48 55
		$ 137 26

with Chas. E. Johnson, Treasirer.　　　　　　　　*Cr.*

1893		
April 1	By credit balance._____ $	49 89
	By amount from parishes and congregations. (See	
	tabular statement) _____	24 51
		$ 74 40
1894		
April 1	By credit balance._____ $	73 18

TABULAR STATEMENT,

SHOWING AMOUNTS RECEIVED FROM PARISHES AND CONGREGATIONS FOR THE FISCAL YEAR ENDING MARCH 31, 1894.

FROM WHOM RECEIVED.	Assessment for Episcopal and Contingent Fund.	Amount Paid on Episcopal and Contingent Fund.	Diocesan Missions.	Relief Fund.	Education Fund.	Church Building Fund.	Bishop's Collection for Diocesan Missions.	Amount Paid on Arrears.	Amount in Arrears.
Asheville — Trinity Church	$200 00	$137 50	$149 50	$	$	$	$50 00	$	$
Asheville — St. Mathias'	11 00	11 00						1 00	
Asheville — Trinity Chapel									
Beattie's Ford — Mission	5 50	5 50					5 48		
Battl — Mission	5 50	5 50							
Battl — St. John's									
Buncombe County — St. Andrew's	3 30		2 25				4 43		
Buncombe County — Grace Mission							2 91		25 80
Buncombe County — Beaver Dam Chapel	6 60	6 60	3 65						
Bowman's Bluff — Gethsemane	10 00						7 75		10 00
Boone — Mission	5 50								
Bryson City — Mission							55		40 50
Burlington — St. Athsius'	52 50	2 00	103 05				30 43	35 00	50 50
— Haw Creek Chapel							87		
Buncombe County — Church of the Redeemer							90		
Chapel Hill	55 00		12 25				5 00		55 00
— St. Peters' Church	250 00		51 07	10 90	18 73	9 51	27 07	75 00	405 00
— St. Michael's	10 00	10 00					2 19		
— All Saints'							4 26	20 00	35 00
Candler's — St. Kent's Church	27 50		5 01				1 75		

Parish								Total
Cunningham's — St. David's	5 50	—	—	—	—	8 60	—	43 50
Deep — St.	5 00	5 00	—	—	—	—	—	14 32
Durham — St. Phillip's	5 50	40 00	15 05	—	—	9 45	40 00	—
Dallas	40 00	—	75	—	—	—	—	—
Enfield — Church of the ...	5 50	—	—	—	—	8 91	—	22 50
Edgecombe — St.	5 50	—	—	—	—	3 74	2 25	14 25
Edgecombe	—	—	—	—	—	2 68	—	—
Salem	5 00	—	—	—	—	—	10 00	10 00
Flat Rock — St. ...'s in the	8 25	—	—	—	—	14 10	—	16 50
Gaston — St. Luke's	—	—	—	—	—	4 91	—	—
Gaston City — the Haven	5 00	—	3 95	—	—	—	—	19 00
St. P ...	40 00	40 00	—	—	—	4 01	—	—
St. Barnabas'	—	—	9 83	—	—	7 04	—	—
St. Philip's	—	—	—	—	—	1 78	—	—
St.	10 00	10 00	—	—	—	2 75	—	—
Halifax — St. Mark's	11 00	—	1 52	1 95	—	8 71	—	58 10
Church of the Holy	82 50	83 00	52 00	3 00	3 00	23 00	—	21 25
Henderson	66 00	55 00	40 00	3 00	3 00	—	—	38 50
County — St.	5 50	—	—	—	—	—	—	38 00
Hendersonville	5 50	—	—	—	—	5 36	—	27 00
Hickory — Ch of the Asion	25 00	—	—	—	—	3 50	22 00	5 00
High Point — St. ...'s	5 00	—	—	—	—	1 65	—	30 00
St. Mark's	150 00	120 00	25 22	10 00	—	—	—	—
St. John's	5 00	5 00	—	—	—	—	—	—
St. ...'s	11 00	—	—	—	—	85	—	50 72
City — Ch of ... or Savior	50 00	50 00	50 00	2 00	—	12 74	—	—
St. James'	20 00	—	—	—	—	4 00	—	60 00
Ch of the	15 00	15 00	—	—	1 00	5 06	—	—
St. ...'s	50 00	50 00	—	1 00	—	7 27	—	70 00
Ch of the Redemption	4 00	—	—	—	—	—	—	—
St. ...'s	60 00	60 00	35 75	—	—	2 92	2 73	—
Lincolnton — St. Cyprian's	4 00	—	—	—	—	—	—	5 27

TABULAR STATEMENT—*Continued.*

From Whom Received.	Assessment for Episcopal and Contingent Fund.	Amount Paid on Episcopal and Contingent Fund.	Diocesan Missions.	Relief Fund.	Education Fund.	Church Building Fund.	Bis p's Collection for Diocesan Missions.	Amount Paid on Arrears.	Amount in Arrears.
En to — Ch d Or Savior	5 50	—	88	—	—	—	5 30	4 50	5 50
En — Ol d he Gs	5 00	—	—	—	—	—	8 58	4 50	5 50
Louisburg — St. Paul's	16 00	16 00	19 00	—	—	—	2 06	—	—
Louisburg — St. Mds'	—	—	1 56	—	—	80	86	—	—
Mn County — St. Agnes'	—	7 55	5 81	—	80	1 17	—	—	—
Mn County — St. John's	5 50	5 50	1 55	—	—	—	—	—	—
M — Mission Gh	5 50	—	—	—	—	—	2 78	—	11 00
Mt. Airy	—	5 50	1 00	—	—	—	10 25	—	—
Mecklenburg — St. Mark's	5 50	—	—	—	—	—	1 19	5 50	—
Mn — St. John's	—	—	—	—	—	—	2 01	—	—
Ma Dale — Mn	5 50	9 50	8 75	—	—	—	46	6 00	—
Arg — Ch of he He y Rest	4 00	—	1 33	4 00	1 39	1 20	4 71	—	4 00
Mn — Christ Gh	16 50	16 50	—	—	—	—	5 37	—	—
He — St. Hs	55 00	13 40	—	—	—	—	4 69	33 25	21 60
Mg an — Ge Gh	112 50	85 03	37 09	—	—	—	2 98	11 56	27 47
Morganton — St. Gs	2 20	—	—	—	—	—	24 43	—	4 40
Oxford — St. Hs	55 00	55 00	53 66	97	—	—	1 36	—	—
Od Fort — Mission	10 00	4 06	1 39	—	16 23	3 73	—	—	5 94
Raleigh — Christ Gh	362 50	362 50	189 83	14 73					

Raleigh — St. Ms	60 00	60 00							
Raleigh — Gh of Gd Shepherd	143 75	143 75	81 60				17 00		
Raleigh — St. Augustine's	25 00	25 00							
...y — Church of the Gd Shepherd	22 00	16 00	2 50			1 50	23 00	6 00	
Ringwood — St. ..s	22 00					7 80	10 00	22 00	
...e — St. Thomas'	11 00					5 87		22 00	
Rocky Mt — Gh of the Gd	49 50		6 73			12 17		59 00	
Rowan Cty — Gt Gh	13 20		1 35			2 44		71 03	
Rowan — St. Andrew's	13 20		1 52			2 65		79 27	
Rowan — St. Paul's			1 71						
Rowan Cty — St. Ms	5 50	5 50				65			
Rutherfordton — St. John's	5 50	5 50	16 19					17 00	
Salisbury — St. Luke's	100 00	100 00	2 00	2 00		9 85			
Saluda — the Transfiguration	5 00	5 00	22 71	1 2		8 05			
...d Nk — ..y Gh	65 00	27 30		2 00	1 06	22 71	35 14	37 70	
...l — St. Peter's						3 41			
Shelby — Gh of the Redeemer	5 00			95	1 14			15 00	
Statesville ..y — Church	27 50	27 48	14 98						
..y — Elkin Mn	5 50				2 10			16 50	
Sylva — Mn			1 05			1 92			
...o — Calvary Gh	220 00		30 91			34 69	26 01	485 70	
Tarboro — St. Luke's	16 50	6 50				7 28	10 00	10 00	
Tilley						2 74			
...n Cty — Mn	8 00							13 50	
Thompson — of the Virgin Mry			50						
...Ha — St. Philip's, Brevard	11 00					4 36		41 25	
...o — Calvary Gh	60 00	45 00				6 52		15 00	
...t Cove — ..st	11 00					3 72		16 75	
...e — Ge Gh in the Ms	20 00					2 45	20 00		
...n — Emanuel Gh	50 00	50 00				9 01			
...n — All Saint's Mn						2 10			
...n ...o — Grace Gh	50 00	25 00				9 01		25 00	
Wil ..o — St. Paul's	8 00	8 00				14 53			

TABULAR STATEMENT—*Continued.*

From Whom Received.	Assessment for Episcopal and Contingent Fund.	Amount Paid on Episcopal and Contingent Fund.	Diocesan Missions.	Relief Fund.	Education Fund.	Church Building Fund.	Bishop's Collection for Diocesan Missions.	Amount Paid on Arrears.	Amount in Arrears.
Williamsboro ------St. John's	$ 22 00	$ ---	$ 9 04	$ ---	$ ---	$ ---	$ 4 72	$ 14 00	$77 50
Wilson ------St.	66 00	65 00	---	---	---	---	8 79	56 00	11 00
Wilson------St. Mark's	---	---	---	---	---	---	2 83	---	---
Winston ------St. Paul's	38 50	38 50	26 21	---	---	---	---	---	---
Wilkes County ------'s	27 50	3 00	6 10	---	---	---	---	11 00	56 60
Yadkin Valley------Chapel of Rest	---	---	---	---	---	---	3 00	---	---
Valle Crucis------Mission	2 20	---	---	---	---	---	---	---	8 80
	$3203 90	$1942 67	$1107 80	$52 72	$45 35	$24 51	$ 577 41	$ 473 94	

REPORT OF CONDITION OF FUNDS IN HANDS OF THE TRUSTEES OF THE DIOCESE OF NORTH CAROLINA, APRIL 1, 1894.

LIST OF SECURITIES.

RAVENSCROFT FUND.

	Par value.
Certificate of Indebtedness W. & W. Railroad___ _____ $	2,000 00
Bank of New Hanover stock _____	2,500 00
Bond and mortgage M. E. Carter (balance) _____	1,712 51
Loan to Fellows of Ravenscroft for repairs of building in 1887	2,000 00
Eighty shares American Improvement and Construction Company_____	4,000 00
	$12,212 51

HICKS FUND.

Missouri Pacific stock_____ $	900 00
Bond and mortgage G. W. Massengill _____	1,500 00
Bond and mortgage E. J. Hardin _____	1,000 00
Bond and mortgage J. W. Gattis _____	1,000 00
Bond and mortgage E. S. Hall _____	1,000 00
	$ 5,400 00

MISS MARY SMITH FUND.

Bond and mortgage W. C. Johnson and wife_____ $	200 00
Bond and mortgage Chapel Hill rectory_____	200 00
Bond and mortgage O. L. Stringfield_____	500 00
Bond and mortgage Joseph Fuller and wife_____	500 00
	$ 1,400 00

Dr.   *Miss Mary Smith Fund, in Account with*

1894			
April	1	To Treasurer's commission on receipts _____	$ 9 49
		To credit balance carried down _____ _____	1,417 81
			$ 1,427 30

Dr.   *Ravenscroft Fund, in Account with*

1893			
April	1	To debit balance ___ _____ _____ _____	$ 428 14
1894			
April	1	To Treasurer's commission on receipts ____ ___ ____	7 00
			$ 435 14
1894			
April	1	To debit balance_____ _____ ____ _____ __	$ 295 14

Dr.   *Hicks Fund, in Account with*

1894			
April	1	To amount paid to Rev. W. S. Barrows, order of Bishop Lyman _____ __ __ _____ _____ ____ ___	$ 300 00
		To cash paid advertising Hardin property _____	6 00
		To Treasurer's commission on receipts _____ _____	6 12
		To credit balance carried down ____ ____ _____	1,613 87
			$ 1,925 99

Chas. E. Johnson, Treasurer.   Cr.

1893		
April 1	By credit balance _____ _____ __ $	1,237 35
	By amount received from Hon. K. P. Battle, Ex'r.	25 00
	By amount received from Hon. K. P. Battle, Ex'r	31 50
	By amount received from Hon. K. P. Battle, Ex'r	39 95
	By interest on W. C. Johnson bond and mortgage.	16 00
	By interest on O. L. Stringfield bond and mortgage	40 00
	By amount received from Hon. K. P. Battle, Ex'r	37 50
		$ 1,427 30
1894		
April 1	By credit balance ___ ____ _____ ___ _____ . $	1,417 81

Chas. E. Johnson, Treasurer.   Cr.

1894		
April 1	By October and April interest on certificate of indebtedness W. & W. R. R. Co. _ _ _____ $	140 00
	By debit balance carried down _____ __ ___ ___ _ ___	295 14
		$ 435 14

Chas. E. Johnson, Treasurer.   Cr.

1893		
April 1	By credit balance_____ _____ _____ __ ____ $	1,303 59
	By proceeds 1 Wilmington bond ____ _____	500 00
	By interest collected on Massengill note ___ _____	122 40
		$ 1,925 99
1894		
April 1	By credit balance ___ _____ ___ __ ___ _____ _____ $	1,613 87

APPENDIX D.

CANONS OF THE DIOCESE AS AMENDED, 1894.

Chapter I, Canon VIII, Section 1, paragraph 1:

In addition to the Standing Committee there shall be elected annually the following Committees, of which the Bishop shall be Chairman *ex-officio*, viz.: An Education Committee, to consist of three; a Church Building Committee, to consist of five; and an Executive Missionary Committee, composed as follows: The Bishop, the Deans of Convocations and the Treasurer of the Diocese, *ex-officio;* four Laymen to be elected by the Convention and an Executive Secretary to be elected by the Committee, any five of whom shall constitute a quorum.

Chapter I, Canon VIII, Section 3, paragraph added:

The duties of the Executive Secretary shall be such as the Committee may from time to time designate. His salary shall be determined by the Committee and shall be paid from the Missionary Treasury

Chapter I, Canon XIV:

SECTION 1. It shall be the duty of every Clergyman of the Diocese to make a collection in the parish or parishes under his charge at least once in each year in aid of the Education Fund, the Church Building Fund and the Relief Fund of the Diocese.

SEC. 2. It shall also be the duty of the Minister in charge of each congregation in the Diocese to obtain, through the agency of the Laity, from every member of the same, if possible, an individual subscription, payable monthly, to the Diocesan Missionary Fund.

SEC. 3. It shall be the duty of the Clergyman, or of some proper officer of each parish, to remit promptly to the Treasurer of the Diocese the amounts collected as herein provided.

Chapter II, Canon I, Section 1, amended by changing the word *four* into *five*, and by inserting *of Salisbury* after the word *Raleigh.*

NOTIFICATION OF PROPOSED CHANGES IN THE CONSTITUTION OF THE CHURCH.

THE GENERAL CONVENTION OF THE PROTESTANT EPISCOPAL CHURCH.

To the Convention of the Diocese of North Carolina:

In compliance with the requirements of Title III, Canon I, Section 3, of the Digest, I would hereby give particular notice that the following alterations of the Constitution of the Church are proposed, to-wit, those comprised in the two resolutions subjoined, said resolutions having been constitutionally adopted by a General Convention of the Protestant Episcopal Church, held in the city of Baltimore, Maryland, in October, A. D. 1892, to-wit:

First—It was by concurrent action of the two Houses of the Convenion (*vide* Journal, pages 338, 118)

Resolved, That Article 8 of the Constitution be amended by striking out the clause "No alteration, etc.," and in inserting in lieu thereof the following: "No alteration or addition shall be made in the Book of Common Prayer or other Offices of the Church, or the Articles of Religion, unless the same shall be first proposed in one General Convention, by the vote of a majority of the whole number of Bishops entitled to seats in the House of Bishops, and by the vote of a majority of all the Dioceses entitled to representation in the House of Deputies, and by a resolve of the General Convention made known to the Convention of every Diocese, and adopted at the subsequent General Convention in the same manner in which it was proposed." * * * * *

Second—It was by concurrent action of the two Houses of the Convention (*vide* Journal, pages 394, 395, 152)

Resolved, That the following changes be made in the Constitution and that the proposed changes be made known to the several Diocesan Conventions in order that they may be adopted in the ensuing General Convention, in accordance with provisions of Article IX of the Constitution:

Strike out the words "Assistant Bishop" wherever they occur, and insert in their place the words "Bishop Coadjutor."

In testimony whereof I have this day hereunto affixed my name.,

CHAS. L. HUTCHINS,
Secretary of the House of Deputies.

CONCORD, MASS , February 14, A. D. 1894

FORM OF PAROCHIAL REPORT.

REPORT FOR THE YEAR ENDING APRIL 30, 189---.

To the Rt. Rev. the Bishop of North Carolina :

(Location)..*(N. C.)*

Church or Chapel of ....*Church or Chapel.*

The Rev. ....*Rector* (*or*) *Minister in Charge*

The Rev. ....*Assistant Minister.*

	WHITE.	COL.	TOTAL
Number of Families			
" Baptized persons ..			
Whole number of persons ..			
Baptisms—Infant			
Adult			
Total ..			
Number Confirmed			
Marriages.........			
Burials.			
Communicants—last reported			
admitted			
received by transfer.. .			
restored			
whole number added			
died.			
removed			
withdrawn			
suspended			
whole number lost			
present number			
Sunday-school teachers			
scholars			
Parish school teachers			
scholars			
Industrial school teachers..			
scholars..			
Other Parish Agencies			
Public services—ou Sundays..			
other days			
Holy Communion—public.			
private....			
Number of Churches			
" Chapels .			
" Rectories .			
" Church sittings			
" Chapel sittings.			

Value of church. .... $ ....
" chapel.. ....
" rectory. . .. .
" endowments. ... .
" other church property . ... | ....

Total ....$ ....

Amount of insurance.. ....
Indebtedness—on property............... ....
" (other).. ... .

RECEIPTS.

Communion Alms. ....
Other offerings at church services. ....
Sunday-school offerings................
From parish societies ....
Other sources .. . .

Total receipts .. ..$..........

DISBURSEMENTS.

Parochial—Alms appropriated . ..... $ ....
Parish Missions ....
Minister's salary paid. .
Current expenses .. ..
Improvements and re-
pairs ....
Miscellaneous. ....

Total Parochial .... $ ....

Diocesan—Episcopal and Contin-
gent Fund ... .
Permanent Episcopal
Fund...........................
Diocesan Missions.. . ...
Church Building Fund....
Education Fund. ....
Relief Fund . ...
Thompson Orphanage..
Convocation . ...
Miscellaneous. ....

Total Diocesan ...... $.. ... ...

General—General Missions . ... $ ....
Domestic Missions... ....
Foreign Missions ....
Colored Missions .. ..
Indian Missions ....
Jewish Missions ....
Theological Department
Sewanee . . ..
Clergy Retiring Fund . | ....
Widows and Orphans
Fund............................
American Church Build-
ing Fund.. ....
Miscellaneous ....

Total General.. .... $ ....

Aggregate of disbursements ....| ... .

SCHEDULE OF ASSESSMENTS FOR THE EPISCOPAL AND CON-
TINGENT FUND AND APPORTIONMENTS FOR DIOCESAN
MISSIONS, TO TAKE EFFECT APRIL 1, 1894.

Parishes and Missions heard from by the Finance Committee in regard to voluntary
increase are marked thus*.

Location.	Parishes and Congregations.	Assessments for Episcopal and Contingent Fund.	Apportionments for Diocesan Missions.
Ansonville	Mission	$ 5 50	$ 20 00
*Asheville	Trinity	200 00	200 00
Asheville	St. Matthias	11 00	10 00
Battleboro	St. John's		10 00
Beattie's Ford		5 50	
*Beaver Dam	Mission	6 60	
Boone, Watauga County	Mission	5 50	5 00
Bowman's Bluff	Gethsemane	10 00	
Brevard	St. Philip's	11 00	10 00
Buncombe County	St. Andrew's	3 30	
*Burlington	St. Athanasius	70 00	50 00
Candler's	St. Paul's		5 00
Cashier's Valley	Good Shepherd		5 00
*Chapel Hill	Chapel of the Cross	55 00	40 00
Charlotte	St. Michael's	10 00	5 00
*Charlotte	St. Peter's	250 00	250 00
Concord	All Saints	27 50	20 00
Cullowhee	St. David's		10 00
Cuningham's	Chapel	5 50	
Durham	St. Philip's	40 00	80 00
Edgecombe County	St. Mary's Chapel	5 50	5 00
Enfield	Advent	5 50	10 00
Fairntosh	Salem Chapel	5 00	
Franklin, Macon County	St. Agnes		20 00
Gaston	St. Luke's	8 25	10 00
Goshen	St Paul's	5 00	5 00
Greensboro	St. Barnabas	40 00	50 00
Greensboro	St. Andrews	10 00	
Gulf	St. Mark's	5 00	
Halifax	St. Mark's	11 00	10 00
Henderson	Holy Innocents	82 50	100 00
Henderson County	Calvary	66 00	75 00
Henderson County	St. Paul's	5 50	
Hendersonville	St. James	5 50	10 00
*Hickory	Ascension	25 00	20 00
High Point	St. Mary's	5 00	10 00
*Hillsboro	St. Matthew's	150 00	50 00
Hot Springs	St. John's	5 00	50 00
Iredell County	St. James	11 00	5 00
*Jackson	The Saviour	50 00	50 00
Kittrell	St. James'	20 00	20 00
Leaksville	Epiphany	25 00	10 00
*Lenoir	St. James	50 00	20 00

LOCATION.	PARISHES AND CONGREGATIONS.	Assessments for Episcopal and Contingent Fund.	Apportionments for Diocesan Missions.
Lexington	Redemption	$ 4 00	$ 10 00
Lincoln County	Our Saviour	5 50	
Lincolnton	St. Cyprian's	4 00	
*Lincolnton	St. Luke's	80 00	30 00
Littleton	Chapel of the Cross	5 00	5 00
Louisburg	St. Paul's	16 00	15 00
Marion	St. John's	5 50	
Mecklenburg County	St. Mark's	5 50	5 00
Middleburg	Mission	5 50	
Milton	Mission	4 00	
Monroe	St. Paul's	16 50	10 00
Morganton	Grace	55 00	25 00.
Nonah, Macon County	St. John's	5 50	5 00
Old Fort	Mission	2 20	
*Oxford	St. Stephen's	112 50	75 00
*Pittsboro	St. Bartholomew's	55 00	50 00
*Pittsboro	St. James	10 00	5 00
*Raleigh	Christ Church	450 00	400 00
*Raleigh	Good Shepherd	150 00	200 00
*Raleigh	St. Augustine's	25 00	12 00
*Raleigh	St. Mary's Chapel	65 00	40 00
Reidsville	St. Thomas	11 00	10 00
*Ridgeway	Good Shepherd	22 00	10 00
Ringwood	St. Clements	22 00	10 00
Rocky Mount	Good Shepherd	49 50	30 00
Rowan County	Christ Church	13 20	10 00
Rowan County	St. Andrew's	13 20	10 00
Rowan County	St. Mary's	5 50	10 00
Rutherfordton	St. John's	5 50	
Salisbury	St. Luke's	100 00	100 00
*Saluda	Transfiguration	5 00	
*Scotland Neck	Trinity	65 00	30 00
Shelby	Redeemer	5 00	
Statesville	Trinity	27 50	15 00
Surry County	Elkin Mission	5 50	10 00
Tarboro	Calvary	220 00	250 00
*Tarboro	St. Luke's	16 50	10 00
*Tryon City	Holy Cross	8 00	10 00
*Wadesboro	Calvary	50 00	30 00
Walnut Cove	Holy Comforter	11 00	15 00
Warrenton	Emmanuel	50 00	30 00
Watauga River	St. John's		5 00
*Waynesville	Grace	20 00	25 00
*Weldon	Grace	50 00	10 00
*Wilkesboro	St. Paul's	8 00	5 00
Wilkes County	Gwyn's Chapel	27 50	10 00
*Williamsboro	St. John's	22 00	10 00
Wilson	St. Timothy's	66 00	50 00
Winston	St. Paul's	38 50	30 00
Valle Crucis	Mission	2 20	

INDEX TO THE JOURNAL

OF THE

SEVENTY-EIGHTH ANNUAL CONVENTION,

1894.

JOURNAL

OF THE

SEVENTY-NINTH ANNUAL CONVENTION

OF THE

PROTESTANT EPISCOPAL CHURCH

IN THE

DIOCESE OF NORTH CAROLINA

HELD IN

GRACE CHURCH, MORGANTON

MAY 15–17

A. D. 1895

RALEIGH
E. M. UZZELL, STEAM PRINTER AND BINDER
1895

CPSIA information can be obtained
at www.ICGtesting.com
Printed in the USA
BVHW041036210219
540828BV00009B/488/P